Tulips for Breakfast

An award-winning children's author, Catherine Bauer is a former journalist and media-communications specialist. She grew up in the suburbs of Adelaide and received her first editorial rejection at the age of eight. Undeterred, she kept on writing. When not working full time as a media adviser, Catherine writes, reads, enjoys theatre, keeps fit, eats chocolate and hangs out with friends and family, including her three sons.

Also by Catherine Bauer

Colourful Memories
Dreaming Soldiers
Len Waters: Boundless and Born to Fly

This story is dedicated to the survivors, far and wide, who shared their stories with me or committed their memories to print – and to those who didn't make it. Their stories and those of other genocides must never be forgotten – especially in times like these.

To my parents, who inspired me to uncover history, to read and to look to the future, thank you always — CB

Tulips for Breakfast

Catherine Bauer

FORD ST

First published by Ford Street Publishing
Melbourne, Victoria, Australia

2 4 6 8 10 9 7 5 3 1

Ford Street website: www.fordstreetpublishing.com

First published 2022

A catalogue record for this book is available from the National Library of Australia

ISBN: 9781922696199 (paperback)

Cover design: Cathy Larsen

Printed in Australia by McPherson's Printing Group

Chapter 1

Someone was in the house. It could not be Ilse Graaf. She had gone.

As for Adelena, brave and strong, she had left long ago, and I may never see her again. I was alone, just Lena.

Alone. Hiding. Like a scared little mouse in a grain barn, waiting for the farm cat to pounce.

Cat-like, the Germans had stalked and hunted us for the past six years and more. And like all half-starved farm cats, their instincts were honed to hunt Jews with a single view to devour and exterminate every one of us.

We were being snuffed out like ceremonial candles in a Hanukkah menorah and the darkness was almost complete. I had come to fear theirs would be the one light left burning across the entire universe.

My own dark hiding place in the cellar muffled the intruders' movements, but my hearing, sharpened by the gloom, helped trace their clumsy steps around the upper storey.

They upended furniture, smashed glass, and broke open doors like crazed children on a scavenger hunt through the house. If searching for a few scraps of food or valuables, they'd find neither. There had been little or no food for weeks and Ilse sold off or traded anything of value months before. A pair of fine gold ear hoops exchanged for a sack of rotting sugar beets; a marcasite brooch swapped for a dozen bitter tulip bulbs. Foods and scraps once only seen as fit for the farmyard had been finding their way into bellies, including my own, across the Netherlands for many months.

I flinched when out of the dark came the sneering taunt, 'It hardly matters to you. You're done for either way. Fallen at the last hurdle.'

'Adelena,' I called into the dark, my voice hoarse from starvation, 'is that you?' I wanted to tell her I was sorry but didn't bother. She would only turn and run again.

I regretted that I only ever paid her scant attention. She was right to mock me now. But sometimes she was too quiet. It was easy to ignore her.

Before my best friend, Hetty Casler, Adelena was my single most important companion and knew me better than anyone. After all, that was the name on my birth certificate, the name my parents chose, but everyone called me 'Lena', or 'Little Lena', even 'Sweet Baby Lena'. They bounced me on their knee and pinched my chubby cheeks.

I didn't want to be 'Little Lena' – meek, mild and mousey. I wanted to be like the girls I envied who had names like Greta, Marlene and Ursula. Those confident girls with easy, irresistible laughs, who spoke their minds and who were invited on outings to the cinema by boys and who brazenly accepted, even though their parents were against it.

I wanted to be Adelena and so I created her in my youngest years from all the best and worst parts of myself and others. When I was timid, she would step forward, finding just the right words; if a boy I liked glanced at me, causing my face to redden and my tongue to stammer, it was Adelena who dipped her chin and smiled charmingly. She was all the things that I wanted to be – confident, brave and knowing. I pictured her as dark-eyed like me, but where I was average height, she was tall; where I had dark springs for hair, Adelena's fell in golden waves around her face. She sounded like me but more measured and grown up.

'Adelena, if that is you, you are right to mock me,' I whispered, my words swallowed by the suffocating darkness.

Interlacing my fingers, I lay them over my eyes. It was something I did when watching the first winter snowfall, enjoying the fragmented vignettes of snowflakes appearing in the spaces between my finger-mask.

As the thudding and thumping continued overhead, my thoughts expanded. I was sure that if I tried hard enough, I could conjure the drifting, dancing crystals, sunlight sparking from their edges as they floated softly to the ground.

If I mustered up all my mental powers, the heavy black wings enveloping me would be replaced with blinding white light. Instead of the nerve-shredding noise of crashing and bumping there would be the excited sounds of the neighbourhood children spilling from their homes, reaching for the snow as it falls like white embers from a heavenly inferno.

Although I tried with every grain of strength, with every cell of my body, I could not block out the shades of night around me. I could not tear down the sky to reveal all this as just a cruel night terror. I knew exactly where I was. Buried under the shelving at the back of the cellar.

Mentally, I walked around the space. A weak light from two small windows penetrated a few metres into the room, infusing the space with a milky light; laundry bags stamped INFIRMARY were piled against a wall next to the two squat washing vats and their wooden batons; a bare globe hung from the ceiling; a broom, wicker carpet beater and an old rug were propped neatly in a corner.

It was all presided over by an ancient beer barrel, long drained of its brew, and the wall of preserving shelves behind which I lay in secret, expecting at any moment to be discovered.

The sound of raised voices, speaking German, continued to reach me from the upper storey. I caught just enough to grasp there was a debate about staying and continuing to search or retreating while they still had time.

'Go, go, go,' I willed them in my mind. 'Run away. Please, just go. Don't wait a second longer.'

Miraculously, as though in direct response to my prayers, the trampling and clattering faded.

I strained my ears, but the silence only rang louder.

My heart lifted. I released the air from my painful lungs. Not in one gasp, but in small, silent puffs.

Maybe I would survive after all. Maybe I would have the strength to pull myself from my hiding place, to crawl from the dank cellar and into the light.

But it was too soon to relax.

From somewhere, a woman's voice shouted, 'Get out before I blow your brains out.'

In moments, the sound of heavy footfalls rose again, this time, closer to my hiding place. My heart sank, my breathing froze.

Where are they? Where are they? Where are they?

My mind's eye followed the thudding steps, imagining the intruders throwing down empty drawers and slamming barren cabinet cupboards, furtive hands tucking Ilse's few remaining pieces of good china deep into pockets and lifting the antique watercolours in the hallway from the walls.

The trampling intruders ran down the side of the house, and stopped suddenly at the low doorway to the cellar.

Finding the entry locked, they shouldered the heavy wooden door, once, twice, three times before the wood splintered.

Someone picked themselves up off the floor.

'*Sei ruhig*!' came the hissed command to 'pipe down'.

'You take that side,' a voice said. 'And you two, over there. I'll check the back. But be fast. We have to move out.'

My head was spinning. I held my breath. I was mere seconds – metres – from disaster. The moments in time that had led to this point began queuing behind my eyes.

I made a minute shift in another useless hunt for comfort, but the damp had made a home in my bones. Those same bones, once covered by a healthy layer of flesh, now poked through my skin. That skin, once plump and tanned, was yellow-tinged and thinly stretched. It was oddly reminiscent of the flayed hides drying in the sun – a grotesque sight that had raised a chorus of disgust on a school visit to a northern farm several summers ago.

How simple life was then.

Before Hitler. Before that morning of May 10, 1940, when the country woke to the swarming of German aircraft engines, marking the start of a five-day battle and the 'Occupation'.

Before then, the biggest decisions my friends and I had to make were whether to picnic at the lake in

Vondelpark or play handball in the street in front of our homes on Merwedeplein.

This is how I first met Hetty. She and her sister Ursula were playing with other Dutch and German children in the street. I watched them from the front window of our house.

For weeks, I ignored Mutti's suggestions to join them. My mother was a talented seamstress and, in addition to helping Papa at our shop, she made dresses and coats for the stylish women of Amsterdam. I enjoyed nothing more than to sit as she worked in our front room, captivated by her quick fingers and delicate creations, running my fingers over the fabrics and threads.

'You have to make friends,' she urged, looking up from her work. But as always, I had an excuse – a sore throat, a headache, a tummy ache, wanting to stay and watch her work or help sort her coloured cottons.

Finally, on a cool sunny morning, she grabbed my hand as I stood by the open window, watching the other children in the street below. 'Come on, I'll go with you.'

I snatched my hand away. 'No. I don't want to.'

'Why not?'

'I don't know what to say to them.' Tears filled my eyes. 'They won't like me. Why did we even have to come here and leave all my old friends behind in Germany? It's not fair.'

'Stop it now. Hush. We have been over it and over it.'

I was about to run to my room when someone called up from below the window.

'Hello there.' It was a pale girl with dark hair. Hetty. 'Come play with us. Lotte's going home, and we need someone else for handball.'

Planting her hands on her hips, she added, 'I'm the leading Under 14s handball player in Europe, you know.'

I was impressed until Lotte shouted over her shoulder, 'Don't listen, she's a fibber.'

I soon found my place in the group and joined in games, cycling expeditions to the countryside and family outings to the beach.

There was no talk of Adolf Hitler then. Not among the children. Our main focus was having fun, getting our lessons done and keeping our parents happy.

Some of the boys in our group were obsessed with aeroplanes and pioneers of the air like the Wright Brothers and Amelia Earhart. On weekends we often got together to build simple planes from balsa wood. The packing boxes from the shop were perfect for this and Papa often gave me one or two to pass on.

The boys built the fuselage and the girls were tasked with whittling the propellers, which we attached to a rubber band. Taking them outdoors, we would line up and launch them into the air and see how far they would fly.

'I won,' Hetty lied, often leading to squabbles and hurt feelings.

'Why do you always have to be the winner?' I asked after one such skirmish that saw Reiner Jansen and Hetty stand nose to nose. 'Even when you're not.'

Hetty kicked the ground.

'It's very annoying.' I wanted her to understand. 'Like when you make up tall stories.'

'I don't know why I do it,' she said, now that everyone had gone home. 'I don't want to be boring. I don't want to be forgotten.' Hetty shifted her feet and played with the buttons on her blue cardigan.

'Boring is one thing you are not.' I looked into her owl-like eyes. 'It's okay not to be first or right all the time.'

'That's not true,' she began, but caught herself and we fell giggling into one another.

Chapter 2

As soon as my parents decided I was responsible enough, I was allowed to cycle to and from school each day.

Meeting my friends on the corner and cycling to class each morning was liberating. I carried my books in a small leather backpack emblazoned with my initials, a gift from my grandparents.

Most afternoons I rode home alone, as many peeled off in different directions to visit grandparents or take private tutorials.

One autumn afternoon, as I barrelled headlong down Amstelkade, keen to get home for some cocoa and cinnamon cake, my breath was visible in the chill air as quick, panting gasps. The skin beneath my bulky dark wool jacket was prickly, hot and damp, as much from anxiety as physical effort.

Despite its distance, I could just make out the Westertoren clock chiming four. Mutti would be looking out for me from our living room window, her lips pursed with worry, her fingers tapping the glass as they often did when Papa returned even a few moments late from an appointment, rushing in the door, his hat pushed to the back of his head and wire-framed spectacles lopsided.

Heart hammering, I pedalled on, not daring to stop to retrieve my red woollen cap when it swept off my head, freeing my dark curls.

The bike's seat springs rasped under the furious strain of the race and the whirring bike chain's oily black grease filled my nostrils.

'Lena!' someone called. 'Your cap.'

But there was no time to stop.

The tall, narrow buildings and the bundled-up and shadowless pedestrians blurred into one as I sped on, parallel to the murky canal and away from my determined four-legged pursuer, Fritz.

Fritz was old Herr Winkler's long-haired Alsatian. And he was fast. While I felt I must be putting distance between us, I heard him closing in, his panting too close for comfort. With no coherent strategy other than escape, I veered blindly into Waalstraat, skidding dangerously on the smooth, slick cobblestones.

'Not now! Not now.' I willed myself to stay astride the bike. 'If he catches you, you're done for. Keep going.'

I rode so hard that the bike tilted crazily from side to side. My legs burned and my springy curls streamed behind me.

'Lena,' someone else called. 'What's the rush?'

A husky yelp spurred me on. I risked a quick look behind and, despite my blind panic, or perhaps because of it, there was a sharp new clarity to my senses, and I could see the Alsatian's great white teeth and his lolling pink tongue. Horror. He was not giving up.

A sharp right turn at the intersection to Roerstraat and once more the bike's tyres skidded sideways on the slippery road. I managed to stay upright and threw a look behind.

Suddenly the sound of metal on metal stifled the sound of the air leaving my lungs. Dread descended as I lay crumpled on the ground next to my mangled, beloved Burgers bicycle, which proved to be no match for the German motorcycle it had collided with.

A tall, grey-eyed, straight-backed German officer strode towards me.

'You're done for,' Adelena, who had been tailing close behind, said unhelpfully.

As the German yanked me to my feet, my peripheral vision caught Fritz loping toward me, his eyes fixed on the prize – me.

'Double done for you, idiot,' the voice in my head taunted. 'Here comes Fritz. Any second now and your throat will be in those jaws. Get ready.'

But unexpectedly, the German took up position between me and the four-legged torpedo, Fritz.

'Sit!' he ordered, raising a commanding arm. Magically, the panting animal obeyed.

As the German lowered his hand, I noticed a

small thread hanging from the sleeve of his otherwise immaculate uniform.

From across the road, Herr Winkler called, 'Fritz, *komm! Komm her.*'

The dog gave me a quick sideways look and obligingly bolted across to Herr Winkler, who scolded him while leashing the downcast animal. Pushing his hat back on his head, he called out from the other side of the street, 'Okay, Lena?'

I nodded, but he was already walking away without waiting for my answer. Fritz trailed behind, tail between his legs, leaving me alone with the German and my battered bike.

Both my palms were grazed, glowing pink and stinging something fearful, and I had ripped the knees of my thick woollen stockings. Mutti would be angry.

'You should watch where you are going, silly girl!' the German snapped. 'Afraid of dogs?'

'Especially that one,' I answered, looking at my feet. 'He's been after me for weeks.'

'That dog is harmless. He doesn't want to hurt you,' he said, perhaps a hint of sympathy in his voice. 'I know these dogs. I suggest you take your bicycle and go.'

'You have a thread.' I pointed at the sleeve.

The words tumbled from my mouth, a nervous babble made all the worse by the prickling heat rising up my neck and spreading to my cheeks. His jaw clenched as I prattled on. 'You better fix it, or the whole thing might unravel. I had a pullover once and that happened. I can recommend a good seamstress – my mother, not far from here.'

Subconsciously, I kicked myself as the words spilled forth. I would never normally speak this way to a stranger, and particularly not a stranger who was also a German officer, recently having arrived with the occupying forces. Not only this, but I also suggested he should come to my home for repairs.

Of course, he ignored the suggestion and pushed his cap back on his blond hair. 'Off you go.' He glanced at the thread. 'Unless you want me to escort you home?'

'No,' I blurted and, seeing this offer for the threat it was, limped away.

As I drew closer to home, wheeling my wonky bike, its dented mudguard chafing the tyre so that the smell of rubber filled my nose, I realised that Herr Winkler had already delivered the news to my mother.

Half-running, half-stumbling towards me, Mutti was still buttoning her coat when I met her a block away from home, Hetty trotting beside her.

'I don't know whether to punish you or kiss you.' Her relief was plain as we turned for home.

As we passed the neat shopfronts in silence, I caught sight of my reflection in the sparkling windows. It was as gloomy as the slate-grey sky overhead.

We walked on. The only sounds were our footsteps on the pavement, the whirr of passing cyclists and growl of car engines.

Mutti broke the frosty hush first. 'Hetty's been looking all over for you.'

Hetty only nodded in agreement, her deep, dark eyes bugging out from her head.

'I sent her out when you were so late from school,' Mutti said. 'Then when Herr Winkler came and gave me the news, I thought I would have a fainting fit.'

Mutti was always threatening me and my father with one of these faints – though we never actually ever saw one.

'Your mother is stronger than she lets on,' my father often said. 'She has the romantic notions of a frustrated actress.'

Back home, and after a thousand kisses and swabbing my palms and knees, Mutti served me and Hetty a slice of spiced cake, a glass of milk for our nerves, and delivered us a telling off.

Holding the exquisitely cool milk glass to my still-fiery cheeks, I shut my eyes and pictured the soldier bearing down on me as I lay sprawled on the roadway.

'All these Germans on the streets.' Mutti's pretty face was stern. Her pearl necklace clacked as she played with the long rope around her neck. 'They are here to stay. They have marched into Holland

and they are taking over. Understand? They are in charge – they have the keys to the city if you like.'

She breathed in. She breathed out.

'Girls, they are looking for anything. Any. Little. Thing.' She slammed her hand on the tabletop, making me jump. 'Any excuse, no matter how small, to pull us up. We must give them no reason. Do nothing to draw attention to yourselves. Do you hear me?'

Catching Hetty's eye, I stifled a giggle. Instead, I nodded, nibbling a piece of the spiced cake, taking comfort in its blend of cinnamon, nutmeg, butter and sugar – my grandmother's recipe.

Hetty, though, was not able to swallow the gulping sound that escaped her throat.

Mutti paused, as though considering her next words before continuing. 'I hope you are taking this seriously, girls. Don't discount anything you hear about the Nazis.' Her voice dropped. 'It's worse than you could ever imagine.'

Chapter 3

As the weeks and months marched on after Occupation, there came a jarring realisation that my carefree existence was slipping away. That, just as Mutti had said, the soldiers were here to stay: watchful and controlling, forceful and disdainful.

Their appearance on the city streets, with their uniforms and their guns, was an affront, jarring and perplexing. There was a collective silent revolt among the citizens' refusal to engage beyond what was absolutely necessary. A few brave souls jeered or shouted, 'Get out, we don't want you here!' before being roughly moved on by the soldiers.

I was unsure how I was supposed to behave, so like the vast majority of people, I looked down or averted my gaze to something else when encountering them on the streets.

Riding to school one morning, I told Hetty my parents were talking about accompanying me in future each day.

'Mine too,' she said. 'What a complete bore. And they told us that life would be better in Holland.'

'Well, I suppose it has been, at least until recently.

I hated the idea of leaving Germany and have never cried as hard as the day Papa told me. He said the Nazis would make our lives "difficult" and it was best to leave and "have a fresh start in Holland".'

'Ha, that's almost the same words my parents used. But I did notice in the time before we left that there was a change – that some of our German friends didn't visit as often. Then, when my best friend Irma wasn't allowed to come over anymore, it felt really strange. Like there was something wrong with me.'

'Yep, I know exactly,' I said. 'My uncle lost his job in the public service and our neighbour, a young German girl, had to call off her wedding to her Jewish boyfriend. I heard she even tried to kill herself.'

'No!' Hetty's eyes were as round as saucers. 'That's too sad.'

'I know, isn't it? But like I said, it's not been too bad here I suppose – until recent times at least. I met you and that's good.'

'Yes, it is very good.' Hetty grinned.

It was true. We had settled well enough into our new home in Amsterdam and lived in a comfortable area with others who'd left Germany. When I did make new friends, despite my awkward ways, I liked nothing more than playing in the streets with other local children.

There were invitations to birthday parties – Dutch, Jewish and German. It didn't matter then in those early days, those days when the name 'Adolf Hitler' was just a collection of black letters on newsprint.

I was happy at school. Papa's shop was doing well and, when I wasn't out playing on the streets or in the park, I helped stack shelves and unpack boxes.

But as Hetty and I discussed, as we rode on that morning, all that was in the time before the Germans barged in with their various impositions.

'Lena.' Hetty glanced sideways. 'I promise I haven't gone mad, but aren't you sort of used to them being on the streets by now and everything?'

My response was an open mouth.

'Well, you know it was a big shock at first with the air raids and all that,' she said, 'but our daily lives so far are pretty much the same, aren't they? And aren't you even just a little bit curious about them?'

Certainly, in the first few weeks after Occupation, the boys in our neighbourhood were fascinated by the pageantry of their parades through the streets, with tanks and infantry vehicles laden with soldiers carrying arms. Those on foot marched in perfect time, their shining boots crunching the asphalt with minute precision. There were military bands, banners and flags.

Hetty, Double B and I, carried away by the excitement, stood like gawping statues transfixed by the handsome, straight-backed young men in their neat uniforms. It was like nothing we had ever seen in real life.

We guiltily admired them. Some of them – even

though German – were quite handsome in their neat uniforms. Tall, blue-eyed and fair-haired for the most part, like movie stars – or so we thought at first. It didn't take long, though, for us to change our ideas.

Often, they just ignored us. In my mind's eye, I thought of them as thick black exclamation marks as they passed.

One slow Sunday afternoon, our friend Willem Walsma, Hetty and I, along with my young cousin Berta Baum – known among us as 'Double B' – managed to convince our parents to allow us to walk to the park for some air and sunshine. We had one hour – strictly. My aunty, Mutti's younger sister and Double B's mother, was most insistent. She had been spat on in the street the previous week by a man who used to buy his tobacco in Papa's shop.

We were used to the sight of the soldiers and thought little of it as we approached an oncoming patrol.

This time, instead of ignoring us as they usually did, they locked their attention on our small group, quickly surrounding us.

'What are you doing with these children?' a soldier asked Willem.

Double B stiffened and I reached down to pull her curly-haired head into my side.

'We're friends,' Willem answered and threw his shoulders back.

'Friends? Interesting choice, don't you think?' one

of the men asked. 'Why be friends with Jews when you have all these other clean and upright Dutch and German children to be friends with?'

'We're going to the park, that's all.' Willem shifted his feet slightly and looked the German in the eye.

How brave, I thought.

Willem wasn't like a lot of the other boys we knew. A true Dutch boy who liked football and all that, but he also liked music and was one of the few boys in choir with us. Our teacher said he had 'a fine angelic voice' and 'innate musical sensibilities'.

We girls would laugh, though, as his voice was changing and it unexpectedly rose to a shriek, or fell, mid-stanza, to a baritone. Even he laughed – something Hetty and I found adorable. Most of the other boys we knew would never laugh at themselves like that.

And here he stood strong and bold, meeting the German's eyes without flinching.

'Well, what if we say you can't?' The soldier's pointed chin jutted towards us and he poked a long pale finger into Willem's shoulder.

His breath was hot and foul.

'You can't stop us.' It was Hetty. I elbowed her, willing her to keep quiet.

'We can do what we like,' the soldier said as the circle around us closed in.

'*Verzeihung*,' came a familiar voice. 'Excuse me.'

Through the forest of soldiers, I could see the

voice belonged to Ilse Graaf, my music teacher and one of Papa's best customers.

The soldiers turned to face the source of this perfectly spoken German, only to behold Aryan beauty, immaculate street clothes, brown leather brogues and a precisely tailored skirt suit.

'Is everything all right here?' she said. 'I've been waiting for you, children.'

'What do you want with them?' one of the soldiers asked.

'They are doing some chores for me,' she said, 'at my home.'

'The boy said they were going to the park.'

'That is true.' She held her head at a haughty angle and didn't miss a beat. 'We are going to the park for kindling on the way. Kindly let us pass, gentlemen.'

Miraculously the circle opened up and we were allowed through.

'But the Jews are to walk in the gutter,' one of them shouted as we walked away. 'They should not be taking up space on the footpaths.'

Chapter 4

One morning, as the Germans became ever more visible, Hetty and I were cycling to school when a pair of German infantry vehicles sped past. A soldier called out something angry-sounding that I couldn't catch.

'What did they say?' I asked, wobbling slightly to avoid the small convoy.

'I don't know. Just ignore them.'

'Easier said than done when everywhere you turn it seems there's a German uniform.'

'True. Everything's changing again, isn't it? We should be planning trips to the seaside, not dodging German transports. Remember last year at Zandvoort?'

'How can I forget it – you almost had me drowned.' I grinned. 'And I injured my shoulder in the process when that wave smashed me.'

'That's not fair.' She scowled. 'How was I to know you couldn't swim?'

'But the rest of the day was good, wasn't it? Apart from that bit.'

Riding on, like a tennis match, we listed the best parts of the day.

'The warm sand,' I said.

'Lemonade and ice-cream,' Hetty threw in.

'The tumbling gulls.'

'Sandcastles with moats.'

'The big ladies in their swimsuits wading into the ocean, trying hard to keep their balance on the soft sand.'

Hetty veered dangerously close as she struggled to contain her laughter.

'Remember my aunty and her little French parasol?' she asked. 'As if that was ever going to give her any shade. And you believed me when I said that the minute our feet got wet, we'd turn into mermaids and be able to breathe underwater?'

Zandvoort. My first-ever visit to the seaside.

The sun's shimmer had bounced off the rippling water, forcing me to shield my eyes. My own small hand sat in one of Papa's, like a just-hatched bird in a nest.

'You were too nervous to go in the water. Such a baby.' Hetty glanced at me with her owlish, intelligent eyes.

Even as we rode along in the morning sun, the memory still stung. I know that she didn't mean to be unkind but as Mutti always said, 'God knows everything, but Hetty Casler knows everything better.'

Maybe if my little sister had lived to take a first lungful of air, if I wasn't the sole focus of my mother's over-protective attention, I would have been more like Hetty.

It was Papa who had told me to follow her into the water.

'You were so worried what your mother would say,' Hetty continued as other children from nearby streets joined behind us, a procession of whirring bicycle chains and wheels.

'I had never even been to the beach before,' I reminded her, recalling the silvery lapping water. 'I didn't know how squishy the sand would be.'

In and out, back and forth; so alive, it breathed.

Without warning, the sand had collapsed under my feet, throwing my balance and sending me flailing for Papa's hand. He was already walking away up the beach, his lean and wiry frame turned away from me.

The rest happened in seconds: a small wave dragged me further into the water, pulling me down and throwing me against the seabed, sending a shard of excruciating pain through my left shoulder.

'You would have drowned if it wasn't for me,' Hetty said.

'Be quiet, will you?' I said, not wanting the others in our convoy to hear.

But it was true. Hetty pulled me up by the front of my new wool swimsuit as Papa bounded into the water in his trousers and rolled-up shirtsleeves.

'Everyone blamed me, of course.' Hetty huffed as

the schoolhouse came into view.

'All's well that ends well, right?' I said, dismounting, even though the incident meant my water-based activities for the remainder of that summer were confined to wading in the lake at Vondelpark.

But Hetty wasn't listening. She was heading to the side of the schoolhouse where a gaggle of noisy students had gathered.

'I'll punch you in the face if you say that again,' someone said from the centre of the small crowd.

It was Jacob Zeit and he was directing the threat at Pieter Bakker, who held a copy of the daily German-language paper *Deutsche Zeitung in den Niederlanden* in his fist.

Pieter's twin sister Anna stepped forward, raising her voice. 'It's true. Our parents say it's because of all you Jews that the Germans are even here. Hitler hates Jews.'

I looked at Hetty, her eyes glowing with hot anger. Feeling a tug on my skirt, I glanced down. It was Double B. I grabbed her hand.

'He hates them for good reason,' someone else piped up. 'Dirty, greedy Jews.'

That was all it took as a melee erupted with pushing, shoving and shouting.

'Stop,' Willem said. 'Don't be a bully, Pieter.'

Pieter shoved Willem in the centre of his chest, sending him to the dirt. 'Jew lover.' He spat a glistening gob at Willem's feet.

I helped Willem up and whispered, 'Are you okay?'

'I'm fine – you?'

'I'm fine. But you've grazed your knee.' Beneath his short, baggy pants; a long stream of blood was trickling down his leg.

'It's nothing. Don't worry.'

Double B burst into shaking sobs. I was about to lead her away when the principal, Frau Eckert, erect as a pin, pushed her way into the centre of the flailing pack.

'Enough,' she shouted above the din. 'That is enough.'

Pieter and Jacob were separated and stood panting as others in the circle sobbed, or remained white-faced and silent.

The principal grabbed the paper from the ground and balled it up. 'This is not a place for untruth and hate. I will be talking with both your parents. The school will not tolerate this behaviour, do you understand?'

No one moved a muscle or uttered a word, except for the little ones like Double B who were still crying.

'Do you all understand?' she repeated, looking around.

A murmured 'yes' went around the circle before we were all dismissed and ordered to get to our classes.

Hetty and I did our best to reassure Double B before handing her over to her teacher. We headed to our own classroom where Herr Meyer referenced the morning's drama by saying, 'We live in uncertain times, but there is nothing uncertain about Pythagoras' theorem. Open to chapter four.'

We all groaned and got on with the day, but not without a sense of unease and a little dread.

I was happy to leave the school gates behind that day to start my chores at the shop.

Dismounting my bicycle at the shop's front door, I saw Papa ripping down posters from the front window, a deep crease running from the top of his eyebrows.

Ilse Graaf – her shopping basket on the crook of her arm, the fair hair I so admired covered by her usual fedora – stood in the doorway, Mutti at her shoulder.

'What's this?' I asked, picking up a torn shred of paper from the ground.

'German posters.' Papa screwed the poster into a ball. 'One of the city councillors made a special delivery this morning, with orders to put them in the window.'

'What are they for?'

'This one –' he pointed to the window '–denounces the black market, and this one –' he thrust the paper ball towards me '–is recruiting for Nazi Youth.'

'Will there be trouble if you take them down, Papa?'

'That's what I said, Jacob,' Mutti said. 'We are enough in the spotlight already and we're losing customers. Not everyone will stick with us. Not like Ilse.' She put her hand on Ilse's shoulder. 'People will see this as making trouble.'

'I am not making any trouble.' Papa's spectacles were askew, the muscles in his jaw working as he reached to tear down another offending banner. 'I put them up as requested and left them there all day.' The sound of tearing paper split the air. 'And now, they are coming down.' He threw the second poster into the gutter.

I also wanted to question Papa's open defiance of the order, but the sight of the torn and discarded posters froze the words in my mouth. I knew this was provocative, a sense confirmed by a commotion that had erupted down the street. I watched in wide-eyed dread as another store owner debated the signage with four German officers.

'Look, Jacob, we will be next.' Mutti pointed in the direction of the gesticulating huddle that surrounded the shopkeeper.

Without a word, Frau Graaf stepped around Mutti, retrieved the posters out of the gutter and whispered, 'Get off the street.' Inside the shop, I leaned against the counter and watched as Papa locked the door and pulled the blind down. A fog of dread wrapped me in its damp arms and we all braced for a knock at the door.

The three quick, sharp taps against the glass were followed by the command, 'Open up!'

'No, Papa,' I whispered. 'Don't open the door.'

'Vera, Lena, get behind the counter.' Papa spoke with authority.

'Do as your father says, Lena.' Frau Graaf, who had removed her hat and coat, stood behind Papa as he opened the door, her shirt sleeves pushed up to her elbows.

'We are closed,' Papa told the two officers on the doorstep, but they pushed past regardless.

Hands on hips, Frau Graaf said, 'Closed for a stocktake. It's all hands on deck, my good sirs.' She smiled her charming smile, her blue eyes sparkling.

'You are not displaying the posters distributed today.' The taller and younger of the two officers stepped forward. 'Why not? It is a requirement, you understand?'

'There are consequences for not obeying the rules,' the other officer added, looking around the shop, observing the contents on the shelves.

I had ducked behind the counter and peered over the edge, fear pulsing through my veins, legs like jelly.

'We have done nothing wrong,' Papa began, but it was Mutti who left my side and stepped forward.

'Gentlemen, our shop needs some reorganisation and we've taken the opportunity to have a good clean up.' This was not true; the shop was always in pristine order. 'We've been working in here all day, and just this afternoon I damaged the posters when cleaning the windows.'

'Perhaps you can deliver another set tomorrow?' Frau Graaf asked.

'We agree, don't we, Jacob? The black market cannot be supported.' Mutti's smile was stiff and didn't reach her eyes, which were fixed firmly on Papa.

'Yes,' he said. 'Deliver us another set tomorrow. Now we must get on with our tasks.' Papa opened the door and gestured towards the footpath.

'Not so fast,' the older officer said. He picked up one of the torn and crumpled posters Frau Graaf had thrown in a corner.

My legs would no longer hold me up and I sank to my knees out of sight behind the counter.

'We require cigars,' the officer said. 'Some of those nice Dutch ones. We will take a pack each and a bottle of wine.'

'We have neither,' Papa said truthfully. 'Supplies are slim.'

The air in the room changed and time stretched in silence. I buried my head in my hands.

'I have something set aside,' Mutti said, 'for special occasions.' She disappeared to the back of the shop, gesturing at me to get to my feet as she passed by.

I pulled myself up, gripping the sides of the counter as Mutti returned with a bottle of Cognac and a long thin box.

She held them out to the officers.

'Ah, this will do very nicely,' the younger officer said, touching his hat.

'Very good.' Papa's voice was clipped. 'Now we must get back to work.'

'We will see you tomorrow with more posters,' the older officer said. 'Be sure not to damage those.'

They left and Papa locked the door, turning his clenched face towards us. We all exhaled and I burst into tears.

Mutti wrapped her arms around me until my sobbing subsided.

'Hush now,' she said. 'It's all right.'

Frau Graaf kissed the top of my head, farewelled my parents and closed the door quietly as she left.

That night, as I lay in bed trying to sleep, I couldn't get the officers out of my mind. The situation sparked all the familiar anxieties that used to rise up when Fritz first began his eager stalking. He had a sixth sense for me. I might have been cycling home from school, on my way to music lessons at Frau Graaf's, running errands for Mutti or playing with my friends, but Fritz would always find me. I seemed to become the focus of his determined attention.

Fritz was placid enough the first time we met. I was shocked when Papa allowed Herr Winkler to bring his furry friend into the shop one Saturday morning. Perhaps mistaking my quick intake of breath for delighted interest, rather than the trepidation it expressed, Herr Winkler led Fritz to where I stood behind the counter.

'He's been with me since he was a pup, haven't you, boy?' Herr Winkler patted the dog's big head. 'Rescued him from a farm up north. Poor thing was harassed by the farmer's children and when finally, he bit one of them, he was tied up, crushing his voice box and leaving him with his odd, strangled bark.'

This story and Fritz's intelligent brown eyes stirred my sympathies, inspiring my trust, despite his gargantuan size. I fed him rye crackers from the pocket of my red gingham shop apron.

I began looking forward to Herr Winkler's Saturday morning shopping trips. While my father filled a string bag with bread and various packets from Herr Winkler's list, Fritz placed his big head in my lap, nuzzling my pocket in search for crackers. As Papa and Herr Winkler discussed the state of the world, Fritz followed me around the shop. He watched intently as I unpacked boxes and restocked shelves with dwindling supplies. Other times he lay with his head on his paws as I dusted the countertops, stepping over him, chattering away, sure he understood every word I said.

When it was time to go, Herr Winkler gave a short sharp whistle. In response, Fritz's ears shot up and he jumped to attention, sharing a quick parting nuzzle before he trotted away behind his master.

He was harmless within the shop walls, with Mutti, Papa and Herr Winkler nearby, but I soon learned he was a different animal out of doors.

One Sunday afternoon, while out bike riding through Vondelpark with Hetty and Double B, Fritz's poor strained bark could be heard in the near distance. Then the rest of him appeared. Streaking across the grass, he was making a beeline for me. I didn't like the determined tone in his bark or the fact that he trampled the flower beds, deaf to Herr Winkler's desperate commands to 'heel'.

My own animal instincts took over and urged me to do the only thing I could and so I took off, with Fritz right behind. Maybe I reminded him of the unkind farm children or maybe he really was a rogue and had turned, but whatever the reason, I wasn't about to stop till I made it home.

On reaching the safety of our building, I dropped from the bike, left it against the portico and took the front steps two at a time. Once safely inside with the door bolted, my hot tears began.

'Stop being a big baby.' Hetty's dismissal of me when she arrived a few minutes later, breathless and pink-cheeked, stung. 'Not even Double B cries like you.'

'What was I supposed to do?' I gulped back sobs. 'Stop and let him tear me to pieces? Anyway, he wasn't chasing you or Double B, was he? He was after me. It's like being hunted by a wolf.'

'A wolf? You're afraid of your own shadow sometimes,' Hetty said. 'You don't climb trees, suddenly you're scared of Fritz, you never talk to people you don't know, you never try new things and you're even afraid of the sea.'

'Stop it!' I interrupted. 'I'm not scared of my own shadow and I don't climb trees because I don't want to fall and break my neck. I bet you'd fear the sea too if you'd almost drowned. And you'd be afraid of Fritz if he came growling and running right at you.'

She smiled, shaking her glossy, dark head in a way that left me feeling even more like a nursery-school coward.

My cheeks flamed, but for the first time, I wasn't silent. 'You must be afraid of something? Worms, the dark, the forest at night, Krampus the Christmas devil?' I challenged her. If I could admit what frightened me, so could she. That's what friends did, so I pressed her to share.

'Nope – none of them. Well,' she spoke slowly, 'the idea of never being able to go outside again in the sunshine and the fresh air scares me,' she said, as serious as I'd ever heard her.

This was a very strange thing to say.

'How can you be afraid of ideas? Things like house spiders, moths, ghosts – and now Fritz, I can understand that. But not an idea.'

'Don't you think so? Or do you only worry about skinning your knees, putting holes in your stockings or being chased by Fritz?'

I didn't know what to say, but she had unlocked something inside.

'I'm scared of my parents not loving me, or leaving me, or dying,' I said. The idea made my throat hot and tight, so that I could only croak. 'That would be terrible.'

'I think so, too,' she said, looking down, and then in a lighter tone, 'but I am definitely not afraid of the water, or dogs – or boys.'

'I'm not scared of boys,' I said, fists clenched.

'Yes, you are! I have loads of boyfriends wanting to visit me or ride home with me.' She laughed. 'You can't talk to a boy without going as red as a beetroot.'

I pinched her arm because it was true. 'What about Willem – I don't blush when I talk to him, do I?'

'Oh, he's different. He's just one of us – you wouldn't want to hold his hand or have him kiss you on the cheek.'

My tears had dried. I washed my face and Hetty went home.

But from that day on, I was on high alert for Fritz whenever I was out in the streets. I began to take other winding routes home along the narrow streets and over the canals just to avoid my four-legged persecutor. These detours took me way off course, but meant that Fritz and I didn't cross paths on the streets.

Chapter 5

After school one afternoon, with a few hours left until dinner time, Hetty and I decided to sneak in to see a Laurel and Hardy film at the cinema without paying, as we sometimes did when *Rin Tin Tin* was showing.

I rushed home to tell Mutti I was going to Hetty's house, and she told her mother she was coming to mine. Hetty and I met Willem on the way to the cinema and he came with us, but it would be the last time we pulled this stunt and not because we were caught.

With each passing week, our freedom was reduced. It was a slow creep at first and each decree was met with, 'Oh, it's just another thing'.

That was until our city became a prison.

Jews were not allowed out after 8pm, or to even sit out in our own gardens in the evening because of the curfew.

Jews could not drive.

Jews had to shop only between the hours of 3pm and 5pm, and then only in shops defined as a 'Jewish shop'.

We had to wear these ugly yellow stars on our clothing.

There was no more cinema for us, no riding on the trams, no borrowing from the public library – the list went on as decree after decree came down.

For several days Mutti was under a self-imposed home detention. 'Surely,' she said, 'we cannot face people on the streets wearing these brands?'

It was easy to forget the star at first and people often rushed out of their homes without it. The Germans knew where everyone lived and who should be wearing a star. And, of course, we had to have our identification papers with us at all times.

When checks confirmed someone wasn't complying with the rules, there were punishments that included increased surveillance, fines, imprisonment and beatings.

'Don't forget your papers,' my parents reminded me and one another before each outing.

'Let me check your star,' Mutti would say after I once tried to hide it under a scarf.

Signs went up around apartment buildings and in private homes with reminders not to leave without the star being displayed on clothing.

I was scolded one afternoon by a German officer for having my star pinned to my coat, rather than sewn on. I much preferred pins as it meant I could still wear all my favourite clothes simply by transferring the stupid star from outfit to outfit.

At first, Hetty and I would walk down the street

with our eyes downcast. It was too shameful to meet anyone's gaze.

But one afternoon, a Dutch man tipped his hat as we walked by, acknowledging us with a sympathetic smile and the words, 'Lovely day for a walk, ladies,' even though there were Germans on the opposite side of the street.

Hetty and I straightened up and walked on. Further along the street, a woman coming out of a shop dipped her chin and smiled instead of ignoring us.

These subtle but powerful gestures became common across the city, but then even these small acts of humanity were disallowed by the occupiers. The face of the city changed as posters went up in public places, shops and restaurants: 'No Jews', 'Forbidden for Jews' and so on.

All Jewish news services were closed down right after Occupation, but Dutch newspapers and news services updated citizens daily with each new decree. And the city's mood was an odd mix of fear and defiance, depending on who you were, or how you looked at life.

In 1941, I had to leave mainstream school and attend a Jewish school. At least I had Hetty with me, but no Willem. Our school was set up by the local Jewish Council and in many ways, once we settled in, Hetty and I agreed that we were rather better off than many of our Dutch friends.

Because Jewish teachers hadn't been allowed to work in mainstream schools for a long time, our teachers were all fresh and eager. We didn't have to witness daily playground skirmishes between Nazi sympathisers and Jewish students, and there wasn't a shred of Nazi propaganda.

'Oh boy, you've got it good,' Willem declared one afternoon as we rode home in a pack. Hetty and I had agreed to meet our Dutch friend on a corner. 'Every single day we have to do physical activity and these sorts of military drills. Then we all have to salute Hitler, and compulsory reading is this Nazi pamphlet.' He rolled his eyes. 'My mother is fuming. "It's propaganda – using our schools to further their cause", she says.'

'She's not wrong, though,' Hetty said. 'We don't have to put up with any of that, do we?'

'No. We get to learn about Jewish history and culture and we even do cooking – as well as the other boring things like maths and grammar.'

'And it just seems a lot calmer, don't you think?' Hetty tilted her head.

I agreed that our school days seemed to pass harmoniously in comparison with the final months in our mainstream school.

'Wish I could say the same,' Willem said. 'There are still arguments about the rights and wrongs of banning Jewish students. There was a huge brawl the other day after our teacher made us go through all the textbooks and rip out pages that had been scribbled with anti-Nazi slogans and cartoons of Hitler.'

Hetty laughed. 'One of those would have been my history book.'

'Which reminds me,' I said, 'the Leidens are collecting for the orphans. I'm going to deliver some of my old books. See you at my place after, Hetty. I won't be long.'

I farewelled my friends and steered towards the Leiden house.

I hadn't been riding more than a few minutes when Fritz rounded a corner up ahead, barking his husky, throttled yelp. Dread hit me in the face like a bucket of ice. And with the dog nipping at my ankles, yet another terror-filled chase began.

I threaded my way through laneways, skidded across cobbles and raced along embankments. Finally, no longer able to hear him, I slowed and looked back. He was nowhere to be seen. Relief. I had managed to lose him, so I rode on more sedately, yet still on alert.

What would Hetty do? The bike bounced across the cobbles. Hetty always had a plan in a dire situation. I couldn't keep running from him forever. But as I cycled on, rounding a bend on Roerstraat, I cursed to myself, for there he was, up ahead on the corner.

My heart hammered and I stopped dead, jumped

off the bike and headed for the safety of Herr Vandervegt's stationery shop. Fritz was closing the gap between us and all of a sudden it was as if the ground had turned to liquid sand because I couldn't lift my feet, and all I saw were his big white teeth and his gaping mouth.

Eyes shut tight, I saw myself being torn to shreds. My poor parents stood crying at my grave and Hetty, beside them, looking guilty, no doubt for making fun of me. She should have taken my fears more seriously.

And then – nothing.

Opening one eye and then another, there he was – Fritz sitting back on his haunches, panting and looking deep into my eyes. He sat forward and nuzzled my pocket. He cocked his head, whined, and nuzzled again.

'He wants crackers, you fool!' I said out loud, flooded with relief. He hadn't wanted to attack and devour me after all.

'I don't have anything for you, Fritz.' I nervously patted his big head. It was then I noticed the German officer at his station on the opposite side of the street. He nodded at me and called out, 'I told you he wouldn't hurt you!'

Hetty came tearing down the road on her bike. Some degree of satisfaction slotted itself into the space between my old terror and new sense of liberation, as I noted the worry around her mouth.

She had gone to my place and waited for me to arrive home from my detour.

'Are you all right? I waited and waited and your mother sent me to look for you. I don't think she's very pleased with you.'

She looked down at Fritz and let her hand rest on his back. 'See? I told you there was no need to be a baby about him. Really, you need to show more nerve sometimes.'

Encounters with Fritz after this moment were entirely different and became occasions that I increasingly looked forward to – especially his visits to the shop where I made sure I had a cache of treats ready for him. He was a bright spot in my existence.

For a while, it looked like my parents would be forced to sell their business. Fortunately, some Dutch-German friends took it over and they stayed open, for a while at least. Nevertheless, my parents' faces took on a tight-lipped appearance and we had regular visits to the shop from the Germans, who helped themselves to the diminishing stocks.

But their anxiety turned to undisguised fear the day Hetty's older sister was called up to register for work in a munitions labour camp to support the German war effort.

After this came hushed, late-night conversations between Mutti and Papa. The Germans began to linger around our shop and the businesses of other Jews. They followed us through the streets and, like a wolf pack, they watched and waited. Mutti was jumpy and teary, and no one would give a straight answer to my questions about what and why all this was happening to us. What had we done and when would it end?

'There is no sense to any of it,' was all Papa said, looking over the top of my head.

I was upset and angry that he couldn't manage anything more reassuring than this.

Fewer customers, even many of the regulars, were crossing the threshold of the shop. Long-standing orders were cancelled and those that did still shop with us were buying one or two items and leaving quickly. It was as though they might catch some terrible disease were they to linger too long, engage in the usual chit-chat over the counter or purchase anything more than the basics.

Herr Winkler stopped by one day to show Papa a leaflet that had been distributed. 'Don't buy from Jews'.

After dinner that evening, Papa threw the leaflet on the centre of the small round dining table, the low hanging light shade casting the rest of the room into shadow.

As we fixated on the piece of paper, the only sound was Papa's laboured breathing and the ticking grandfather clock in the hallway.

'We will have to close. There's nothing for it,' he said.

I hated seeing him upset and tried to be reassuring.

'It's only words, Papa. Remember you said that words can't hurt you.'

'Well, I was wrong. The Nazis are using words and hateful lies to hurt us.' He leaned over me with dark eyes. 'The Germans hate us. Hitler hates us. This so-called Führer says we are the cursed race and the cause of all the world's misfortune.'

Hitler was a mad man – that much was clear even to me for I had eavesdropped on enough adult conversations in the shop.

'He says Germans are the superior race and the line must be kept pure at all costs.'

'He is setting up breeding programs, can you believe?'

'He says that Jews want to take over the world.'

'He says that all Jewish children should be sterilised and not allowed to reproduce.'

'I read that the Germans are planning to take over England by coming through the Netherlands. That's their plan.'

'I read there are plots inside his own party to kill him off. I hope they succeed. He has to be half-mad.'

But I had thought they meant he was an annoying zealot, a bit like scary old Jorgesson who used to stalk the canals warning that anyone who did not repent their sins would 'burn in the fiery furnace'. I thought it wouldn't be long before people woke up to it and put him in a hospital, like what happened in the end to Jorgesson.

'You think things are bad now?' Papa said. 'You think that posters of Hitler in your classroom, having to wear these bloody stars and the streets overrun with Germans is as bad as things will get?'

I had never seen my father like this before. He paced across the patterned rug as the words flowed freely, his footfalls so heavy, the glass-beaded fringe on Mutti's table lamp bounced and jangled and the candles in their brass holders quivered.

'Sit, Jacob, please.' Mutti gestured toward his favourite armchair, the leather seat and armrests soft and thinning from years of wear.

'How wrong we've all been,' he went on as though he'd not heard. 'There is no escaping them. We could flee to the furthest corner of the world and they will find us.'

'Hush.' Mutti placed a soothing hand on his arm as he passed, but he brushed her off.

I was alarmed that Papa was somehow drifting away, like a canal boat that had broken its mooring.

'The Steins have relatives in America,' he said. 'They say they are hearing of Nazi experiments on babies – abominable stories of families being taken at night, old women and men being beaten, family treasures destroyed or stolen. Hitler is stampeding across Europe leaving ghosts in his wake – in bedrooms, dining rooms, boardrooms, in gardens, hospitals, shops, banks and schools, in nurseries, kindergartens and universities.

'Nowhere is safe.' His eyes shone. 'The Nazi blackness is creeping. They are not only going after Jews. They go after their political opponents, Catholics, gypsies, anyone with a disability – in fact, anyone different is transported like cattle to camps, where they are starved and tortured.'

'Stop, Jacob! That's enough.' Mutti's hands played with the pearls at her throat. 'You're scaring her.'

But there was no stopping him.

'It is time she realises how bad things are.' Papa's face was red with anger, his thin-rimmed glasses slipping down his nose. 'If this news is what is coming out, just imagine what we don't know?'

He sat across the table from me. 'Wake up. This will not disappear.' He spoke more evenly. 'You must not put yourself in their path. Do you understand me? Do you understand why it's more than words? It's why people aren't coming to the shop – they are afraid, and they have every right to be.'

'Yes, Papa.' My voice sounded thin.

The following morning, after a restless sleep, I shuffled into the shop. I found the familiarity of the space with its shelves, boxes and advertising signs of everyday, mundane household items comforting.

The tinkle of the bell on the door signalled someone's arrival.

It was Ilse Graaf.

She insisted I call her Ilse, but I used to call her Frau Graaf. She was my violin teacher and our favourite customer. She came to the shop every other day, often with a treat tucked in her pocket for me – a coin, a polished river pebble or a homemade toffee.

I had not seen her since the day Papa took the German posters down from the shop windows, and as always, I was awed by her Aryan beauty.

German? Yes. A bigot? No. And one of our most steadfast customers.

Like me, she was also born in Koblenz but left her entire family behind to make her home in Amsterdam when she married her 'very own tall and handsome Prince Charming' Johannes in the spring of 1935.

Ilse's brother was a soldier in the German Wehrmacht. She told Mutti that he was pressuring her to return to Germany to care for their ageing parents. But she didn't. Lucky for me.

'How is Little Lena today?' she would ask. 'What have you been up to, Little Mouse?'

Once our family had caught the Germans' attention, a few of our neighbours moved away and others stopped saying hello on the street.

But not Ilse. While the shop was still open, she came in every other day as usual, her golden hair tucked under a stylish fedora.

She kept coming even after Papa had to start barricading the shop. At closing time, he covered the shop windows with boards. It stopped the windows being smashed, but not the vicious 'Don't buy from

Jews' and 'Jewish vermin' slogans and posters from being put up overnight.

After a while, he gave up trying to stop me and Mutti from seeing the dirty words.

As Frau Graaf rushed through the shop door, a gust of wind blew some dry leaves in behind her.

'So sorry to be last minute. And I've made a mess.' She stooped to pick up the leaves but Mutti scolded her and swept them aside with an old broom.

'I'll be quick,' she said. 'I don't want to get you in strife for trading after hours. I just need a few things on the list here.' She handed it to Papa who disappeared behind the counter to retrieve her order.

'How are you today, Little Lena? All well at school I hope?'

I nodded and smiled.

She picked up a packet of gingerbread and placed it in her basket. 'I love gingerbread, don't you?' she asked.

'Not as much as chocolate,' I said.

'What about marzipan?'

I screwed up my nose.

'What do you like?' she asked. 'Do you like pancakes and hot cocoa?'

'Oh yes.' I nodded and reeled off all my culinary likes and dislikes as she paid close attention.

Papa handed her basket back and after a cheery farewell, she left.

Just as Herr and Frau Casler told Hetty, my parents insisted it was now best that I go straight home from school and not dawdle on the street with Double B and our old school choir friends. Not even if Fritz was with us, which often, he was these days, unlike Adelena, who was more elusive than ever and who made unexpected appearances only when it suited her.

After school one day, and with my parents on one of their increasingly common 'important errands', I went back to Hetty's. Double B tagged along as usual and Willem joined us, while Fritz left the group at the front steps.

We ran upstairs, dumped our school satchels in the dark hall, drank lemonade and mooched around, speaking of nothing important.

The Caslers' apartment and living room were decorated in a similar style to ours with curtained windows facing the street. Framed family photos hung on the walls, a radiator sat under the waist-high windowsills and a handsome old mantel clock sat atop Frau Casler's china cabinet.

Between a pair of sturdy armchairs, Herr Casler's bureau was piled high with local newspapers and cuttings from English newspapers sent by relatives and friends living overseas.

I walked across the plush Persian carpet to one of the three tall living room windows to see if Fritz was still waiting downstairs in the street. Unlatching the lock, I pushed one window open and leaned on the sill. Hetty joined me and we stood a few moments watching people pass below on the footpath.

Someone in one of the nearby apartments sang along to the radio and we could hear the shouts of our Dutch schoolmates playing in the park across the street.

On the other side of the square, a truck had broken down and the driver was revving the engine to try to get it going again, carrying the smell of diesel through the window.

'Close the window will you, Hetty?' her mother asked.

'In a moment.' Hetty turned to us. 'Ha. I know what we can do.'

She came up with one of her ideas for a game. We each took it in turns to call out silly things in funny voices, and then ducked away as confused pedestrians looked up from the pavement below.

We were in hysterics, crouching down on the floor, hiding just below the window line.

'What are you all up to?' Frau Casler called from her sewing room at the end of the hall.

'Nothing, Mummy. Willem's showing us how he can burp the alphabet.'

'Hetty – you're an idiot.' Willem laughed. 'But a funny idiot.'

I didn't want to be left out and was struck by my own bright idea.

'Where are you going?' Hetty asked as I ran to the kitchen.

'You'll see – I've got the best plan.'

I returned with a water basin so full that it sloshed all over the floor, splashing Double B's shoes.

'Careful of the carpet,' Hetty scolded. 'It's me who'll be told off – not you.' But she was already opening the window wide. Staggering under the swilling weight of the basin, I corkscrewed my way towards the opening.

'Stop!' Willem shouted, a new edge to his voice. 'Are you two crazy? Both of you – stop, don't. You can't do that.'

'Don't be such a goodie-goodie,' Hetty said. 'It's just for a laugh. A bit of fun – won't hurt anyone.'

'Lena,' Double B said. 'My new shoes – be careful. Mutti will be angry. I'll tell her it was you.'

Hetty helped me hoist the basin to the windowsill. We were weak with laughter and screeched as we upended it, sending an icy waterfall to the pavement – and all over the head and shoulders of a German patrol officer.

Willem was white-faced, but Hetty, Double B and I thought this was hilarious.

'Again?' I asked, once I had my breath back. But before anyone could answer, there was a knocking – no, a pounding – on Hetty's front door.

We four froze as the fist hammering the front door continued.

Frau Casler entered the room, a frown between her brows and her tape measure slung over one shoulder.

We watched her back as she disappeared down a set of steep stairs to answer and moments later was followed up by a tall German officer, his shoulders sodden and his high peaked crusher hat under his arm.

Double B burst into tears and wet herself at the sight of him.

I didn't cry at first but had to catch myself from falling as my knees buckled. I flattened myself against the china cabinet, making the glassware inside clink. For a moment I even considered crawling inside.

'What have you all been doing?' Frau Casler demanded.

'It was just a bit of fun,' Hetty said, so pale she looked sick.

Double B was hysterical and pressed her wet face into the heavy material of my skirt.

'We didn't mean anything . . .' I was also sobbing. 'The water was my idea.'

Willem, Hetty and I had all discussed the various snatches of adult conversations we'd overheard and put together whenever we met. Stories that in some parts of the city, Jews were being forced into ghettos, others herded into cattle trucks and sent to camps, where they were made to work and were being starved and beaten.

'Ha, silly girl, your time has come.' I couldn't silence Adelena's voice in my head. 'Really, what were you thinking? He won't even give you time to pack a bag or say goodbye to your parents.'

'*Ruhe, bitte*!' The German's voice cut through the chaos and bounced off the walls of the confined foyer. 'I said, quiet!'

Convinced he was going to drag us away right then and there, Hetty, Willem and I could only stare at one another.

Frau Casler's bird-like bones were visible as her hand gripped the stair post. She stood in front of the towering German. He peered over her shoulder and inside to where our four terrified faces stared back.

'Ah, so these are the culprits,' he said, one eyebrow higher than the other.

'Culprits?' Frau Casler could not disguise the tremor in her voice.

'Can I suggest that you keep a closer watch on the children?'

Was that a smirk on his face?

He retreated a step, turned his back and, spreading his arms, revealed the full extent of the drenching. A large dark water stain ran the length of his coat, like spreading blood.

I coughed hard to disguise the hysterical, frightened laugh building at the back of my throat.

'Please accept my apology. The children will be punished, let me assure you of that,' Frau Casler said.

'How old are they? Ten? Twelve?' he asked. 'I have a little sister who also likes to play tricks. I don't want to have to speak to you again – do you hear me?' he said over Frau Casler's head. 'You are lucky I convinced my fellow officers that I come up alone.'

We nodded and, as he returned his hat to his head, he touched his hand to the brim. A small and disarming courtesy. That was when I saw the thread hanging from his coat sleeve – it was the same officer. He had not yet had it fixed and I noted the seam was coming apart very slightly.

A bead of sweat ran down the centre of my back and I panted heavily, as though I'd run laps of the Vondelpark lake.

'Thank you,' I blurted as he walked away. 'Thank you so much. We won't do anything like that again.'

Hetty pinched my arm but I swiped her hand away as Frau Casler closed the door.

'What are you thanking him for?' Hetty asked.

'Well, he could just as easily have fined us or something,' I said.

'He could have done much worse.' Frau Casler sank into a chair and sobbed. 'Oh, much worse. Wait and see now. Because of this, they will be watching us even more than ever. They will see this as an attack on their dignity!'

Hetty was deathly pale. 'We didn't know they were going to walk under the window, did we? We can't have any fun anymore.'

'Don't argue,' Willem said under his breath.

Frau Casler rounded on her daughter. 'I wonder sometimes if you have lost your senses. What more do we have to do before you children understand that this is not a game?'

She rose from the chair and grabbed a bundle of newspapers from the bureau, thrusting them in our faces and sending clippings raining through the air. 'Look, read. There is a war – the Germans are advancing across Europe. There is no stopping them. Soldiers are fighting and dying – young men, not much older than you, slaughtered and blown up. Bombs are being dropped and ordinary people – just like us, like you – are dying in droves.'

I was used to seeing my parents upset and angry these days, but I had never seen Frau Casler anything but warm and composed. I could not take my eyes off her, not even to glance at my friends.

'Other countries are trying to stop that Hitler. England, Russia, Australia and France among them. The whole world is involved.'

She paused to catch her breath and looked around at our gaping faces before slumping down into an armchair. 'All our lives are under threat every minute of every day.' She lowered her voice. 'And what do you do, Hetty? You stick your hand into the wasp nest. You will have us all killed.'

Hetty sank to the floor and put her head on her mother's knee. 'I am sorry, Mutti,' was all she could say through her tears. 'Please don't be sad. Don't be angry.'

After this, things changed yet again, and we were all on an even tighter rein.

Hetty and I played it low key from then on. Absolutely no pranks, no fooling around in the street, nothing at all that would attract attention and definitely no straying from the new rules. That meant staying out of the library, no visits to the cinema and wearing our hated yellow '*Jood*' star visibly and correctly, sewn just below the left collarbone.

Nevertheless, despite all these efforts, my path soon crossed once again with the officer's.

Chapter 6

A week or so later, I was tasked with watching Double B for my aunty, yet another one who was off on some 'special errand' no one would elaborate on. Papa was out and poor Mutti had a terrible head cold and had to stay indoors. She gave me a package to take to the post office down the street. My instructions were to post the package and come right back.

As it was heading towards the evening hour, I pulled on my once favourite light-blue coat. I had loved that coat. It was ruined by an ugly yellow star stitched to the front.

I stood in front of the hall mirror and absent-mindedly draped my scarf over the badge. Before I had time to adjust it, Mutti spun me to face her and arranged the scarf so that it didn't hide the star.

'I can do it myself,' I said. 'Anyhow, how do they know if I'm supposed to be wearing one or not? Do I look that different from other girls my age? Other girls who aren't Jewish.'

'Don't talk back,' Mutti said. 'You know exactly why. You might get stopped and asked to show your papers. It happens all the time. Look what happened to Frida.'

Frida Klein was a local teenager. She stitched several stars to her coat. She said she thought they were not only pretty, but she was not ashamed of her Jewishness and would happily shout the fact from the rooftops. I admired this bravery and defiance. Naturally, the Germans did not. Angered by her outright insolence and open mockery, a patrol took her from her home. She was held for two days and so badly beaten that she was hospitalised.

'Her poor mother,' Mutti said.

'Her poor mother?' I asked. 'Don't you mean poor Frida?'

'Never mind,' Mutti said. 'Just make sure you are properly dressed. Double B, come here. Let me check you.'

Anyway, off I went with the package, Double B tagging behind. Fritz crossed the street on seeing us and together we made a happy little band. Shop street stands were being dismantled and carried indoors as shopkeepers closed up for the day. Only the fixed newspaper stand remained open for business, the little interior light casting a comforting glow into the chilly afternoon air.

I made sure I always had a small stash of broken crackers when I went out. I tossed one in the air for Fritz to catch. Double B was chattering away about a fairytale book she'd been given for her seventh birthday. It had enchanting coloured pictures printed on glossy paper. Even though I was nearly twelve, I still liked to think that fairies and fairyland existed just beyond the edge of our sight. That little flicker at the corner of your eye early in the morning, the tiny sounds heard while sitting out in the garden at dusk – fairies, I always told myself.

As directed by Mutti, we went straight to the post office and turned for home. Passing a public park on our return trip, Double B followed Adelena, who had been walking ahead on the other side of the road, towards one of the shaded walkways. They wanted to look for fairies.

'No, come on.' I tugged on Double B's coat collar. 'Remember what Mutti said? Post the parcel and come straight home.'

'Please, please, please. It's a perfect time – it's quiet and we have Fritz with us. Just five minutes?'

'Double B, you'll get us both into big trouble. Come on – pleeease.'

But she was already skipping away.

'I'll leave you here by yourself, then. Goodbye!'

My bluff failed and she kept walking away from me. She continued along the path, late afternoon sun hitting her fine light-brown hair. It reminded me of the delicately spun toffee sugar confections in the window of the French patisserie.

Fritz was shepherding us, so I decided five minutes

wouldn't hurt. And we might just see something.

I followed Double B into the park, which was by now more or less empty, except for a couple of cyclists making their way home and a young couple on a bench.

The smell of the recently laid flowerbeds rose up in the cooling evening air and overhead, starlings and swifts fussed as they nestled in the branches of the darkening tree canopy.

Dappled late light trembled across the path as a groundskeeper walked towards us pushing a barrow. Noting our yellow stars, he nodded and told us not to stay too long.

'We won't – just having a quick look for fairies,' I said, nodding towards Double B and rolling my eyes to indicate that such a babyish pursuit was beyond me.

We walked towards a small pond with Double B talking away about it being the ideal place for water sprites. Indeed, it was the perfect spot and, making ourselves as discreet as possible, we watched the tantalising sway of pond reeds for the glimmer of a wing or any hint of a slender arm.

We lost track of time and I only realised the fact when I saw two German patrol officers striding towards us. My spine stiffened and Double B grabbed my hand.

I squeezed it and whispered, 'You hush.'

'This time surely you've done it,' Adelena scoffed.

'Fairies? Really? What were you thinking? And now you're in another pickle.'

Fritz gave a warning growl and kept close.

I relaxed just a little on recognising one of the officers – the one with the coat and the grey eyes. Hot blood rushed to my cheeks. The other officer had a pointed nose and looked even younger than the officer we already knew.

'Ah – we meet again,' he said. A half smile spread over his face. 'Up to new mischief?'

My mouth immediately went dry and I couldn't speak.

'What are you doing?' the pointy-nosed officer demanded. 'Curfew is approaching.'

With my heart racing, I managed to croak that we'd been to the post office and my cousin wanted to stop to look for fairies.

'Puh – fairies? Stupid little Jews!' he said.

'Adler!' my grey-eyed officer said to his younger partner and then to us, 'you must get home immediately. Haven't you been in enough trouble already, or do you want us to take you home to your parents?'

'Wait one moment,' Adler interrupted. He pointed his nose right in my face. 'What did you post?'

'I don't know. Something for my mother,' I said.

'And where was it going?' Adler demanded. 'Who was it going to?'

'I have no idea,' I said, my voice trembling. 'I didn't even notice.'

My face was hot and I felt Double B nestle closer to my side, gripping my own damp hand in hers.

'Well then,' Adler sneered. 'What was the size of this parcel? Show me with your hands.'

I demonstrated the approximate size with shaking hands, telling them it was the size of a book.

'How much did it weigh?'

'I don't know,' I stammered. 'It wasn't very heavy at all.'

'Adler,' my officer interjected. 'We have to get back to the station.'

But Adler turned his attention to a terrified Double B.

'What about you?' He loomed over her and she burst into tears.

'I don't know, I don't know,' she howled.

'Liar,' Adler spat. 'Little lying pigs.' He reached for the collar of my coat and I jumped back.

Fritz growled long and low. He took a step forward, his teeth bared.

'Shut your dog up. Or I will.' Adler reached into his coat and withdrew his service revolver. 'I should save a couple spaces on the wagons, too. What do you think, Hass?'

I had never seen a gun before, and the terror must have been clear.

Hass, I repeated in my head. So that's his name. Officer Hass.

'Adler – enough,' Hass said. 'Put it away, or I'll report you. They're just children.'

'Jewish children. Jewish children who grow into Jewish adults. And report me? For what? Exterminating a couple of vermin?'

Double B was crying hard. I was about to do the same, ignoring Adelena's voice in my head urging courage and strength. Fritz continued to make threatening sounds and I had wonderful visions of him launching himself at Adler's throat.

Adler's revolver was still in his hand. He levelled it at Fritz. Whether he was going to shoot him or us, or just wanted to scare us, I will never know, but now I heard my own voice call loud and clear, 'What are you waiting for? Go! Run.'

I grabbed Double B's hand, yanked her off her feet and dragged her after me until she realised what was happening and began running, too. We headed back in the direction of the street, loyal Fritz keeping pace.

The two officers' raised voices died out as we raced away.

For the second time in recent months, I didn't know what my parents wanted to do more: punish or hug me on our return home.

We were peppered with questions. Why were you so long? Where have you been? You've been crying. What happened?

'Germans,' Double B gasped through her sobbing. 'They – they were going to shoot us.'

'Shush, Double B,' I said. 'Let me tell Mutti.'

My recount led to more tears, angry outbursts and even higher emotion. It was a repeat of what happened with Frau Casler after the water prank at Hetty's.

'They were going to shoot us, Tante Vera,' Double B repeated, finding her voice again and eliciting another moan from my mother.

'When will you understand?' Mutti demanded. 'Wars have no ethics, no compassion. People get trampled. Do we have to keep you locked up night and day?'

'Perhaps we do,' Papa said. 'Perhaps that's just what we have to do.'

'What?' I stamped my feet and at last it occurred to me. 'This' was a real thing – not like a living, breathing monster from my fairytale book.

My parents had shielded me from most of the news reports in the papers and on the radio. A lot of it was censored anyway. At home, from the safety of our heavily curtained sitting room, our radiogram picked up BBC World transmissions to get the 'real news' as my father said, but I'd heard enough talk on the streets and experienced enough changes in my own small life to know this wasn't some fantastical adventure like in the movies. This was real life. My real life.

I just hoped it would soon be over.

Later that night, after dinner, we sat around the radiogram as usual, Papa in his armchair and Mutti and I on the green velvet-covered sofa. I went to turn on my favourite jazz music program, but Mutti reached for my hand, moved it away from the dial and held it between her own.

Her fingertips were ice cold and I was struck by her pale skin and red-rimmed eyes.

Papa leaned forward in his seat and I asked, 'What's wrong? Is Oma sick?'

'No, it's not that, darling,' Mutti said, looking over my head at Papa, keeping hold of my hand.

'Things are getting more and more dangerous,' Papa said.

'Yes?' I said, as more of a question than a statement. 'I know.'

'We have to move away from here. There are too many threats,' he said.

From then it was as though the air had been sucked out of the room. Gasping, I snatched my hand away from Mutti. For a moment I was back at Zandvoort, the sand collapsing beneath my feet, the waves tossing me against the seabed, only now there was no one to pull me to my feet.

'There are many who have done the same and your mother and I have been planning for some time.'

'But where will we go? To Switzerland or America? For how long?' I was looking between my parents, trying hard to stifle my growing panic. It was as though a black hole had opened under my feet and I was being dragged towards it.

'Until the war ends,' Mutti said.

This was my fault. My fault for giving in to Double B the other day. My fault for being a baby too and looking for fairies in the park instead of coming straight home. My fault for putting us under the Germans' spotlight.

My questions tumbled into the deathly silent room. When are we going? How will we get there? Who else is coming with us? How long will it take?

'Look, it's best that we don't go into all the detail now,' Papa said.

'You don't trust me?' I cried. 'This is because of what happened in the park, isn't it? It's all my fault. Please, I won't do anything stupid like that again. I promise you.'

'No, little one.' Mutti reached for me, but I jumped away. 'It's nothing like that. It will be the best thing for all of us if we go away – if we hide. It won't be forever.'

'When are we going? You have to tell me – tomorrow? Next week?'

'It will be soon. That's all I can say,' Papa said, his voice flat. 'No one – absolutely no one – must know.'

For the first time, my parents were unable to offer any reassurance, any comfort or confidence.

Their lips were moving but the words were muffled. They were my parents but what they said made no sense to me. They were supposed to care for me, but couldn't they see every word tore away a piece of me?

Papa said leaving was the smart thing to do. The only thing to do, Mutti said. Herr Winkler had gone, leaving Fritz behind with local Dutch friends. The Baumanns, the Kleins and the Habers had gone, too.

Gone where?

No one apparently knew.

And what if we didn't go?

Mutti started crying again and that was the end of that.

I wanted to go to Hetty's but it was far too late, so I went to my room and refused to come back out.

Throwing myself on the bed, I reached for my doll Lottie and, gazing into her glassy blue eyes, pulled the colourful blanket, knitted by my grandmother, over my legs. The comforting smell of Lottie's hair and weight of the blanket reminded me of home.

At least here in my rosy painted bedroom, surrounded by familiar belongings, the book of folktales on the nightstand, the French armoire, the floral-covered reading chair and small wooden drawing desk, I felt safe.

'Leave her,' Papa told Mutti on the other side of the door. 'If we are scared, Vera, imagine her thoughts. She will come to us when she's ready.'

I fell asleep in my clothes.

The next day – a Sunday in July 1942 – I ran to Hetty's apartment. I just had to see her. But no one answered. I peered through the narrow window beside the door, into the hallway and the sitting room beyond. It all looked the same. But there was an eerie stillness.

She had been there yesterday.

A neighbour, arriving home with a basket of shopping, said not to bother calling out. Her face was hard and her eyes cold. 'They've left.' And then to my uncomprehending stare, 'Gone. No one's there.'

'What?' My voice rang along the corridor.

'I saw Frau Casler late yesterday afternoon. I know I did because we exchanged a few words,' the neighbour said, her eyes softening at my distress. 'And then this morning someone from Herr Casler's office stopped by with some papers, but . . . as you see, empty. Someone from number ten said she heard from someone that the family had moved to Switzerland, or were on the way to England. They wouldn't be the first, you know.'

And with that, she disappeared behind her front door. The click of the lock made me feel desolate.

As I stood outside Hetty's abandoned apartment, the questions came in a rush. Gone? Hetty had gone? Why hadn't she said goodbye? When did she leave and when would she be back? How could she just vanish without a word?

It was too much to process.

My heart sank even further that evening when, after dinner, Mutti once again began to cry.

Papa gestured and I followed him into the sitting room, and I knew by his stillness that something was wrong. As Mutti trailed behind, I fixed my gaze on the face on the portrait of my fierce-looking grandmother and listened as my father explained that he and Mutti were both moving away until the war was over.

'Where are we going? America? Please say America,' I asked, playing with the collar of my dress. 'I didn't like the idea of moving away again, not at first, but now I think it would be exciting.'

Mutti was still crying and I tried to comfort her by telling her that really, I wasn't bothered by the idea anymore.

'Did Herr Casler tell you where they've gone?' I tried to sound upbeat. 'Hetty and I want to write to each other.'

'Lena,' Papa interrupted, placing both his hands on my shoulders. 'Stop and listen to me. Mutti and I are going together and we're leaving you behind – for safekeeping – here with Frau Graaf. You are our treasure, and we don't want to risk losing you. We can't risk that.'

In the few seconds it took for Papa to speak those words, something inside me changed forever.

For a moment I was still struggling to breathe. I watched the scene as if from above. Me, standing in the centre of the room in a plain dark blue dress and stockinged feet, my father kneeling before me and

Mutti, on the lounge, head in her hands, not even mopping at the tears making dark wet marks on the lap of her grey dress.

Gradually the room stopped turning. I was full of questions, angry protests and burning tears. Didn't they love me? Didn't they want me anymore? Didn't they care?

'But you can't just go off and leave me,' I pleaded. 'Don't do this – please. You can't be serious?'

'It is not forever – the war cannot go on forever. Remember that.' Mutti covered my face with broken-hearted kisses. I noticed how the small gold watch pinned to her dress rose and fell in time with her sobs.

'Papa and I will be together. Travelling is too risky these days and we want to keep you safe. You, our Sweet Baby Lena. Frau Graaf will take the best care of you. Please understand, we want to protect you.'

The discussion, my begging and recriminations went on well into the night and at the end of it all, Mutti tried to smile, and Papa embraced us both in a hug I never wanted to end. We all cried. There was nothing left to say.

Until this moment, I thought I knew the feeling of fear. It was being chased by a large Alsatian; it was being punished by my French teacher for barely passing a test; it was being dragged under by the sea.

I was wrong. Fear was not a thudding heart, racing mind or gripping panic. Fear was being told your parents are sending you away and they don't know when they will see you again. It was being punished for a crime you didn't even know you had committed.

My heart didn't race. It stopped altogether. My soul drained through the bottom of my feet, and I became so small that the wind may have picked me up and carried me away and I felt no one would even try to catch me.

Maybe this was how poor Adelena felt when I put her aside in favour of Hetty and my new Amsterdam friends. I wished I had paid her more attention and not been so careless. She might have had the words to help me make sense of all of this.

Mutti placed a hand on my shoulder. Her trembling fingers resounded deep inside, folding around my heart until it hurt.

Without a word, I was guided towards my bedroom, where Mutti perched on the edge of my bed and drew me to her. I wanted to climb inside her, never to be parted from her shelter and safety.

We wept and she hushed my protests. My head on her shoulder, I breathed in her scent as she buried her face in my hair.

Papa came to the doorway. 'It's time. We have to beat the curfew.'

I had no idea what I was supposed to take so, dropping to my knees, I reached for the small suitcase, the one I used for holidays.

'It's not there,' Papa said. 'It's already been

packed and delivered to Frau Graaf's house. All your favourite things, your books, your pencils and scrapbooks and your dolls.'

Mutti helped me into my coat and placed a hat on my head.

'Come, quickly, you two,' Papa said, holding the front door open.

I didn't even think to take any last looks or make a farewell to the house as I clung blindly to Mutti's hand and headed into the darkening, quiet street.

The throaty sound of car engines, the smell of woodsmoke from stove fires and yellow squares of light from the surrounding houses told of local families who were oblivious to our fight for life going about their nightly rituals.

The streetlights cast our bodies as small silent shadows as we hurried beneath their cold white haloes, our footfalls click-clacking on the pavement.

'Not so fast,' Papa said, as a patrol passed through a T-junction in the distance. 'We are merely on our way home if asked.'

'But Jacob, we are going in the opposite direction. What if they ask for our papers?'

I didn't want to hear any of this. It hadn't even occurred to me that we may not make it to Frau Graaf's.

'It's not far from here,' Papa said. 'Just keep going. One foot in front of the other. Act casual.'

The next few blocks were excruciating as

collectively we fought the urge to run the rest of the way to our destination. We tried to make small talk, as though heading home after taking some air, all hoping no one would notice our absolute terror.

Finally, there it was. Frau Graaf's home was in view. I wanted to break away and run. But at the same moment, the patrol we had seen earlier turned into the street ahead of us.

In an instant, Papa had dragged me into the open gate of a dark and silent house. Mutti followed and pushed me down behind a thick hedge, her hand around mine hot and shaking.

The patrol's engine grew louder and approached with a slow growl.

'What are you talking about?' a German said. 'You're seeing things again – too much schnapps.'

'Shut your mouth,' someone answered. 'It was around here. I'm sure I saw a group.'

The vehicle idled and a dog barked in the distance.

My throat was dry and swallowing was hard. Surely they would hear my heart pounding against my ribs.

I could just make out the whites of Papa's eyes in the gloom where the streetlights didn't reach. He put his hand over my mouth, a firm message not to make a sound.

Mutti had not let go of my hand.

'There's still ten minutes to curfew,' someone else said. 'So what if you did see anyone out walking?

They're probably inside now eating their kosher food and counting all their gold. Come on, let's keep going.'

'That's the attitude that will lose us the war,' the persistent one said, but moments later the vehicle drove on and soon the street was again silent.

Finally, I exhaled and Papa's hand on my mouth grew slack.

'We wait a few minutes longer.' He was barely audible.

In different circumstances, I would have looked on this as a game. In different circumstances, I would have been with Hetty, Willem, Double B and Fritz enjoying a summer evening game in the park.

But here I was crouched behind the fence of someone's home, waiting as the minutes ticked on for our fates to play out.

At last Papa deemed the silence meant it was safe to emerge back on to the street and walk the final few metres to the safety of Frau Graaf's tall and narrow house, its gable roof just a little higher than its neighbours.

The journey to this house had been both too fast and too slow, but there was a bittersweet sensation as we walked towards the front door.

Even before we knocked, Frau Graaf had opened the front door and ushered us inside.

'Welcome. Come in, please. This way,' she said, drawing us into her cosy *Küche*.

'I saw the patrol,' she said. 'I knew you must be

close. I've been watching from the window. My heart was in my mouth.'

'Ours too.' Mutti was still a little out of breath. 'Lucky for us there was an open gate and we just fell into it. The house seemed empty.'

'Ah, I know the place,' Frau Graaf said. 'That's Frau Achterberg's – she'll be at bowling. I hope you didn't trample her flowerbeds. She'll be complaining for weeks.'

'I'm sorry, we didn't intend –'

Frau Graaf interrupted Mutti with a smile and told her not to worry.

'As long as she has something to worry about, that woman is happy. Please sit.'

After everything that had gone on that evening, there was a warm comfort to be found in the *Küche* smelling of apples and cinnamon.

There was a tiled wood-fire stove in one corner, like the one at home, and a handsome sideboard along one wall. My parents and I sat on the bench seat that extended along the opposite wall, behind a long narrow table set with a small supper none of us had an appetite for.

'Well, we made it safely in the end and that's the main thing,' Papa said.

'Indeed, it is.' Frau Graaf's fingertips touched mine across the table and I quickly withdrew them, as though I'd plunged my hands into a fire.

Mutti leaned in heavily, almost slumping on the

tabletop. 'Thank you for what you are doing for us – for Lena. You know how grateful we are.'

'Yes, yes,' Papa said. 'I hope you never know what it's like to feel that there is no one who can help. Who wants to help.'

'Vera. Jacob.' She looked at my parents with soft eyes, a hand at the base of her long neck. 'Please, it's no trouble. We've discussed this and planned for months. As humans, we all have a duty to help one another where we can.'

So, they'd been discussing and planning for months and I had no idea. The fact stung.

I turned to my parents. 'Why didn't you tell me? Why didn't you prepare me at least?'

'Because,' Papa said, 'it was too much of a risk. No one can know.'

'And because until this afternoon we weren't even sure the plan would actually go ahead,' Mutti said, looking into her lap.

'Why? Why can't we be together?'

Frau Graaf came to sit by me, but I tried to move away. 'Go away. I don't want to be here. I don't want to stay here.'

A sound escaped from deep inside my mother. Shrill, yet guttural, deep and long. It was the sound of a breaking heart.

'Jacob,' she croaked. 'Maybe we –'

'Stop, Vera.' Papa brought his hand down. 'We've discussed this over and over and we have agreed.

Best we go before it gets any later.'

Sensing the discord between my parents, I asked Papa, 'Why don't you want me anymore?'

'Lena.' He raised his voice. 'I told you at home what the plan is. This is not forever. It's about keeping us all safe until this is over.'

He rose from his seat and gestured to Mutti to follow.

Frau Graaf, who had remained silent throughout, took my hand in a warm, firm grip and led me towards my parents.

Mutti held me so tight that it hurt my bad shoulder and at that moment I felt like I was drowning and flailing against something that was bigger and more powerful than me.

'See you soon. I know we will see you soon. You will be safer here with Frau Graaf.' I sensed she wanted to say so much more. I desperately wanted to hear more from her – something more reassuring, more cheering.

Then it was Papa's turn. His great big hands trembled, and his eyes were wet behind his wire-rimmed spectacles.

'Be brave, *meine Kleine*, and remember little one, this is not forever.'

'But where will you be? Where are you going? Please don't leave me, Papa. What have I done? Why can't I come with you, Mutti? I'm sorry I didn't come straight back after the post office. I'll eat all my vegetables from now on, no complaints. Don't you love me anymore? Please, please don't leave me.'

Mutti choked down a sob as Frau Graaf tried her best to comfort her with an arm around her shoulders.

'This is not a punishment. It is because we love you that we are doing this,' Papa said. 'Please try to understand and trust me when I say to you that it is for the best that we don't discuss the details.'

'What if something happens to you?' I asked.

'Nothing will happen. Please, darling, don't cry.'

'I will kill every German I see,' I said. 'I hate them for this.'

'Stop. Stop it,' he said. 'Please don't worry, my darling. I know you will be a good girl for Frau Graaf and do everything she asks of you.' He paused before inhaling long and deep and uttering the only words he could manage, '*Tot ziens*. See you later.'

I said nothing. Not a thing. I couldn't form a thought, let alone a word, as my parents and Frau Graaf exchanged hugs and hushed words.

But suddenly, I blurted, 'You don't love me – you can't love me, or you wouldn't be doing this. You just want to get rid of me.'

'Oh, Lena, stop!' Mutti begged. 'Jacob – must we leave her, really?'

But it was Frau Graaf who spoke. 'Come,' she said, in a tone that immediately said she was in charge. 'It's precisely because your parents love you that they're leaving you with me. You are like a big diamond that the royal family keep in a vault for safekeeping. They don't want to, but it's safer this way.'

She looked right into my eyes. 'You are big enough to understand what's going on and that the Nazis are taking people away to camps. This is a much better option, and it will mean your parents can move faster if necessary.'

'Yes.' Papa stepped forward and pulled his shoulders back. 'Of course, we can't bear to think of leaving you, but we will be back together – some time before too long, I am sure.'

Mutti and I clung to one another before Papa said, 'Vera, come. We must go.'

Then they were gone.

First Hetty, and then my parents.

My next thought was for Double B. But it was too late to ask. Without knowing where I was going, I ran to a room at the front of the house and tried to open the window to call after them.

'I need to tell them,' I cried out, pressing my hands against the glass. 'I need to get them back.'

Frau Graaf came after me and pulled me away. 'Let them go. You can't call out.'

'I didn't say goodbye properly. I didn't tell them I loved them, and what about Double B? She's going to be so lost without me.'

Guiding me back to the *Küche*, Frau Graaf said Double B and her parents had also gone to be somewhere safer. 'In Hiding' is what the adults all called it. Like it was a place.

She knelt so that her eyes were level with mine.

'I will love you as if you are my own little girl,' she said. 'As though I am the keeper of the Queen's diamonds.'

I burst into confused tears.

Arms around one another, we sat in silence until the hall clock chimed midnight, signalling the start of the first day of my new life . . . in hiding.

Chapter 7

I followed Frau Graaf up the stairs and into a small bedroom off a hallway. Its pale rose-coloured walls and heavy curtains reminded me of my own room and the familiarity only made me more confused and sad.

The wooden floor creaked and a small clock ticked out the time on the painted white bedside table.

The traditional box bed was enclosed on three sides and built into the wall. I had always wanted one of these cave-like beds. The heavy and overstuffed eiderdown was layered with the zig-zag striped blanket knitted by my grandmother. Lottie, known to all as my 'second favourite' doll because of her missing shoe and broken hand, lay on top of my nightdress in the middle of the bed.

'How did all this get here?' I stroked Lottie's blonde head, the smell of my own bedroom still in her hair.

'Your parents have been bringing everything, all these little bits and pieces, over the past few days,' Frau Graaf said.

With that, she opened the small pine cupboard and

there on padded hangers were some of my clothes – my blue winter coat with its hideous yellow star, two dresses, two skirts and a few blouses. Pullovers, a pair of long pants, wool stockings and underwear were neatly folded in the drawers which smelled of fresh pine needles.

Books and a box of new pencils were arranged on a small wooden desk in the corner.

'I hope you like it,' she said. 'I want you to like it here – as much as you can under the circumstances.'

'I want my parents. And if they don't come for me, I'll just go and find them myself.'

'Listen.' She plumped some cushions on a rickety reading chair and straightened a small watercolour on the wall. 'Don't you understand? This is your home now – this house and a few rooms in it. You will not be going to school anymore; you cannot go outside. No one, absolutely no one else but your parents and I, knows that you are here. If you are discovered, you will be sent to a camp. I'm sorry, but there is no other way to say it.'

A sickening, fluttery feeling enveloped me.

'You must be as quiet as possible, especially during the day,' she said. 'You must stay away from the windows and when anyone visits, you must immediately run down to the cellar. Come over here and let me show you.'

With that, she showed me a little hatch under the desk. I watched, intrigued, as she lifted the lid, revealing a set of steps leading down into the dark. I peered into the darkness, my skin prickling with curiosity and alarm.

'I'll show you more in the morning,' she said, and plonked down on my bed.

'How long will I be here?' I asked. 'A year?'

She reached for my hand and took it between her own. With a deep sigh, she drew me toward her and spoke in a gentle voice. 'It might be even longer.'

'I want my Mutti. I want my Papa.'

Frau Graaf pulled me closer, and I tried to wriggle away.

'Stop it,' she said. 'It's me – you know me. You know you can trust me.'

'But you're a German!' I twisted from her embrace. 'I don't want to be here for a night, or a day, or a week. I'm not staying here for a year. Take me to my parents.'

Overwhelmed by the same sense of panic that overtook me on that day Fritz first pursued me on my bicycle, I pulled my clammy hand from hers and fought the urge to drop to my knees.

'Look at me and listen.' She gave me a sharp look. 'Everything will be okay. We'll get along fine and soon all this will be over. Not all Germans are Nazis. Don't you ever forget, they also killed my husband.'

She put her arm around me again. 'Come now, this way to the bathroom.' Frau Graaf shepherded me along the hall. 'Wash your face and time for some sleep.'

I did not move. I did not speak. I could not utter a word.

I stood my ground in silence, twisting my hands and staring at my shoes. I could make a dash for the door and be down the stairs and into the street within a moment. I could open a window and call for help.

But the reality of my situation squashed any futile escape plans and suddenly I was exhausted.

I followed her to the bathroom and changed for bed, but while her back was turned, I peeked between the curtains and out into the street. I wondered where my parents were, where Hetty was. As I turned away, I caught a glimpse of Adelena standing under the streetlight. Her hair was covered by a red woollen cap, much like the one I had lost during my bike race through the streets during my escape from dear Fritz.

It seemed like such a long time since I had even thought of Adelena. The sight of her came as a surprise.

'You're going to have to work this out for yourself,' she mouthed when our eyes met. She turned and walked into the dark.

I wanted to call after her, tell her to come back and get me, but it was too late.

I pulled on my nightdress and Frau Graaf tucked me in, pressed the eiderdown under my chin, and kissed me on the cheek.

'I'm sorry for what I said, Frau Graaf,' I mumbled.

'I have forgotten it. But no more Frau Graaf. From this point, I'm Ilse. Okay?'

I burst into another deluge of tears. 'I want Mutti. Please, can't you get a message to her and ask her to come? I didn't even say goodbye properly. I couldn't say anything. I should have told them. I need them to know. They don't know I love them. I told them they wanted to get rid of me and didn't love me.'

'Oh, Little Lena.' She sighed and sat on the side of the bed. 'Believe me, they do know. They are your parents, and they know. Hush. We might be grown up and appear to be very old to you, but we do remember what it is like to be your age. They know.'

'But what if something happens to her and Papa? What if I never see them again? Why did they have to leave?'

'Move over a bit.' Ilse lay down on the bed next to me. 'Try to think of something good. You are here because your parents love you so very much. You are their princess – you know that. Leaving you was so hard for them, but sometimes you have to do what feels hard at the time if it means that in the end, it will be all right.'

She stroked my head and finally my tears dried.

Eventually, she moved to leave.

'Don't go. Stay a bit longer,' I said, my voice thick

with tiredness, and I felt her relax next to me once more.

The noisy clang of the Westertoren clock rang out as it struck one in the morning. Where were my parents laying their heads? And what about Hetty? I could only hope and pray they were safe, like everyone said they would be.

After a heavy, dreamless sleep, I woke the next morning to the confusion of being in an unfamiliar place. I had a tight, heavy feeling in the middle of my chest. I opened the curtains and looked out the window. The sun was not yet risen, and I squinted into the dark of the pre-dawn.

'No! Stop, Lena,' Ilse shouted. She had slept on the small daybed on the other side of the room. I jumped away from the window. Shocked tears stung my eyes.

'No, don't cry. I'm sorry,' she said. 'For now, you must stay away from the windows, remember? We spoke about it last night. No one can know you are here. I live alone. If anyone notices someone else inside, they'll start asking questions. If the German soldiers find you, we'll both be in terrible trouble.' Ilse faced me squarely. 'I don't want to scare you, but this is how it is for the moment.'

For someone who didn't want to scare me, she had me completely terrified.

After washing and dressing I went to the *Küche*

where Ilse, who had changed into a pretty pink house coat with a blue floral print, was making warm cocoa. She cut a large slice of buttered honey breakfast cake. I was ravenous and made short work of the dark rich and spicy slab and its comforting flavourful blend of honey, cloves, treacle, ginger and aniseed.

'You have a healthy appetite – that's a good sign you are not too sad.' She smiled, smoothing her hands over the front of the cotton coat.

'Oh, I just . . .' I stammered, my thoughts immediately turning to my parents. 'Mutti used to make this every week. I wonder what they are having for their breakfast.'

'I am sure they are also enjoying something hearty to start their day.' Ilse cut another slice. This one I only nibbled at before setting it aside. But she didn't scold me for wasting perfectly good food, like my parents would have.

'Remember what we said last night? It won't be like this forever,' she said, her face soft.

'Do you really think the war might go on another year?' I asked.

'I don't know. I wish I did.' Something dark passed behind Ilse's eyes and then she brightened, announcing she had something for me.

While she was reaching into a small box by the stove, I was told to close my eyes. 'Sit still and no peeking.'

I heard her moving across the *Küche*.

My breakfast cake sat like a brick and my stomach began to feel unsettled.

'She's German, you idiot.' Now it was Adelena that I heard, clear as day. 'It's a trap.'

I opened one eye.

'No peeking.' Ilse laughed. 'Just one more minute.'

It sounded as though she was struggling with something.

'All right – but please hurry,' I said, fighting the urge to open my eyes.

'Be patient. It will be worth it. Trust me.'

'What could be worth losing your head to an axe or a bullet between the eyes?' Adelena said. 'Good luck. I'd be running for the door.'

I shifted in my seat.

'There – all set,' Ilse said. 'Keep your eyes shut until I say.'

I squirmed.

She was standing right in front of me. I opened my eyes the tiniest bit and, through my lashes, saw her brown lace-up shoes.

Any moment, my rampant anxieties told me, any second, the cold axe blade will slice into the back of your neck.

I felt lightheaded and moved in my seat once more.

'Keep still. Put your hands out.'

'Please hurry.'

'One. Two,' she said, drawing out my anxiety so

much that I wanted to scream. 'Three. Open your eyes.'

My eyes snapped open as Ilse placed a small black twitchy bundle in my lap. A baby rabbit with a red satin ribbon tied around its neck!

'She is quite tame. She's yours. But she's a little wriggler. I had trouble getting that bow on her.'

I touched the rabbit's soft coat and her little triangle of a nose twitched.

'She's adorable,' I said, a little louder than I should, relieved that it was a rabbit in my lap and not my head. In an instant, the stone in my gut evaporated.

'Shhh.' Ilse put her hand to my mouth. 'Hush.'

I scooped the rabbit up. 'Sorry,' I whispered. 'She's beautiful and so small. What's her name?'

'You decide.' Ilse tensed her jaw. She darted to the window and peeped out through the curtains, fingers to her bottom lip as she checked the street.

'Beatrice,' I said. 'Very French and glamorous, don't you think?'

'Perfect.' She sounded relaxed. 'She is a very glamorous-looking little rabbit.'

The small ball of warm fur fitted neatly in the crook of my arm, her little nose twitching as her tiny heart raced.

'Quick! Follow me while the sun is still low.' She beckoned me to the outside door. 'Quiet. Come and see the garden.'

Given all the serious warnings about the need

to remain hidden and silent, this invitation was unexpected, and my ever-sly anxiety stirred once more. It pulsed through my veins, savage and ferocious, I could hear it throb and surge like it had the day I dumped the basin of water on the German below Hetty's window.

Noting my hesitation, Ilse lay a hand on my shoulder. 'I promise you it's okay. Put Beatrice back in the box for a moment. You have to trust me, as your parents have trusted me and as I also have placed my trust in you.'

She was right.

She had to trust me as much as I had to trust her. If not, we each could betray the other, mutual destruction guaranteed. Somehow, her plea for trust conjured an impression of my German officer: he was supposed to be my enemy and yet he had somehow been an ally.

I set Beatrice back in the box and tiptoed after Ilse.

'I thought you'd like to explore the garden a bit.' She whispered this so quietly, I wasn't quite sure what she was saying.

The rear plot was rather small. In the growing dawn light, I could see it was a secret world with walls on all sides and a canopy of tall trees overhead. I couldn't tell in the dawn-dark if there were any other buildings close by.

'Maybe now and again you can come and spend some time out here,' Ilse said, her voice low. 'But we will have to be very careful and you must never go outside on your own – do you understand?' She looked me straight in the eye. 'There will be times when I will have to leave you here alone, so you must promise me. You have had some lucky escapes lately. We cannot risk being discovered by being careless or forgetful. Understand?'

I nodded. Slow. Serious.

There was also a pond off to one side. I'd always wanted a garden with a pond. I was just able to make out the golden fish gliding beneath the surface. Three fat-bellied stone gnomes stood at the water's edge. One was smoking a pipe, another fished, while the third serenaded them on his squeezebox. I imagined that if there were any fairies in this garden, this is where they would meet. There was a low wooden bench nearby. The perfect spot, Double B would say, to sit and wait for them to come out and dance in the evenings.

This garden held secrets. I could feel it.

I picked up a pebble and threw it into the dark, still water. It made a delightful 'plop' as it swallowed the stone, making me giggle.

'Shh – remember, quiet as a mouse,' Ilse whispered. With the sun on the horizon and the pipits and robins beginning to stir in their nests, she guided me back indoors for a 'grand tour' of the house.

I was well familiar with the outside of the tall, narrow house with its jaunty, lopsided gable roof, but apart from the music tutorial room, its inside was an intriguing mystery.

Like many of these former merchants' houses, this one had been modified over the years and the floor plans were a higgledy-piggledy mess.

As we moved through the rooms, I began to get my bearings. The *Küche*, or kitchen, was located at the back, overlooking the garden. Next to this was the *Stube* – a small sitting room with chaotically stacked bookcases either side of the fireplace and a radiogram in the corner next to a blue-and-white patterned armchair. From there, via a short hall, was a small and neat music room where Ilse taught local children the violin.

Both the *Stube* and music room fronted the street and so, Ilse said, for the sake of normal appearances, the curtains in the front rooms must be opened and closed at the expected times.

She explained that she also took in laundry that she boiled in the cellar to supplement her income. 'But I'll tell you all about that later.'

A steep, narrow staircase led to the two first-floor bedrooms – Ilse's and the room that was mine – and the bathroom. Ilse's room was large and airy but must have once been even bigger, as part of it was partitioned to create a separate smaller nursery room.

None of these rooms' interiors could be seen from the street. Nevertheless, she said, I was never under any circumstances to go near the windows and should not use these rooms at all during the day – and especially on busy weekdays when the street was full of passing foot and vehicle traffic.

Though lovely and comfortable, these rooms that I could not enter at certain times, let alone was not supposed to leave, felt stifling, still and airless.

I tried to shake the feeling as we headed up another steep ladder-stair, this one leading to the attic room.

'This was my husband's room,' Ilse said. 'His study.'

It was cold up here now. A thin shaft of sunlight speared through the gable windows, but I imagined that it would have been a perfect spot to curl up and read, cloistered in the compactness, with the little stove going. The steep pitch of the roof meant it was only possible to stand upright in the centre of the space. There was a utilitarian metal desk. One wall was lined with low bookshelves filled with leather-bound books; the rich comforting smell reminiscent of my grandfather's study. Stacks of files and papers lay on the floor. An old-fashioned safe stood like a squat and unsmiling policeman against the tallest part of the opposite wall, and framed photos and a dried bunch of flowers were placed in a dusty vase on a small circular table. This was Ilse's wedding bouquet.

'He was a sentimental man.' She smiled, fingers brushing the paper-like petals.

I leaned in to smell the faded blush of dried roses. The faintest hint of fragrance still clung to the buds, transporting me to the busy flower markets Mutti and I so loved to visit.

A violent sneeze escaped me.

'Sorry!' I clapped a hand over my mouth. 'What was he like?'

'Johannes was a wonderful mix of whimsy and seriousness,' she said. 'I like to come here and sit, just to drink in the feel of him. His books, papers, the smell of his untidiness – it all makes me feel close to him.'

On the opposite side, two leather armchairs sat tucked under the pitched ceiling of the front wall.

I had been starting to think, in my own naive way, about romance. Hetty and I sometimes spoke about which boys at school we thought were the most handsome and who we would marry one day. While we both liked Willem, he was just a boy. Hetty said she wanted to marry someone who looked like Errol Flynn and danced like Fred Astaire. I wanted someone with Clark Gable's eyes and Heinz Rühmann's hair for my future husband.

We both looked forward to being swept off our feet one day and our husbands would support our careers – Hetty as a journalist or business owner, and me maybe as a musician. I still wasn't sure.

'Did he sweep you off your feet?' I asked. 'Mutti says Papa swept her away on a pink cloud.'

'Yes,' she said, grinning. 'I suppose he did. We eloped. My mother was very cross with me, but she got over it.'

'That's so romantic. What happened to him?'

'He died at the Waalhaven airfield, two years ago. May 10, 1940 – the day of the blitzkrieg. It was so fast and fierce; the airmen didn't stand a chance.'

'It must have been awful,' was all I could think to say – but I meant it.

'It was. I was expecting our baby and the doctors said it was bound to be the shock. The baby died – a little boy.'

I took her hand and kissed it.

'*Wunderbar*.' She laughed. 'We will be very happy, you and I.'

She closed the door, briefly leaning her head against the wood before descending the steps.

Next, standing in the narrow hall outside my room, Ilse told me to get down on my hands and knees.

I thought it very odd, but recalling my father's request to be obedient and our earlier conversations before going into the garden, I did as she asked.

'We – you – have to stay out of sight. Remember?'

'How can I forget when you remind me every five minutes?' I rolled my eyes and shook my head in good-natured disdain.

'That's the spirit.' She beamed, reading my confusion as I crouched on my hands and knees.

'Follow me, it will make sense – I want to show you a way down to the cellar.'

But mention of the cellar sent me into a mild panic. It made me think of my grandparents' cellar in Germany. Horst, the terrible boy next door, locked me in there one day. It was cold, pitch-black and smelt damp. He said an old Rumpelstiltskin-like character hid in there and would kidnap me if I didn't show Horst my underpants. Thankfully, my Oma overheard his threats, and she took to him with the carpet beater.

Cheered again by the image of Horst running down the street, clutching his carpet-beaten bottom, I followed Ilse and we slunk across the floor towards the hatch under the desk.

A solid-looking set of the narrowest steps I had ever seen – and I had seen plenty in my years in this city of tall narrow buildings – led straight down before being swallowed by the dark.

Ilse explained they led down, inside a space between the walls, from this level past the ground floor *Stube* and music room to the cellar. She and Johannes stumbled upon the secret ladder when they pulled up some original flooring that had rotted.

Johannes' great grand-mother, Beata, told him a little-known story that a network of secret tunnels lay under this and other nearby homes, but no trace had ever been discovered.

'I have often wondered if somehow the little secret tunnel in our house is connected to this old story,' she said as she stepped onto the first rung.

Inside the walls, it was just a rough grid of wood and old plaster and as we continued downwards, I asked Ilse if she thought the tale about the tunnels could be true.

'Who knows? Anything is possible,' she answered. 'But as it doesn't look to be very well known and there have never been any reports of their actual discovery. I suspect it was just an old lady telling a little boy a marvellous fairytale.'

We reached the cellar. Cold damp air hit my face right away, sucking the breath out of me.

'You stay there,' Ilse said. 'I'll get the light on.'

I heard her feeling her way along the walls in the thick dark. Soon a dull *click* was followed by a dim light which spread over a warren of small, separate storage spaces.

Whoever built this house in the late 1700s had been smart, for it was constructed over a spring, Ilse explained. In addition to giving running water, it also helped keep the cellar cool for food storage.

The low ceiling was arched and shelves built into the walls contained jars of jam, pickles and preserves. There was a barrel of potatoes and great washing vats filled with sheets and other laundry bags, stamped 'INFIRMARY'.

'These I will tackle later,' she said, a sigh escaping her.

'Already they have come in handy. The Germans have been looking at suitable local houses to accommodate troops. When they came here a few weeks ago, I explained these sheets came from the isolation ward and they soon turned on their heels. One thing they fear, nearly as much as a Jew, is infection.'

I scoffed at her distasteful comparison, glaring hard at her.

'I don't mean to offend, but you would be surprised. Some – not all – but some Germans have learned to see things differently, as have a few Dutch around here who, I'm sorry to say, sympathise with the Nazi view. It's opportunistic.'

I asked what she meant.

'People see that perhaps they can gain something by falling into line and ignoring their own feelings about things or overlooking what's right,' she said. 'They are the ones keeping the good jobs. Their businesses are doing well, and their bellies remain full. With some, it has surprised me, but others, it does not – like that busybody Frau Achterberg from down the street.'

Oddly, I noticed a disconnect between her words and expression. Ilse, rather than appearing repulsed, looked amused.

'Oh no – we don't like her either,' I said and screwed up my nose. 'She's nutty, *bekloppt.* Mutti says she's nothing but a viper and thinks she's better than everyone and she was very pleased when she stopped coming in as soon as the Germans arrived. No one wants anything to do with her.'

I paraded around the cellar in a parody of the hoity-toity Frau Achterberg, back ramrod straight and nose in the air.

'But Papa said he believes that people are acting out of fear. They just want to follow along, so they don't attract attention. Like Sussan Volder – she used to be my friend and then Liesel said I had a "big Jew nose" and she joined in and stopped being my friend.'

Ilse nodded. 'Your Papa is right. And may I say, you have a very nice nose.'

I smiled and curtsied, all mock refinement.

'Now, back to important things,' she said. 'Look here.'

I watched as she crouched beneath the lowest shelf and showed me how the back of the sturdy cabinet slid across to reveal another hatch in the floor. In turn, this also slid across to expose a snowhole – about the size of a fat man's coffin, I noted.

'Gosh, you would never know it was there,' I marvelled. 'And so why is it there?'

'Clever, isn't it?' We exchanged a grin at the ingenuity of the city's former inhabitants. 'I suppose it was for hiding important stores long ago or maybe family treasures.'

Suddenly she became serious. 'There will be times you will have to spend time down here and you may well have to hide out in this secret spot.'

Her directions were clear.

I was to make my way here either directly via the hatch in my bedroom or the less likely route, via an exterior entry under the *Küche*.

I was to head here if Ilse was out and someone came to the door.

Or if anyone broke into the house. My eyes widened at this prospect. But it was a real threat, she warned, as desperation on the streets increased.

I was to be noiseless during her violin tutorials and whenever anyone else was in the house. She would aim to keep social calls to a minimum, but for appearances' sake, some would be unavoidable.

She also had to keep to her usual routine to avoid arousing suspicions. Sunday mornings it was church, Wednesday evenings *kegel* – a social game of nine-pin bowling – and, of course, she would have to go shopping and on errands.

Ilse repeated yet again the outdoors was off limits to me, but that if she judged it safe, in time she would consider allowing me out into the garden under cover of darkness, for the sake of my health.

All these instructions had the effect of making the walls feel too close again. But I also appreciated the level of planning that had gone into taking me in. So there was a tinge of shame that I had thought she could be a spy, about to remove my head from my shoulders.

'You really drew the short straw with me, having to think of all these things.'

'Little Mouse, I have nothing left to lose and everything to gain in helping you and your family make it through this. I want this over as much as you do. I want you to be free again.'

At the end of this discussion, she handed me her little flashlight and made me practise getting up and down to the cellar and into my hidey-hole by myself. It felt like a game. Hiding was a challenge I rather enjoyed and completed without any fuss, apart from the annoying whisperings of Adelena who shadowed me through the gloom, telling me to be careful of the ghouls lurking in the dark and waiting to pounce.

I wanted to tell her to either go away and leave me in peace and to stop teasing, or to decide if she was going to be a real friend and reveal herself, but she had the annoying habit of slipping away whenever I turned in her direction.

Chapter 8

Eventually, the days settled into a routine. While I missed my parents and my old life terribly, I saw Ilse as my guardian – a real angel. I believed this was only short term and my life would soon return to normal. Until then, all this was an adventure.

We shared an early breakfast each day, after which I washed, climbed the steep stairs and sat with Ilse in Johannes' sun-filled attic study where we went over my school lessons.

My parents had thought of everything and made sure most of my school materials were delivered in the days before my arrival. This great consideration of my education meant there was no escape from sums, grammar or history.

We lunched together on soup, followed by a meat and vegetable dish and then, if there were no small chores to help with, I sat in my curtained room and made drawings at my desk or lay in the cocoon of my bed and read.

My favourite book remained the German illustrated classic *Max und Moritz*, cautionary tales of two naughty boys and their antics. They were devilish in their pranks, but I admired their pluck. They would annoy the community with tricks such as sawing through a footbridge, stealing roast chickens, putting gunpowder in their teacher's pipe and placing bugs in Uncle Fritz's bed. Naturally, as in all cautionary tales, the pair came to a bad finish and ended up in the local baker's grain grinder.

My new life wasn't ideal, but I didn't live in dread. It was a bearable existence, and I was ever hopeful that the war's end was just a few months away.

For the first few weeks, Ilse's outings were few and never more than an hour.

But once Ilse left me alone for more than a short while I was frozen with fear and crushed by the anxiety that I would be alone, truly alone, for the first time in my life.

I lay on my bed with Beatrice and drew its curtains around us. In this shell, I saw myself as sealed safely in a box within the box of my room, all packed within another box that was the house itself.

I was sure time began to slow, to stretch, as though Ilse had set her metronome to *Larghissimo* beat. It was excruciating to watch the clock hands move, as though through treacle, taking ever longer to circuit its cold white face.

I turned one way, then another. Lying on my back, I stretched my arms above my face, examining my blue veins and oval fingernails and the small spots the doctor had told my mother showed that I wasn't getting enough iron.

I listened to the small sounds of the house – the tick-tock beside my bed, water pipes contracting, the floors cracking, the birds chirping in the trees outside the windows I couldn't look out from. I could hear Dutch children in the street below, laughing and playing hopscotch or some other after-school game I couldn't join. Laying my hand over my heart, I felt its even rhythm and had to remind myself that I was lucky just to be breathing.

As August and September 1942 slipped past, I grew more comfortable being left to my own devices. I began to drift through the house as noiselessly as a shaft of light passing through a pane of glass. Often, I spoke to the framed photo of me with Mutti and Papa, telling them how I'd been passing my time. When Adelena was in a good mood, she listened to me read or we'd talk about the old times.

Sometimes Ilse returned from her outings with a small trolley cart, bundled with the heavy red-lettered 'INFIRMARY' linen bags.

She said people cleared the path for her as she approached, especially the German soldiers. This, she suspected, was due to the fear they would be contaminated in some way by the bags' contents, rather than as a courtesy.

'People see me coming and they cross the street,

or sidestep me,' she said. 'But good – I don't want to get involved talking mindless gossip with people. The less I gossip, the lower the risk to us. See?'

I did entirely, for there were plenty of times I had avoided people because I wasn't in the mood to talk. I told her it was an inventive plan.

I helped fill the great zinc vats in the cellar with water so that Ilse could boil the sheets and turn them with a sturdy wooden paddle. After washing, she lugged them up to the garden where they hung out in the sun. In cool weather, we strung up a line system in the warm *Küche*.

I enjoyed wash day. It was often a full five or so hours of filling vats, heating the water, washing, wringing, and hanging, then repeating the process. I liked helping and passing the hours in discussion or happy silence. Ilse assured me, despite other people's fears, there was little or no risk of falling ill by coming into contact with the bed linen, which was from the general wards and not from isolation, as she led others to believe.

'But sometimes it doesn't hurt to plant a few small seeds of half-truths,' she said to me as we worked side by side. 'It doesn't take long before they bloom and grow into great truth-choking weeds.'

Meddling Frau Achterberg, one of the city's greatest gossips, had been the first to query Ilse about the contents of the bags.

Ilse seemed to dismiss her as a harmless fool. I wasn't so sure and considered her a genuine threat. I would have to make sure to remind Ilse at every opportunity.

'Of course, she was very polite about it.' Ilse imitated busybody Frau Achterberg and her feigned interest in the young widow's wellbeing. 'I explained that in order to help make ends meet, I am supplementing my tuition from lessons by taking in washing that others were not inclined to deal with.'

'But you are not worried about catching some dreadful disease?' Frau Achterberg had asked. 'Surely, it's not safe?'

'I reassured her that contamination was highly unlikely, and she need not worry about me in the slightest – I gave a sickly cough for dramatic effect and then I grabbed at the collar of my blouse, as though it were too tight. You should have seen her face!'

Ilse demonstrated and we both fell about laughing.

'Shhh,' Ilse whispered, tucking her hair behind her ears. 'But it was very funny, I must say. She bid me good afternoon very quickly and our conversations in the street these days are blessedly short. I don't mind. Suits me well and good. I don't want her calling in here and poking around.'

'No. She might be a silly gossip, but Papa always says you can't trust people like her – they are often hiding something under the veneer, he says.'

'Your Papa is right.' Ilse smiled. 'I will remember that.'

'I wonder what they are doing now? Mutti and Papa I mean. I wonder where they are.'

'I'm sure that you think about that all the time, Little Mouse.' Her voice was soft and her eyes crinkled at the corners. 'I do as well. I'm sure that they are thinking of you at this very moment and that they are happy you are safe. They're probably planning a big party for when everyone's reunited.'

'Do you think so?'

'I'm sure of it.' She ruffled my hair. 'A party with cakes and ice-cream.'

'And a band and decorations.'

'Of course, that goes without saying. Come, we mustn't get distracted from our task.'

We filled the steaming water vat, washing, pummelling and scrubbing until our hands were pink and wrinkled and our brows damp from the effort.

Next, muscles straining, we fed the laundry through the mangle, taking it in turns to wind the handle as the two wooden rollers squeezed water from the tortured material.

Ilse took down the clean and dry items from the rope line that hung across the room. Between us, we folded sheets, towels and swabbing material. Ilse would often sing a folksong and I even liked to hum some of the traditional tunes I'd learned back in Jewish school.

Several sets of sheets were kept back in the cellar for display purposes should any unwanted visitors stop by.

These we deliberately stained with black tea and dark yellow nettle juice. They looked putrid, by all appearances, as though marked by foul and fetid infectious matter.

We needed to make up a few more for Ilse to place inside the laundry bags.

'This is a very clever trick,' I said, peeling beetroots for boiling, my hands stained a gruesome dark red. 'I would definitely think that these sheets were covered in something disgusting.'

'I will take that as a compliment.' She laughed and wiped some of the splashed juice from my cheeks.

'I'm sure that you could get work making sets in a theatre if you ever wanted to stop teaching music.'

'Hmm, I'll think about that. Which reminds me, I'll have to watch the time. Liesel is coming later – even though she's always late, it could be the one day she's on time or, Lord forbid, early! Once you've finished with the beets, set them aside and help me get these sheets in the vat. I've already added the nettles.'

We unfurled several snow-white sheets, flapping them out in the air. For a moment they floated in space like the sails of a great ship. But as soon as we pressed them beneath the surface of the vat, the nettle juice began to bleed into the threads, turning them a swampy green.

Our already overworked muscles protested as we lifted the soggy mess from the water, slapping it down on to a trestle. The next task was to rub tea leaves and coffee grounds into patches.

Starved of interaction from others of a similar age, I wanted to know as much as possible about Ilse's music students – Dutch children who had all the freedom in the world, it seemed to me.

The one who played most stutteringly was a gangly girl I knew from my old school named Brigitte, and the one who showed weekly improvement was Joep.

The student whose playing was truly joyful was Pim.

'He's your favourite, I think?' I teased Ilse.

'Oh, I can have no favourites.' She playfully flicked me with some water. 'But yes, he is a very good student. A real talent. I've known him since he was a little boy. His father worked in the cloth industry and his family moved to the street behind us here when Pim was just starting to walk.

'His big sisters coddled and fussed over him and he got all grumpy and tried to fight them off. He received a small violin from his grandparents one Christmas and that was it – he showed immediate empathy for the instrument. His mother predicts he will be a great maestro – and she may very well be right.'

I was intrigued by this boy Pim and quizzed Ilse for anything she could tell me about him.

'He's a pretty typical-looking Dutch boy, truth be told,' she teased, offering no other information.

'Go on, what else?' I poked at the vat.

'He is thirteen and has thick sandy-coloured hair.'

'His eyes? What colour?'

'Blue. No, green. Or perhaps you could call them hazel. I never know.'

'And how tall?'

'Tall for his age, though he used to be quite short as a toddler.'

'His complexion?'

'Tanned and freckled, with a few spots here and there.' She wiped her top lip with the back of her hand.

He sounded pretty much like any Dutch boy, indeed, like plenty of boys at my former school, but I knew from my eavesdropping upstairs that he had a pleasant mature tone to his voice and was well-mannered.

'As for Liesel.' Ilse rolled her eyes. 'She is so rude and never on time for her lessons, and always has an excuse for not having practised.'

'Liesel Doesburg. I was in her class at school – she was the same there too, with the excuses and bad time keeping.'

'It doesn't surprise me a bit.'

'Lazy Liesel, we called her. She's the one who made fun of my nose. Never has a smile or a kind word to say about anyone or anything. She lives a short walk from the school gates, but still she was often collected in a chauffeured car.'

Ilse raised her eyebrows and shook her head.

'Well, that's a reason not to like her, I suppose.'

'And despite her complete lack of talent, Liesel was often front and centre at school musical events and recitals,' I went on.

'That's unfair.'

'Even though Willem and I were a lot more harmonious – even Hetty – we were stuck to the side or back of the chorus. We could see the audience's faces, forced to sit through her torturous playing. I had to make sure I didn't make eye contact with Hetty or Willem for fear of collapsing in hysterics.'

'I think I was at that last concert and I did tell her parents that perhaps Liesel might try another instrument.' Ilse raised her eyebrows. 'They didn't agree. She is rather timid deep down.'

'That's hard to believe.'

'Her parents are very overbearing, I think.' Ilse emptied the water from the mangle tub into a drain in the floor. 'Her family, I'm sorry to say, is one of those who's been entertaining high-ranking Germans in their home and while many city residents are growing thin, her father grows increasingly prosperous. Her older sister is seeing a young officer, I believe. She has always been boy-crazy, that one. I tutored her just before the war and she was always chasing some boy or other.

'So, is this boy from school – Willem – is he your boyfriend then?' Ilse took a sidelong glance in my direction. 'Or is he Hetty's boyfriend?'

Hetty had lots of boyfriends – or 'boys who are friends', as she liked to say, I explained.

'He's definitely not her boyfriend as such,' I said. 'I do like Willem. He's got a good sense of humour, even though he's a bit of a bookworm too.'

Ilse smiled as I mused, adding, 'It sounds like you do like him quite a lot.'

There was no more time to continue with that particular discussion as the allotted time for Liesel's arrival approached.

'I must tidy myself up and get ready for Liesel,' Ilse said, checking her dainty wristwatch lying on the table.

'She's so lucky she can get to play – shame she's so awful,' I sulked.

'Later on, I promise, you can.' She guided me towards the ladder to my room.

I was grateful it was time for Ilse to tidy herself up before her lessons. Laundry work was long, hot and steamy.

'Good work today,' she spoke to my retreating back. 'I don't know that I have the energy for lessons to be honest. But on we go.'

I dragged my weary body up the ladder and to the bathroom where I tried to scrub the beetroot stains from my palms and the green gunk from under my raggedy nails.

Several minutes later and after almost scouring my hands raw, I secreted myself in my room where I happily threw my tired limbs on the bed. Not long after, the first strains of a violin began, signalling lessons had begun downstairs. I always knew in advance, of course, when Ilse's students were due. I retreated to my bedroom, or sometimes sat out of sight at the top of the stairs.

I missed my own violin playing and practising and Ilse sometimes allowed me to play her instrument in the evenings, mine not having come with me. We would go up to the attic, close the door and then make sure the roof windows were sealed. As I was not nearly as accomplished, we had to be mindful of being overheard in case someone – namely Frau Achterberg – noting the sudden poor standard of what she would have thought was Ilse's playing, came snooping.

I was never quite able to make out any conversation from where I sat in my room during the lessons, but I listened to each student as they arrived and he or she was shown through the hall and into the music room.

I looked forward to Pim's lessons and began to leave my bedroom door open just to listen.

I wished I could watch his bow glide over the strings.

There was a near disaster one afternoon when Beatrice hopped off my bed and raced out through the bedroom door.

His playing had lured me out of my room. I lay flat on my stomach on the stair landing. In my blissful state, I didn't notice the rabbit flip-flopping her way down towards the ground floor.

'Wake up, idiot.' Adelena's voice kicked me into action. 'The rabbit.'

I sparked into action and made a clumsy grab for Beatrice, but she was out of reach. I half-stumbled down several steps, making a terrible racket along the way as I made my failed grab.

The playing stopped, and I heard Ilse's voice as the music room door opened.

'It's all right, Pim,' she said. 'You keep going. I'll check. I put some potted herbs in the stairway window this morning. It sounds like they've fallen.'

The sweet strains started up again and a pale-faced Ilse strode into my room with Beatrice under her arm.

She put her fingers to her lips and I held my breath, gesticulating at Beatrice and trying to demonstrate that she'd gotten away from me and loped downstairs.

Without a word, Ilse frowned and left, closing the door noiselessly behind her.

'You are asking for trouble, aren't you?' Adelena

said. 'You're a careless brat. What if that boy had seen you?'

'Shut up, will you?' I snapped. 'I'm fed up with you being negative and sniping all the time. Leave me alone.'

Later that evening over our dinner of bread, cheese and sausage, I felt glum and silly.

'I am sorry, Ilse,' I said, before she had the chance to bring the matter up. 'I know I was careless. I lost track. His playing is so magical. I didn't even think of Beatrice.'

'It was careless,' she said, her eyebrows almost meeting in a frown before her tone softened a little. 'Look, I know it's hard for you. You are a healthy young girl. It must be terrible being cooped up and not being able to make a sound, not to be able to run around in the fresh air and be with other people. But it's dangerous to take risks.'

To emphasise her point, Ilse told me what she had heard about a Dutch law student on the other side of the city. 'It was just behind the Royal Palace.' She pointed vaguely towards the windows. 'He was dragged through the streets several days ago when four Jews were found huddled in a secret compartment in his attic.'

'That's terrible.'

'Someone informed. The student was executed, along with the four.'

My eyes widened and I looked at my feet.

'I only tell you this, Little Mouse, to impress upon you that this is not some kind of hide and seek game. You and I must remain on high alert at all times.'

I nodded and stroked Beatrice's silky ears. 'When will it be over? It must be over soon?'

She smoothed the front of her apron and sighed, shaking her head. 'I don't know.'

For the first time, I noticed the fine lines around her eyes were deepening and a few strands of her hair were greying at the temples.

'Music!' she said, removing her apron and placing it on a hook in the *Küche*. 'That's what we need.'

Following her into the living room, I turned on the table lamp, picked up a cushion from the lounge and took up a spot under the lamp's warm glow.

Searching through the static, Ilse tuned the radio to Radio Oranje just as the announcer began his report about a fearful battle raging in Stalingrad:

> Stalingrad has entered its thirtieth day of battle with Germans gaining control of somc streets of the Russian city at great cost. After ferocious fighting amongst the city's blazing ruins, German infantry, supported by one hundred tanks, pressed Soviet units back and succeeded in holding several streets. Heavy anti-aircraft artillery has kept German bombers high over the

> city but the damage they are inflicting is described in messages from Moscow as major.

As always, we sat in silence listening to the news. I could only picture the angry orange flames and streets in wreckage. Ilse leaned forward, fingers playing at the edges of her lips.

'Surely they must run out of bombs and bullets at some time?' I asked.

'Ha. They have big factories. And they are taking workers from all over Europe to make more and more weapons it seems.'

'I often wonder if our old house in Germany is still standing. We had a beautiful garden in such a pretty street. I hate to think it's been destroyed.'

'I suppose buildings and gardens can all be replaced, right? Memories can never be taken away, though. Always remember that.'

The Jazz Hour followed, and we set aside our worries while Ilse teased me about my crush on Pim and I asked her about the first boy she fell in love with. It was Hans Peters, once the best-looking boy in the school, she said, but who was now a thickset shopkeeper living in Berlin with thinning hair and a gold tooth.

Chapter 9

More than five months in hiding, and the days and weeks slipped towards Christmas and December 4, my thirteenth birthday. I had been on my best behaviour and on constant watch not to be noisy or ask too many questions Ilse couldn't answer.

I still longed to meet Pim and continued to lurk near the top of the stairway during his lessons. For that hour when he was in the house, I could be a beautiful lady with glossy hair, like the Hollywood star Veronica Lake, and he and I would dance and romance one another in the city's most glamorous cafés and restaurants.

On December 4, I opened my eyes to a grey and bitterly cold dawn. This came as a cruel contrast to the dream I had just been enjoying. In my dream, it was a Friday afternoon with evening closing in. Drawing the curtains on the outside world, Mutti and I prepared the house for *Shabbat*, setting the table with the best china and arranging fresh flowers, roses, snowdrops, poppies – whatever was in season. Mutti sang traditional songs and Papa and I made fun of her terrible voice. Intently, I watched her beautiful face as she lit the two candles signalling the start of *Shabbat*. I knew later we would gather as Papa recited a prayer over the braided loaf of sweet, eggy *challah* bread. Afterwards we sat together in cosy peace, Papa in his armchair puffing away on his tobacco pipe, its pungent but not unpleasant smoke filling the air. Mutti sat under the big lamp with some sewing and I spread out on the floor with my movie star magazines. My beloved Fritz, my bitterly missed four-legged friend, also crept into this dream and lay next to me, his chin flat on the floor.

A bird flew into my curtained window and startled me awake. Overwhelmed by stinging disappointment, I pushed my face into my pillow and whispered, 'Oh, Mutti, Papa, Fritz. Where are you? Please come back to me. Please.'

I traipsed down to the *Küche* where Beatrice met me, dressed up for the occasion in her red bow. Ilse had been up early to stoke the fire and guided me to the long bench seat, which was a clever contraption. The hinged seat lifted to reveal extra storage space where Ilse stowed old newspapers, wood for the stove and sacks of vegetables.

After I had taken my place, she proudly set an iced chocolate cake in front of me and it even had a few shards around the sides. She had been stockpiling the rationed ingredients for months. Grateful tears stung my eyes and I cried as much at the realisation of her effort and planning as I did for the missing of my parents on this day.

'No tears on your birthday – you are a young lady now. Happy birthday, Miss Lena.' Ilse hugged me tight and kissed my damp cheeks. 'I'm sorry. Just get up for a minute again.'

She opened the seat and brought out a bundle of prettily wrapped presents which she set down in front of me with a flourish.

All bound with ribbon, the tissue paper wrapping was printed with stripes, flowers and kittens. As always, I resisted the urge to tear the paper, carefully peeling the package open and setting it aside for later. From Ilse, a knitted sweater and a little leather purse.

Mutti and Papa had left a card with her to pass on all those months earlier and a small square box, tied with blue satin ribbon. Inside lay a fine silver bracelet and a pair of dainty enamelled earrings. There was also a brooch and a tin container of chocolates, a copy of *Tales and Legends of the Netherlands* and best of all, a camera obscura, like the one Hetty received for her birthday earlier that year. They had remembered!

I opened the card. 'Best Wishes on your Birthday' was printed on the front, and a colourful bunch of flowers underneath.

Knowing my parents had touched the note, I ran my fingers over Mutti's elegant, looped writing.

'To our darling daughter Lena on your thirteenth birthday,

We are sure this finds you well and happy. We will be together soon.

All our love,

Your proud and loving Papa and Mutti.'

I couldn't stop the tears. I still felt bad that I didn't say a proper goodbye and tell them I loved them.

'I've told you before, that's because you're a spoiled and self-centred brat who thinks only of herself.' Hearing Adelena's voice shocked me. I had not even thought of her once in recent weeks and pushed the idea of her to the back of my head again.

Once I had composed myself, I turned my gaze to the third package which, Ilse said, was from Pim.

This made no sense and I told her so.

Ilse said she had quizzed him about girls. I was amazed at her daring in even raising the topic with him.

'Ha! I have been teasing him about different things for years,' Ilse said. 'He is always complaining about his two older sisters. He says just about every member of the female race, as far as he's concerned, is silly, giddy and empty-headed – and that's a direct quote.'

I took the news as a personal insult and could only stare at the floor to hide my disappointment. I don't know what I had hoped to hear, but it wasn't this complete dismissal of the female race.

'I asked him about the girls at his school – but he

just blushed and shook his head.'

He told Ilse he did not have time for girls, but when he married it would be to a sensible and brave girl, who liked music as much as he did. He would buy her books and gramophone records and they would travel the world together.

'Someone like you, no?' Ilse grinned. 'So, this is the gift he would have given you if he knew you.'

I tore open the paper. It was a world atlas. 'So, you can start planning your travel routes,' a beaming Ilse added.

I reached up and threw my arms around her neck, feeling the lightest and most hopeful I had in a long time.

More's the pity it was a short-lived joy.

***

At the end of December, I was fossicking in the old scraps bin looking for some carrot tops for Beatrice and had to move some old newspapers aside.

There, amongst the pile, was a recent copy of an illegal Resistance newspaper.

'Mass Jewish executions' the headline blared. I froze and re-read the words over and over before being able to move on to the article reporting that a week before Christmas the British House of Commons had been told of mass executions of Jews by the Nazis in camps dotted around Europe. Men, women and children. Housewives, doctors, accountants, shop keepers, students, babies, the aged and infirmed. It was indiscriminate.

I sat, shaking and too numb to cry, on the floor of the pantry until Beatrice nuzzled at my knee. Scooping her up, I took the paper to where I knew Ilse was in the cellar with her laundry bags.

'Why didn't you tell me?' I asked, thrusting the paper under her nose.

'Because I didn't want to upset you.' She took the paper out of my hands. 'What is the point? It is hard enough as it is.'

Ilse said the sickening facts were greeted with widespread horror, not just across the city, but across the free-thinking world.

'In some good news at least, the underground radio reports that the Allies declared the crimes would be avenged. They are strong and powerful and they will redouble their efforts, I am sure. We must take heart in that.'

No wonder with this news coming out that the Germans had been confiscating citizens' radios. However, like many locals, she read articles on how to make a homemade set using a few basic materials and, ever resourceful, she managed to hook one up to her radiogram speakers.

I told Ilse I wanted the Allies to hurry and smash those Nazis to pieces.

Until the crackling confirmation over the radio one evening, I had not been fully aware of the extent of the attempts being made to exterminate all Jews. All because of our Jewishness. No more, no less. I had thought that many of the horror stories doing the rounds early in the war and many of my parents' tales and warnings were over-imagined, just to scare children like me into behaving. I was wrong.

Apart from several stolen moments with Ilse up in the attic, I had not even glimpsed the open sky in months, not felt the sun on my face, walked out in the streets, played in the park, or any of the other simple daily activities I'd previously taken for granted.

I missed Mutti and Papa so much that I could somehow feel it in the middle of my chest, like something heavy sitting there. I missed the smell of Papa's pipe, the comforting feel of my small hand in his. If only I could hear the sound of Mutti's voice, the way she sang me to sleep when I woke from a bad dream. Then there was Hetty, Double B, Willem and Fritz. I even missed the routine of going to school and having a purpose to my days.

For now, my only focus was to stay alive. That meant staying invisible and noiseless, extinct to the outside world. I had become less than a shadow, not even a silhouette. I was transparent.

It had been five months since I had spoken to anyone other than Ilse and Beatrice – but she was a rabbit and Adelena didn't count.

For weeks I had been speaking directly to Adelena in the mirror. I stared into her eyes, studying me intently above the washbasin.

'No one will ever want to marry you,' I said, cupping my hands and splashing water on my cheeks. 'You look awful.'

The water had saturated my blouse.

'Damn it.' I pulled the shirt roughly over my head, brushing my chest in the process. The pain made me flinch and my hands went straight up to the small budding mounds.

My chest was developing and would get awfully sore. Out of the blue, I would get angry or sad, but I put it down to my nerves. One evening I got the most terrible pains in my belly, which was blown up like a balloon. Doubled over, I managed to walk to the toilet and sat, only to be horrified by the sight of blood in my underpants.

Stifling a scream, I knew I was dying. I must have had a tumour or perhaps my appendix had burst.

I rushed to find Ilse and through my tears told her about the pain and the blood.

'You are growing into a woman, Lena, that is all,' she said.

That night after I bathed, Ilse showed me how to use the napkins to catch the blood. She brushed my hair and we had a good talk, nowhere near as awkward as it might have been with Mutti. Ilse also cleared up some of the schoolyard stories about how women get babies.

After the shock of the blood and the pain came

the realisation that my body was suddenly capable of carrying a new life.

'Why do I feel so sad?' I asked her as the brush ran through my hair.

'Well, it's a big thing,' Ilse said. 'It means that you're not a little girl anymore. Those days are over. Now you are a woman. I felt sad for a bit too when it happened to me. But try to look at it as something exciting and momentous, okay?'

I agreed, but couldn't shake the heaviness that overtook me as I climbed into bed that night. I slept badly and had vivid dreams of my parents, Willem, Double B and Hetty. We were sitting around our dining room table sharing a birthday cake, or they were all calling out for me from some dark place and I couldn't find them, or we were all on a train travelling to Switzerland and sharing lunch in a first-class dining car with Fritz.

I sat up, rubbing my eyes. It's only a dream, I told myself, reaching for the water on the nightstand before laying my head down again.

No sooner had I closed my eyes, I was riding my bike along the beach at Zandvoort. It was lovely and warm, the sand smooth and the riding easy. The sound of rolling glass-like surf was overlaid by the barking of a dog and I looked behind to see a great black beast gaining on me, but as I pedalled faster, the sand turned into a bog and the wheels barely turned. Looking for a way out, I faced the water – it had transformed into a dark green and pitching wash. I was trapped between the black beast and the tossing depths.

In a sweaty panic, I woke to the curtained reality of my box bed.

Chapter 10

A new year and January 1943 brought the news that the Americans had bombed Germany, followed a few days later with the Germans surrendering Stalingrad in Russia – surely the beginning of the end, we thought.

But the news Ilse managed to pick up here and there was mixed.

I had to work hard to fight the urge to get out of bed each day and tear open the curtains, throw open the windows and fill my lungs with fresh air. I wanted to run down the stairs when I knew Pim was in the house for his lessons. I wanted to sneak out of the house in the dead of night just to walk down the street. I longed to run through a field of grass, or climb a tree, or jump on a tram and trundle into the city centre. Sometimes, I stood back from the high attic window and watched people in the distant streets, including Adelena, who had started wearing a green beret, making her stand out among all the other drably dressed pedestrians. I knew she enjoyed taunting me with her freedom and I hated her for it.

I wanted to call out in a funny voice and then

duck away, the way Hetty, Willem, Double B and I had done. I wanted to do all the small, unimportant things I once enjoyed without a second thought.

The one thing that stopped me was consideration for Ilse's safety and wanting to be reunited with my family. One day soon, I kept hoping. Those thoughts and Adelena – the realist, the wet blanket, the sensible, grim one – kept me in hiding.

And to be truthful, I had little energy for silly pranks. Some days I wanted to do little else than lie on my bed. I often felt tired and heavy. This always happened before the blood came. I cried often and not always in secret. The tears crept up and spilled forth at random as I sat in the bath, read a book, or helped Ilse with the laundry.

Aware of my despair, dear Ilse – my one friend and the one without whom I would not survive – brought me magazines and the occasional black market chocolate bar.

During the day, when it was busy on the streets with people going about their business against the noisy din of traffic and trams, we would go down to the thick-walled cellar and Ilse and I played violin together. This hour of music became a happy relief and distraction.

After we had cleared away the evening meal one night – July eleventh, Hetty's birthday and a day I was feeling very low – we were preparing to play a card game, when Ilse told me unexpectedly to go and fetch my outside shoes.

Reading the questions on my face, she told me she had a surprise.

It had been almost a year since I had worn the outdoor shoes and they were uncomfortable and tight. When I came back downstairs, Ilse was waiting for me at the open back door to the garden.

It was around 8pm – curfew for Jews, I reminded myself – and I smelled the garden's unfamiliar greenness from where I stood.

'Come on. Quiet,' she said, beckoning with her finger. 'We still have at least an hour or so before sunset.'

'Really? Outside? I can go out? But my shoes don't fit. I can't go out.'

The early summer evening was warm and fragrant. It called me and yet as I stood on the threshold of an opportunity I had longed for and dreamed about, I was paralysed.

I picked up Beatrice and held her tight.

Didn't being outside spell danger to me now? What if someone came to the house? What if we were surrounded by spies and informers? What if someone suspected I was there and was just waiting for this chance to pounce and drag me away?

But surprisingly it was Adelena who pushed me through the door.

Ilse took me by the shoulders. 'You need this. It will be all right. Let's take our shoes off. I can see yours don't fit anymore.'

So, we sat on the doorstep and took off our indoor shoes and then wandered, barefoot, along the pathways before arriving at the pond.

After months indoors, it was a revelation and I gorged my senses on all of it, every blade of grass, petal, leaf and twig. The sight and sound of the breeze moving through the trees and low shrubbery. The smell of wood smoke that wafted from houses along the street and the grumble of the occasional passing car or a tinkling bicycle bell.

Other than the very top gable of a neighbouring house – Pim's, Ilse said – no other sign of human life was visible from this green and fragrant seclusion. I craned my neck and caught sight of Adelena sitting boldly astride Pim's gable, smiling with approval.

It was as if we were in the middle of the countryside. I lay on the grass under the spreading awning of the chestnut tree and revelled in the sight of the soft blue summer sky. Its beauty was just visible through the lattice of the chestnut branches. An energy rose up through the ground, cracking its crust and running up the length of my spine, rejuvenating me.

Ilse leaned down and kissed me on the forehead. I closed my eyes, unable to speak my gratitude. I had been wasting away and wallowing in misery. I had been selfish. I was one of the lucky ones and had someone who loved and cared for me. My reality could have been quite different.

We sat out an hour on the little wooden bench, tossing breadcrumbs to the fish, watching them dart to the surface and flash away back into the cool dark depths.

When we spoke, it was only just audible.

We returned inside and, as we often did of late before turning in for the night, sat with my birthday atlas spread open and discussed various exotic locations we might visit one day – Australia, Brazil, Africa or the tiny islands around Asia and the South Pacific.

'Thank you,' I said to Ilse when it was time to say good night. 'I am alive.'

That night I slept deeply, with no dreams of my parents, or Hetty, or strange train trips into the borderlands.

Chapter 11

Noting the simple joy and immediate lift in spirits the garden visit had given, the trips became an occasional part of our evening ritual into spring. When most Dutch families promenaded through public parks and gardens, Ilse and I – shadowed as always by Beatrice, and often openly watched by Adelena from the gable top – sat out, barefoot, in her fairyland garden. We leaned our backs against the great trunk of the chestnut, and we would 'just be', as Ilse described it.

Just be.

If we spoke at all, it was always softly as we shared observations of the garden – an old bird nest, the colour of the flower beds, the garden's small seasonal variations, how there could be so many different shades of green or what foods we most missed under rationing.

For me it was chocolate, while Ilse missed fruits and vegetable varieties. Food supplies in general were growing scarce across the Netherlands as the war raged on. Thankfully, Ilse's cellar was well-stockpiled with jams, loaves of black bread and pickled vegetables, and we used them from time to time to supplement our own very plain and basic diet.

'I wonder what Mutti and Papa are eating where they are,' I mused out of the blue one evening as we sat under the chestnut tree. 'And Hetty and Willem? Where do you think they are, Ilse? I feel like all my friends will forget about me.'

'Oh, Lena.' She sighed, drawing close to me as we leaned back against the sturdy trunk. 'I don't know where they all are. But I can bet they're thinking of you too and they will be believing you are safe and sound, even if they can't see you for a while.'

'I miss them – Mutti and Papa. I can't remember the sound of Mutti's voice. And sometimes I think of all the times I was rude or disobedient and I feel so bad. I think of all the stupid things I've done. The time I threw water on the German soldier and he came to the door.'

Ilse tried to comfort me. But I would have none of it.

'I could have got us all killed then and there, couldn't I? I remember the times I thought mean things about Hetty or when I got impatient or cross with her over something silly. What if I never see her again? What if the Germans drop bombs on us and we get blown to bits and I never get the chance to say sorry?'

'Shhh.' Ilse grabbed my hand. 'Don't. I know it's

hard, but we must stay hopeful and know that no one – on either side, I am sure – wants this to go on. Everyone is suffering and we must believe that the goodness inside people will overcome all this darkness. Do you think your Mutti wants to think of you being sad and regretful? We can't change what we've said or done in the past, so try not to worry about it.'

I nodded slowly and Ilse looked at me steadily as though deciding whether to continue.

'After Johannes died – and the baby – I wanted to die too. I thought of all the stupid arguments we had ever had. I saw it as wasted time and energy. I was distraught – mad with pain and loss.' The colour drained from her face as she paused. 'I ran up the attic stairs. I pulled a chair up to the window, climbed up on to it and opened the glass. I was ready to throw myself down. I could not face the idea of the world without them in it. Then something stopped me.'

She hesitated.

'What? What made you stop?' I asked, eager for the answer.

'I heard some children in the street, laughing and shouting.' She smiled at the memory. 'You and Hetty came flying around the corner on your bicycles. Fritz dashed after you. Hetty called out to you to slow down. You stopped and gave the dog something from your pocket. He wagged his tail madly and jumped around you both. I could see you were all so carefree and full of joy. I'm not sure just what it was about that, but it gave some small sense of hope.'

'I'm glad then that we came around the corner at that moment,' I told her. 'Fritz – I was so scared of him until I realised he just wanted to be friends.'

'I'm glad you did, too. We have to stick together. We must stay hopeful. These hard times will pass, they will. I know that as well as anyone.'

'I'm sorry that happened to you. It happened to my aunty. She was all ready for her baby to come and then a few weeks before it was supposed to come, it stopped growing.'

'It's one of the hardest things that can happen to a woman. It's a hard thing to tell people, so you really are the only other one who knows.'

I squeezed her hand in reply.

But nothing could have prepared me for what she would share in the days to come.

***

When one of her more accomplished students failed to arrive for a lesson one sunless morning, Ilse was at a rare loose end.

'Game of cards?' She raised an eyebrow.

'Mmm, no. I don't feel like cards.'

'Charades?' she asked, referring to one of our regular evening games.

'But what shall we do after supper if we can't play that game?'

'I know what we can do.' Her eyes lit up. 'It's time.'

'Time for what?'

Ilse signalled to follow and we headed upstairs. At every step, my curiosity burned brighter.

First floor.

Second floor.

Attic.

Opening the door and only hesitating to flip the light switch, Ilse made a beeline for the desk, pulling open several drawers before finding what she was after. A bunch of jangling keys.

Choosing one key, the largest, she thrust it at me.

'Here. You do the honours. You open it.'

Not understanding, I didn't move.

'Open the safe,' she said. 'I want to show you what's inside. The old lady, Johannes' great-grandmother Beata, was a great collector. Some of the items in that safe have been in the family for many generations.'

This was like a thousand birthdays at once. I put the key in the lock, my fingers prickling with excitement.

This was not a simple domestic strongbox for the safekeeping of wills, a strand of pearls or stocks and bond certificates. This was a sturdy, thick-walled fortress in the shape of a cupboard. There must have been something important inside – maybe jewel-encrusted goblets, diamond necklaces, emerald rings and shining silver plates.

Gripping the key tightly, my fingers trembled in

anticipation. The key turned in the lock and, seizing the cold metal handle, I tugged at the door.

Stuck fast, it wouldn't budge. My heart sank.

'Let me try,' Ilse said. 'It hasn't been opened in a long time.'

It only took two more attempts before the door gave way, ready to give up its secrets and my heart lifted once more.

But rather than a tinkling, sparkling slew of jewels and coins, a wad of old picture postcards fell with a thud to the floor. Ilse reached in and removed a child's moth-eaten stuffed bear and a selection of cheap embossed metal tins.

I couldn't hide my disappointment and allowed a hollow sigh to escape.

'There's more.' Ilse pushed the tins aside. 'I'll show you these later. This is what I want you to see.' She sounded triumphant.

Reaching to the back of the safe, she carefully removed two violin cases. One was a rather ugly and bulky wooden case and the other, with an animal hide covering, was embossed with brass studs. They were ungainly and cumbersome looking.

I couldn't see why she had been so keen to share any of this old stuff with me. What a huge let-down.

Ilse unlatched the wooden case first and, with the tenderness of a new mother, lifted the violin enclosed inside. 'This is a masterpiece,' she said, eyes lit from within. 'It's an Amati.'

Amati? This meant nothing to me, and I couldn't conceal the fact.

'The Amati Family were Italian instrument makers. This violin is about three hundred years old and is still as good as new.' She waited for me to react. 'Can you believe it?'

'Gosh, that is old.' I was dumbstruck.

'And this one,' she said, turning to the cowhide case, cautiously flipping open its fastening. 'This was made by Antonio Stradivari – you must have heard of him?'

Indeed, I knew the name of the greatest violin maker ever. Anyone who had ever learned the violin knew the name Stradivari. My interest in this treasure hunt was reignited.

'Can I touch it?' I asked, gazing at the revered instrument – an icon, the stuff of music legend.

Her answer was to hold the long-necked beauty before me.

I took it, gazing at its elegant lines, admiring the smooth, rich wood and the fine horsehair of its bow. I could barely breathe, terrified I might drop it. I tried to hand it back.

'Play it.' Ilse sat back on her heels.

'Oh, no.' I was appalled at the idea. 'What if I damage it?'

'You won't – it's survived hundreds of years. I trust you.'

'My playing won't do it justice.' I felt awkward,

thinking of the many expert hands this instrument must have passed through over time.

'Oh, don't be silly. Here, let me tune it for you.'

With great reverence, I handed the instrument back. She tweaked the violin's tension and ran the bow across the strings. Soon, the discordant sounds came together as the violin began to sing with resonance and longing.

'Go on.' She handed it back. 'Try the Tchaikovsky Serenade – that's lovely and joyful.'

'Here? Now?' I asked, brows raised. 'But what if someone hears?'

'It will be okay. Look, Erica didn't show up. If anyone asks, you are Erica. Just do the opening before the cellos come in. We are up high here and all the windows are closed.'

Even though that part only took about thirty seconds to play, I paused for a long time with the bow over the violin's waist. The first stroke of the bow invoked ancient incense-filed cathedrals, prehistoric forests and vast mountain ranges. Love, delight, bliss. There was a sweetness of sound and while far from dazzling, there was a new quality to my playing.

I was unable to speak for several moments, gazing down at the superb instrument.

'Bravo,' Ilse said, and smiled. 'See? You did very well.'

'Well, it wasn't disastrous, I suppose.'

'You could be a very good musician if you put your

mind to it.' She poked me in the ribs. 'No. You are already a very good musician. But you really could be outstanding.'

'That would require at least two things though,' I said, grinning.

'What would they be?' She tipped her head to one side.

'A desire and the ability to practise freely – neither of which I possess.'

'Well, yes, I see. At the moment, perhaps. But we do our best,' she said.

We spent the next hour tinkering with the two treasures, discussing their history and how they came into the family's possession.

'The story goes they were gifted to the Graaf family by the Stradivari family,' Ilse said. 'Antonio Stradivari was an apprentice to Amati, also great early violin makers. Amati saw great talent in the young craftsman. And as we know, their faith was worthy.'

I nodded, trying to keep up.

'The Graaf family would take summer holidays in the Fiemme Valley in the Italian Alps,' Ilse continued. 'They had a very gracious chalet and sizeable woodland forest – one of the woodlots where Stradivari sourced the wood for his violins. They didn't charge Stradivari for the wood, something he was eternally grateful for. He willed the instruments to the family on his death.'

Sentimental and almost priceless heirlooms to be protected, Ilse summed up, they may only be passed from one generation to the next, and they must never be sold.

'But they must be worth a fortune then?' I asked in wonder.

'Indeed they are, but that's the arrangement and it's been respected for generations.'

I helped return the cherished violins to their respective cases.

'I want you to have these one day,' Ilse said, her voice quiet and solemn.

'No. I can't. You must keep them in the family. You will have children one day and they must have these.'

'I won't have children,' she said with certainty. 'There will never be anyone else for me. And you are my family. But you must retain them and never sell them – promise me?'

All I could do was nod and we embraced, her hand cradling the back of my head and my face pressed into her cotton blouse.

Ilse was the first to break the embrace, looking relieved and much brighter. 'Now,' she said. 'There's more.'

'Not possible.' I giggled. 'This is all too much.'

Turning her attention to the cheap metal tins scattered on the attic floor, she handed them to me, one by one. They contained an array of stamps,

Roman and medieval coins, weighty gold brooches, delicate silver rings, diamond earrings, unset rubies, emeralds, and giant black pearls.

'These are all worth a small fortune.' Ilse beamed. 'Beata had a keen eye and collected throughout her entire long life. The stories include that she charmed the rare stamps from a desperate suitor – yes, she did end up marrying him! Some of the jewels were bequeathed to her by her godfather, others her husband accepted as payment from traders, and the coins, I believe, were a smart investment made to celebrate the birth of her first child.'

Once again, I was unable to speak and gaped at the hoard before us.

'When all this is over, when the war ends, I want you to take your pick – as much as you like, just leave enough for me. What do you think?'

'I think you are just amazing.' I shook my head in wonder at the boundless goodness of this woman.

'Excellent, that's all agreed then,' she said, slapping her hands against her lap. 'Look at the time. Let's pack this all safely away and think about lunch.'

Chapter 12

As 1943 wore on, I was inspired to be bolder with my violin practice and rather than wait until Ilse had the time and focus to take me up to the attic or down to the sound-swallowing cellar to play, I sometimes took the instrument on my own and ran the bow lightly across the strings.

However, the worst thing possible happened late one afternoon. After all this time I thought it would never happen, but an unexpected visitor called at the house when Ilse was out.

Ilse had left to collect a load of hospital washing and I had slipped up to the attic with my violin when the rattling of the old iron street gate made my heart jump. Any minute they would be at the front door. The gate was so old that it often stuck, but Ilse deliberately didn't have it fixed as it was a good early warning sign that someone was approaching.

I froze, my right arm suspended mid-air and my breath stalled in my lungs.

It wasn't long before the rattling gave way to a scraping noise as the gate was forced open and the sound of the buzzer. Had someone heard me? Had

I finally pushed my luck too far? Had my parents confided in the wrong person and had they also been betrayed? It was Adelena's voice I heard firing the questions.

The persistent buzzer cut into my immobility and forced me into action. Dropping to all fours, I crawled across the attic floor towards the stair ladder, terrified of making a sound and willing the floors not to creak and crack beneath me.

'Go away, go away,' I thought, trying to will whoever it was to leave.

With my foot on the top stair, I began my descent, wanting desperately to get to my room and the safety of the cellar hatch. Ilse thankfully still drilled me from time to time on getting down and into my hidey-hole; I had mastered the entire operation, getting it down to just under ninety seconds.

I made it down to the hallway outside my bedroom, when whoever it was began knocking on the door.

'*Guten tag. Ist jemand zu Hause?*'

German!

I knew my heart would burst or stop at any moment.

'Good afternoon. Is anyone home?' a clipped male voice rang out again.

I caught my white face in the hall mirror before crouching to inch my way across the hard bedroom floor, careful not to be seen above the open window lintel as I threaded my way towards the hatch in the corner.

Then, Ilse's voice broke into my rising hysteria. It was calm and even, but I knew it well enough to pick out a slight edge.

'Good afternoon, Herr Officer,' she said.

How did she do it? Not a stammer, no frenzy.

We never discussed what actual discovery might be like. It was always just there in the background. I wished we had speculated more. Would we both be taken away at once or just me? Should we try to resist? Did Ilse have a gun in the house?

And here it was – the moment I had hoped would never come, but always feared would. I would never see my parents again, or Hetty, or Willem, Double B or Fritz. I wouldn't get to meet Pim or travel to Australia, America or Africa. I'd never picnic in Vondelpark or feel the Zandvoort sand under my feet. And because of me, something terrible would happen to poor Ilse.

'How can I help you?' Ilse asked. 'I've been at the infirmary. Let me get these filthy bags out of your way and I will be with you.'

What a huge bit of good luck she had just returned from a washing run from the hospital. I pictured the German sidestepping her little trolley of filthy sheets and putrid medical linen. Nevertheless, I was sure he was about to demand a search of the house and I continued my crawl across the floor.

'I am Officer Kaufmann,' he said. 'I am told you are a teacher of the violin?'

'Yes. I am Ilse Graaf. I teach local children the violin and I do a laundry service for the local infirmary – as you can see.'

'Your German is excellent,' the officer complimented her. 'You speak with no accent whatsoever.'

'I was born in Koblenz and we moved later to my mother's small village outside of Essen, not so far from the Dutch border,' she answered, no hint of the nerves I knew she must be wrestling.

'Essen? What a coincidence. My wife and daughter are there now. I expect you are glad not to be there at present,' he said. 'They have suffered terribly in the March air raids. So much damage and death. I am in the process of bringing them here in the coming days – I feel it is safer. Forgive me, you must be wondering why I am here . . .'

Their voices faded as I opened the hatch under my desk. I crouched on the ladder, closed the hatch again noiselessly above my head and quickly, carefully, made my way down inside the wall and toward the cellar, catching the sleeve of my light jumper on the splinters of rough wood beams as I went. I was truly thankful to the cautious merchant who had constructed this secret escape route. Maybe he was a smuggler or slave trader, I mused as I stepped down and down, guided by instinct and the faint yellow beam of torchlight.

On reaching the cellar, there it was – the familiar cold and rich damp smell. Quickly, I slid open the secret bottom panel on the wall of storage shelves and, in turn, the sliding lid on the 'fat man's coffin', as I always thought of my hidey-hole.

I lay still and wide-eyed in my small dark nook. The illuminated hands on my wristwatch told me that the minutes were passing. This was the first time I had really used my hidey-hole properly. I kept the torch off, as Ilse had said, to preserve the battery.

It was pitch black and I fought hard against the rising panic sitting on my chest. My mind went back to horrible Horst and his tales of the sinister man hiding out in my grandparents' cellar. I imagined him here somewhere, lurking, hunched and yellow-toothed, all wizened skin and foul breath, claw-like fingers reaching for me in the dark.

With every passing second, I also expected the German upstairs to push past Ilse and rampage through the house, hunting for me. She would scream and protest, but he would slap her away. I was sure he would be upon me any moment, dragging me out, parading me and Ilse through the streets and shooting us in the main square.

Close to hysteria, I pressed myself against one of the walls and waited for the inevitable. I pressed my fingernails into my palms, hoping it would help quell the overwhelming desire to jump up and give myself away. This was something I often did when playing hide and seek. I couldn't stand the anticipation of waiting to be found and often couldn't ignore the impulse to reveal myself and get it over with. Hetty always teased me about it.

I would have opened the slider had I not, at the very moment I reached up, heard Adelena. 'No, stop. Think of Ilse. Do you want to kill her?'

Seconds passed and I heard nothing more but the beating of my heart and the blood pulsing past my ears.

Five minutes, ten minutes. Almost fifteen minutes. Agony. Then came muffled voices overhead and my heart was off and racing again.

Someone was in the back of the cellar, which also had a separate exterior entry. Straining my ears, I was able to pick up enough through the crack I had opened.

'Really, there is no need,' Ilse said. 'Be careful of your clothing, Herr Officer.'

The laundry trolley wheels squeaked and there was a scraping sound that I assumed was the laundry bag being dragged across the floor.

'It's no bother,' the German said. 'I will just leave the bag here by the vat?'

'Thank you. Most kind.'

I heard his quick steps retreat to the cellar door

opening and away from the dirty mess contained in the bags.

'It's settled then. You will let me know if you can find room on your list for my daughter, won't you? She has shown some small talent and her mother would like her to pursue her violin studies while we are stationed here. Girls of twelve can be difficult to occupy.'

'Yes, they are. Don't I know it?' Ilse said. 'My mother used to say the same thing about me at that age.'

He laughed and bid Ilse a good afternoon.

I heard nothing more but was too frightened to move, so remained still and quiet in the dark. Several more minutes passed before I heard the hatch slide across and Ilse's gentle tapping on the wood followed by her whisper, telling me to go back up to my room.

Doing as instructed, I emerged from my hiding place. She kept her back to me and remained busy with the laundry bag, clearly acting the part of washer woman should the officer return as unexpectedly as he had arrived. Following her lead, I didn't say a word to her and headed upstairs, huddling on my bed with the curtains drawn.

Ilse's light footsteps, like sweet music, approached a short time later. She hugged me so tight, her heartbeat could be felt strong and quick through her thin chest.

'That was the moment we have been preparing for,' she said, the adrenaline clear in her voice as she raced on. 'You did very well – as I knew you would, Little Mouse. I will have to stop calling you that, won't I? You are no mouse – you are a brave girl with the heart of a lion. That was close. What a shock to see him on the doorstep. And you must have been terrified.'

I reassured her that I didn't have to think too much and that all our training and practice had come to good use.

Later that evening, Ilse poured herself a shot of cherry schnapps from the bottle on the dining room sideboard. I followed her into the sitting room with a cup of hot milk and nutmeg.

'How have your nerves settled?' she asked, draining her shot glass. 'My goodness, I am still a little fluttery inside.'

'I thought that was it.' I took a gulp from my cup. 'I don't know how I didn't explode with terror.'

'You did so well – we both did!'

'We did. I can't believe it.' I prickled with exhilaration. I had not panicked and given myself away – I had done what I knew I needed to.

'Ilse, if you had told me a year ago that was going to happen and I – that we – lived to tell the tale, I'd never have believed it. What did he really want?'

'Officer Kaufmann simply wanted tuition for his daughter. I truly don't think it was a ruse for snooping around, or he would have forced his way in.' She turned the empty glass in her hands and placed it on the small table at her side. 'He said he'd pulled strings to get his wife and child out of Germany. I would take that as a clear signal the tide must be turning against the Germans if officers want to take their own families out of the homeland.'

'You can't have a German coming here for lessons.' I was incredulous.

'No, he wants me to go there. To his home,' she said, rising to pour herself another half-shot of schnapps. 'I told him I already had a full list of students, of course. He said he'd pay well and I felt I couldn't refuse. I couldn't come up with a plausible reason. He is a German officer and I am just a violin teacher. To deny him could create even more trouble, you see?

'I am in an impossible situation, don't you think?' She raked her hands through her thick fair hair and then pinched her bottom lip between the thumb and index finger of her left hand. 'I don't want to be in the presence of these people and yet if I don't . . .'

We both knew that she could not risk the consequences that could come with refusing his request, even if she herself was German. Heightened attention from the occupying forces was something we did not need.

In the following days, Officer Kaufmann called for Ilse in a big black car and drove her to meet his daughter. Her name was Gerda and Ilse said she was a shy and sweet child.

It was decided Ilse would teach Gerda every Monday and Friday afternoon between two and four. With travelling time, this meant she would be away from the house for up to three hours. Then there were the weekly farm trips, though Officer Kaufmann said he would happily have her driven out to the farms for produce.

'You know, I think that he saw the look on my face and understood because he said, "I would not want to make things difficult for you with your neighbours, Frau Graaf – of course I am aware of the prevailing sentiments among parts of the population. I was only offering assistance. Perhaps it's better you keep to your usual practice". At least that shows he has some sensitivity, perhaps.'

'Or maybe this girl is a real terror for her mother, and they will do anything to make sure she is kept busy. Or maybe they want the best teacher for her – you.'

If only Officer Kaufmann knew that his daughter's German-born teacher was also harbouring a Jew under her roof.

This new turn of events meant I was to be left on my own more often and so my hiding drills increased to daily practice and we went over and over the rules.

'In the event I am ever away longer than expected,

there's food in the corner of the vegetable storage bin and if anyone –'

'Comes to the door, go straight to the cellar. Ilse – I know. Don't worry.'

She paused and a quick smile outshone a little of the seriousness that had come, adding years to her eyes.

***

At least once a week, Ilse rode her bike into the countryside with a neighbour or two, to visit the farms in search of fresh vegetables for our table. The irony was that while those of us living in the cities were suffering from lack of food, the farmers had mountains of grain and produce, but were finding it increasingly difficult to get it to market due to interference from the German forces.

The trips took several hours and where once I had felt scared and nervous being alone in the house, the precious solitude was an opportunity to stretch my newfound wings. As the number of weeks I'd been in hiding grew, so did my desire to test my growing need for independence. And so, one afternoon when Ilse was away from the house, I decided to go out into the garden on my own.

'What on earth are you thinking?' It was Adelena at my elbow now as I lingered near the door to the garden.

She flicked her curls behind her shoulder and

looked me dead in the eye. 'Are you completely mad? What if someone comes to the house?'

I was a teenager and no longer a child. I wasn't really that unlike Adelena these days. I had changed. A few minutes out there by myself wouldn't hurt.

Surely not.

I turned away from her.

My heart hammered as I opened the back door and stepped outside on my own for the first time in longer than I could remember.

I tiptoed towards the pond, my eyes darting around the garden. The swaying tree branches cast sinister shadows and the shrubbery trembled with hidden dangers. Sounds were amplified. I could hear the rustle of every leaf, the chirp of every bird and the sound of my footsteps seemed like the tread of a giant. I willed myself to go on and finally made it to the bench, but only for a moment before being overwhelmed by a panic that sent me slinking back inside, exhilarated and thrilled.

Adelena, who had not come out with me, smirked. Back in the familiar safety of the house, I leaned against the *Küche* door. The subsiding panic was replaced by a thrill that I had done it – I had stepped out, albeit briefly, all on my own.

In the weeks that followed, I gained more confidence and whenever I could, headed out stealthy as a cat, guilty as a child caught red-handed in the biscuit barrel. Each time, I spent a few more furtive moments out in the open. Eventually I would spend ten or fifteen minutes at a time outside.

Lying on the grass on one of these covert garden outings, I took it into my head to climb up among the swaying green chestnut branches. As I stared up at the tree, I wished Hetty and Willem could see me.

Whenever we went to Vondelpark, the pair of them scaled the trees like squirrels, whereas I preferred to keep my feet on the ground. They teased me about it. But I did try once. However, the higher I climbed towards Willem and Hetty, the more fearful I became of falling, or that I would freeze in terror and get stuck halfway, like Jacob Bresler.

Jacob was the spoiled eldest child of wealthy parents and the source of plenty of jokes among other children, for he had an annoying and undeserved swagger. Jacob liked to drink apple cider out of a beer glass, pretending it was beer and he smoked cinnamon sticks as though they were cigarettes.

He also tried to emulate the look of the boy we called 'Sporty Simeon', whose sleek physique and top lip would glisten with a fine layer of sweat after completing some fabulous athletic undertaking. Jacob would lick his top lip and wipe at his dry brow with a damp handkerchief he kept in his pocket.

One late-winter morning, we all played a game of chicken and stuck our tongues against the icy iron railings outside the law courts. I, of course, never won this game, but did compete, only ever holding my tongue out for a few seconds at a time. Willem was most often the winner, despite Hetty's claims otherwise. Not to be outdone one chilly morning, Jacob strolled up and thrust his tongue against the black railing, holding it there for what seemed like an eternity. Of course, his fleshy pink tongue froze against the railing and he got stuck there.

What a fuss – he hollered and blabbered, with difficulty, and his mother had to rush down with a hot iron and hold it near enough to melt the ice, freeing Jacob's cracked and bleeding tongue.

But the following spring, last winter's mortifying 'chicken' challenge had faded so that when Jacob materialised in Vondelpark one afternoon and saw Hetty and Willem scaling the ancient chestnut tree, he ordered me to 'stand aside' and up he scrambled.

Jacob, who as his mother said was 'strong for his age', or in other words, pudgy and tubby, soon tired and at the halfway point became too scared to move either up or down. Hetty and Willem were caught higher up in the tree and could not climb down, either past or around poor Jacob, despite their best pleading and encouragement for him to move.

'Just put your foot on that branch to the left,' Willem said.

'It's so close,' Hetty said, in her best coaxing voice. 'You can make it easily.'

'It's too far,' Jacob moaned. 'I can't.'

'Just try, you won't fall,' Hetty said.

This went on for an age and I was sent for Herr Bresler who came with a ladder – all to no avail, of course.

In the end, as the sun began to set and the wind chill picked up, Frau Bresler and Jacob's grandfather were called to beg the boy to climb down the ladder. But this was unsuccessful too, as were promises of no school for a week. In the end, Father Visser was called to tell Jacob that if he didn't obey his parents, he would more than likely spend an additional six months in Purgatory.

Though he was clearly tempted by the idea, it was not enough to get a result.

Hetty's parents had arrived at the park and soon there were raised voices and I heard Herr Casler say, 'This is what happens when a child is overindulged.'

'That's a fine thing for you to say, Herr Casler,' Frau Bresler countered. 'There's no more precocious a child in all of Amsterdam than your Hetty.'

'Stop this silliness,' Frau Casler's voice cut in. She scribbled a note onto a piece of paper in her pocket diary and sent me running to the fire warden's house.

He took me to the station with him and together, with two other firemen, we were soon rattling along in a shiny red truck to Vondelpark, where Jacob was eventually charmed from the tree and down the long ladder with the promise of a trip to the cinema with the fire warden's pretty daughter.

Hours after the whole ordeal began, we were

walking through the darkened streets towards home, a hot meal, and bed.

Now, as I stood at the foot of the magnificent tree in Ilse's garden, it all felt like a lifetime ago.

I peered up into the treetops and girded myself for the climb. Getting up to the lower branches wasn't difficult. I sat for almost fifteen minutes, enjoying the view across the garden. I could just get a glimpse over the high wall into Pim's plot.

More than ever, I wished I had ignored my fears and shared the Vondelpark treetops with the others. Maybe I wouldn't have felt so inexperienced. I only had Beatrice and Adelena to bear witness to my new adventurous streak. Beatrice nibbled the grass at the base of the tree while Adelena made it known she was not even a bit impressed.

Here I was, shielded in my airy room, hidden by the thick vegetation that shivered in the breeze. Double B would have been able to tell me just which tree sprites lived among the chestnuts. I felt them all around me and was comforted by their presence because they reminded me of her.

The minutes ticked away and while I had grown adventurous, I had not yet become reckless and felt I had better not test my luck too.

However, getting back down was not so easy.

I was wearing a dress and could not shimmy down as easily as I had on the way up, so I decided to jump.

'Stop!' Adelena shouted. But it was too late.

The moment I hit the ground with a thump, a terrible pain shot through my ankle. I hobbled back inside, Beatrice hopping behind. I'd also torn my dress.

What if my ankle was broken? No way could Ilse take me to the hospital. Maybe it wasn't broken. There were no snapping sounds. But what if it was and I got gangrene and, in that case . . . it would have to be cut off.

By the time Ilse returned I had worked myself into a panic. Unable to hide my pain, I told her I had twisted my ankle after tripping on the loose step on the attic ladder.

She accepted my lie without question.

'I am so sorry, little one,' she soothed, checking the swelling. 'I should have fixed that – I have been so lazy. Johannes used to look after all those jobs. I'm afraid I'm not very good with tools.'

She checked the ankle, asking me to wiggle my toes and to turn my foot this way and that.

'It's not broken at least,' she said. 'You'll just have to wear a bandage and be careful the next few days. Here, put it up for a bit.'

My injured foot propped on a cushion, I felt even more guilt-ridden, and my conscience nudged me to confess. 'It's not your fault at all, Ilse. I am sorry, I have been so . . .' I stumbled over the words, so ashamed of my outright defiance. 'It's just, I need to say . . .'

'Look, I should have got to it months ago.' She placed a hand on my shoulder. 'One of us was bound to take a tumble – I am just sorry it was you. Anyway, Little Mouse, there is news.'

'Tell me. What news?' I demanded, happy for the distraction.

'There is word the Allies are gathering strength. Let's not have false hope, but it does feel that the mood is lifting.'

She bandaged my ankle and asked what I had been about to say.

'Nothing important,' I said. 'I was going to say I have been very clumsy lately and not to worry about fixing the step.'

'You're growing so fast. I remember I was all arms and legs at your age and was also clumsy, spilling and dropping things wherever I went.' She laughed. 'My mother never let me near her good cups and plates.'

I limped around for the best part of a week, feeling cooped up again and guiltily accepting Ilse's sympathy and frequent reminders to elevate my foot.

During those days of recovery, I veered from vowing that this was a warning to never break the rules again to scolding myself for being superstitious. It was my own fault for jumping down instead of taking greater care. And furthermore, if I had worn trousers it would have been far easier to climb up and down.

And so, tree climbing was back on the agenda, as

long as I dressed properly and took greater care.

Up there in the shimmering greenery, my thoughts always wandered to Mutti, Papa and Hetty, Willem and Double B. I wondered where they were and what they were doing at that moment.

And Pim, of course. I would think of him and whether he was on the other side of the wall, enjoying the fresh air and pondering, just like me, when the war would end. I had already decided that when the war was over, I would go and introduce myself.

Chapter 13

Flexing the more adventurous side of myself had sparked an even greater hunger for the return of my old life. At times it felt impossibly far away and at other times – at the smallest piece of good news, or if Ilse managed to obtain some black-market chocolate, I felt overwhelmingly positive.

One November afternoon, I had been half-heartedly working on my French grammar when I heard Ilse bounding up the stairs, half-frightening me to death. She showed me a copy of the underground *Vrij Nederland* which carried reports of a large Allied air raid on Berlin. 'Good news,' she said. 'Finally, things are turning in the right direction.'

I scanned the newsprint reading that the raid had been significant and damaging.

'They are closing in then, you think?' I asked. 'The Allies are making a dent?'

'I think we can all be cautiously optimistic, yes.' She did a little jig in the centre of the room.

After lunch one day, and not long after Kaufmann's visit, I said goodbye to Ilse, who was leaving for her usual lesson with Gerda.

I read on my bed for a while but, being unable to focus, wandered around the house, before ending up in Ilse's bedroom where I succumbed to the temptation to look through her wardrobe. There was a soft blue wool wrap, a fox fur with the head still attached, jaunty felt hats and berets and a sumptuous long black velvet gown. Holding it against my slender shoulders, I admired the way it set off my pale skin. I wondered if she'd danced with Johannes in this dress at some glamorous dinner dance at De Silveren Spiegel and I floated around her room with the dress until I was dizzy.

Ilse's words 'cautiously optimistic' circled inside my head. 'I think we can all be cautiously optimistic'. I was definitely feeling a little more optimistic and decided I had to take my chances, to live a little, to taste the little freedom that lay within reach. I may never get to dress up in a long velvet gown and fox fur, but I could lie under a tree, watch goldfish dart and dash and drink in the fresh air.

When I had exhausted many of my usual indoor distractions, and no longer able to ignore my hankering for the outdoors, I ran downstairs, pulled on a pair of Ilse's old garden shoes that stood inside the door and a cardigan from the coat hook. Despite our rationed diet, I continued to grow out of my own clothes.

Beatrice sprang out the door ahead of me to root around in the bushes while I took my place in the branches, enjoying the cool afternoon breeze on my face. Stretching my arms above my head, drawing in the fresh air, my eyes searched the higher canopy. It beckoned me upwards, into its green embrace. I climbed to a point that I was able to see over the fence into Pim's garden. Adelena sat with me. She was quiet and didn't utter a word of reproach.

My snooping revealed the usual neat flower beds, a well-plundered and bedraggled vegetable patch and a tumbledown summer house, or store. The roof had fallen in and the way it sagged reminded me of the decomposing cat carcass Hetty, Double B, Fritz and I discovered down along the canals one afternoon. The flesh had all collapsed around the ribcage, and we screamed and ran at the sight of a host of writhing maggots working away inside.

The decrepit building had several windows boarded up in an attempt to stop someone breaking in, or was it to stop escape from within? The overall impression was one of abandonment and quite at odds with the rest of the neat grounds and adjacent house.

My speculation was interrupted by a violent scuffling in the bushes at the back wall of the garden. As I always did now when taken by surprise, I stiffened and stayed that way for what felt like forever. It stopped. Then just as suddenly, started again. Snapping my head around, all but losing balance, I grabbed hold of the sturdy trunk. Craning my neck for a better view through the branches, a small cloud of dirt rose up around the bushes by the garden boundary. The tip of Beatrice's ears told me she was responsible for the commotion.

It was time to go inside anyway. Worried she had come to some mischief, I climbed down to investigate. She was tangled in a dense blackberry thicket and I worked quickly to free her.

'Careful next time, Beatrice,' I said, brushing her fur and holding her little face against my cheek before I let her free again and dusted myself off. She bounded away towards a small dry pile of branches in a corner against the wall, another favoured spot for rooting around.

I followed and discovered that my little Beatrice, who had been working away back here on and off, had dug up enough divots to reveal the corner of a wooden plank beneath a layer of old tree cuttings. Flicking her glossy ears, Beatrice then loped away into the gloom.

'*OPPASSEN*' was printed across the plank in peeling red paint.

'BEWARE? Of what, I wonder?' Adelena echoed my own question.

Hands shaking, I pushed the cuttings aside and experienced the same prickling thrill I had upon my first sight of the beach at Zandvoort years earlier. The earth was hard and dry, and the cuttings crackled and snapped as I stepped over them. I winced at the sharp cracking sounds, freezing for a moment before returning to my task. Little effort was needed to push several brittle planks aside, though I earned a thick splinter in the thumb.

Checking my watch, I knew there was less than half an hour before Ilse was due back.

Standing next to the pile of planks, I peered down into a ditch extending several feet into the earth. Whatever I had expected, it wasn't this.

A broken ladder led downwards. I set my foot gingerly on the first rung, testing each one's strength as I went and being sure to nurse my tender ankle. The earthy smell wasn't wet like the cellar, but rich and fertile. Several steps ahead, there was an iron gated grille set in cement, its thick bars weathered and rusted, blocking me from going further. A few straggly ferns had taken root in the cement and dangled at the top of the grille which was just higher than the top of my head, I peered past the bars, but only a few feet were visible before darkness took over.

Adelena clapped her hands to my mouth to stifle my exhilaration. The tunnels did exist! It wasn't just an old lady's fanciful tale.

A wooden trolley cart and a thick rope were positioned in the entry just beyond the grille. I stuck the toe of my shoe through the bars and kicked at an old oilskin, causing a flint and matches to fall from its folds. Next to this sat a flame-blackened hurricane lamp, like the one Ilse and I used during the increasingly common power blackouts.

I pushed against the gate, but it didn't budge. But yanking it towards me, the time-stiffened hinges gave way, creaking and protesting the way Great Aunty Tilda did when we visited on her birthday and she was forced to get out of bed. I was worried the noise might draw attention, but nothing was going to stop me from investigating.

The tunnel was just high enough to stand in without bumping my head on its uneven ceiling. I stood wanting, but not daring, to move forward. Glancing over my shoulder, Beatrice peered over the top of the ditch, nose twitching. I stepped back up the ladder, tucked her under my arm and placed her on the ground.

She snuffled around in the dirt for a few moments and loped away into the tunnel's gloom.

'Go on. What are you waiting for?' Adelena stood at the top of the broken ladder. 'Scaredy cat! This could be the chance you've been waiting for.'

I wanted to tell her to shut up, but aside from the fact that it was too dangerous, I couldn't speak.

Neither could I stop myself from pushing on, so I took a few steps forward. The light from the entry was soon swallowed by the dark. My whispering to Beatrice yielded no result. I was afraid. I retreated a few steps, scraping my shin on the trolley and trying to move it with my foot, only managed to push it an inch or so. Picking up the stiff oilskin, I brushed away some of the dirt and plonked down on the cart. Taking the rough rope between my hands, I gave it a sharp tug. Just as the time-worn gate had, the cart fought me at first but soon yielded and inched forward.

Remembering the lamp, I took a match and struck it against the flint, held it to the wick and right away my dancing shadow was cast against the walls and ceiling. In the yellow light, I saw the rope was attached to a winch, like the one we used to hoist bulky goods from the street to the attic above Papa's shop. Only this one ran horizontally. The cart itself, with half-metre-high sides incorporating narrow shelves and storage compartments, seemed to have been designed to carry small goods.

The ceiling was trussed at regular intervals by sturdy wooden beams and the whole thing appeared solid despite clearly being abandoned some time ago.

Tugging the rope, I inched along the tunnel, the rusting wheels making the going tough and progress slow. Eventually they gave way enough for me to move slowly along the dark stretch, until a small resistance on the rope indicated I had arrived at an incline. I had to pull quite hard to move on.

Something about the journey reminded me of a family trip to Heidelberg Castle and its rattling funicular railway that crawls its way up and down the castle's steep hillsides, like a fly on a windowpane.

Sweat dripped down the inside of my shirt as I

searched for the secret doors and treasure chambers I felt must be there.

Ilse would return soon. Maybe she was already home.

I should go back.

Must go back.

I convinced myself to continue a few moments more, until the track ended abruptly. I was faced with a disappointing and roughly hewn dead end, and Beatrice already burrowing industriously.

Raising the flickering lamp, I discovered a wooden hatch above my head.

Where did it lead? What lay behind? Who lay behind?

An uncomfortable mix of fear and temptation prickled through every drop of my blood. I wanted to flee but at the same time, so wanted to push against it.

The sound of wind and dull thunder from the tunnel entry called me back, warning me not to proceed. I scooped up Beatrice, who was sniffing around in the corner, into the trolley for the return trip. She nestled into my lap as I grabbed the scratchy rope between my hands and tugged.

This time, the trolley's long-disused mechanisms were more cooperative. I made a note to later use some axle grease I'd seen in the cellar to remedy this.

My curiosity was well and truly stirred as to what lay beyond that trapdoor: long-lost treasure; a warehouse of stockpiled foods; a cache of weapons; or perhaps it was just a pile of canal rubbish, dead barges and ruined boats.

As we reached the other end of the tunnel, the howl of the wind extinguished these daydreams, and my focus turned to getting back across the dark garden without being caught.

With Beatrice clutched under one arm, I made it to the *Küche* door just as an unseasonal storm hit and only minutes before Ilse ran in through the scraping iron gate.

Chapter 14

The following ten days were bleak. We and many others were imprisoned by icy winds, rain and snow. The weather was both a blessing and a cause for bitter frustration.

On countless occasions, driven by guilt, excitement and lack of anything else to talk about as a result of being stuck indoors, it was on the tip of my tongue to tell Ilse about my discovery. But this would mean revealing I had disobeyed the rules, jeopardised our safety and destroyed all the thought and planning that had gone into keeping me safe and alive.

And selfishly, I liked having a secret. It made me feel somehow safe and in charge.

Ilse was relieved to know that most others across the city were also in the same situation and would only go out if they absolutely had to. That meant far less likelihood of anyone dropping in unannounced, no students calling and not having to go out to Gerda's tutorials.

I couldn't believe my bad luck. Until recently I had grown grudgingly accepting and somewhat content with my small world: the cosy *Küche* and my little room and its books; eavesdropping on the music lessons; undertaking my own tutorials; keeping up with my studies; listening to evening radio broadcasts; the occasional supervised – and my own more frequent – trips to the garden.

The tunnel discovery had started me wondering what lay the short distance beyond my walled-in world and all the possibilities that were passing me by in the outside world.

The garden's seasonal budding and subsequent decay marked the passing of time.

I too felt somehow changed. Not only did I have bigger feet, but also longer arms and legs. How had my friends changed? Would I recognise them still?

Were my Dutch friends still riding their bikes to school in the mornings, climbing trees in Vondelpark on Sundays, playing handball on the footpaths outside their homes?

The tunnel took up all my thoughts and I was sure that Pim's broken-down summer house and the tunnel belonged together, united in some thrilling mystery. Perhaps it led to a secret diamond stockpile, an ancient escape route to the coast, or it led the way to a long-forgotten smuggler's cave, filled with stolen treasures and relics?

Each night I cursed the howling winds and the icy white drifts of snow they dumped on my world – so like the pale dunes at Zandvoort, yet so different at the same time.

Every morning I woke, my goose down quilt and woollen blankets tucked under my chin, and knew the cutting air at the back of my throat signalled another day inside, either drawing, writing and reading, or trying to find new ways to beat the boredom. Ilse, too, was housebound, the roads being iced over and banked with snow.

She brought a game of quoits up from the cellar, along with Johannes' old dartboard. We played charades or our own version of Pin the Tail on the Donkey with a homemade poster for Pin the Nose on the Cat.

I wrote long letters to my parents and to Hetty. Letters of course I knew I'd never send. But I enjoyed the daily scribblings and found myself confiding my activities, fears and hopes to the white paper.

> Dear Hetty,
>
> I hope you are keeping well and not stuck in some awful place. As for me, I sometimes think that I'll explode or die of boredom if this doesn't end soon.
>
> I am living – or should I say 'hiding' – with Ilse Graaf. I don't know where my parents are – they didn't tell me anything when they left me. Everyone seems to be slinking around or hiding away and trying to stay out of trouble.
>
> I for one, have become so sneaky! More and more I'm plotting to make

the most of the time I get to spend by myself. This happens whenever Ilse has to leave the house on errands. I have actually been going outside into the garden! AND I have found a tunnel – a hidden tunnel. I don't feel too bad about it anymore. I've decided that if I can't be free to live in the normal world, then at least I can be free to take some small liberties in my world of hiding.

The food shortages are getting worse. Sometimes I take food from the pantry and hide it for later. I have half a block of chocolate hidden in my school satchel, a bowl of dried figs at the back of my underwear drawer and some pumpernickel bread in my cupboard.

I almost fainted last week when I found Ilse dusting around my desk. Stupidly, I had all these letters stuffed under my desk blotter. I absolutely froze when I saw her.

I knew if she found out about any of it . . . I just can't think about it!

Anyway, she was getting closer and closer to my hiding spot, and my heart almost stopped when she leaned on my desk to reach up to a shelf. Her fingers were inches from the blotter so I just rushed over, grabbed the duster out of her hands and told her that I should really be cleaning my own room – like I used to at home.

She was more worried in that moment about me running in front of the windows, but I just had to stop her. I couldn't go through that again so after searching for a place, I've hidden the letters behind a loose skirting under my bed. Maybe I should burn them?

I suppose, knowing you, you're keeping up with your lessons. I'm trying to because I don't want to be too far behind when we get back to school.

So that's all for now. I miss you and can't wait to see you again soon.

Your very best friend

Lena

When I wasn't writing letters I knew were most likely never going to be sent, I was wandering around the house, or reading, or Ilse, Beatrice and I huddled around the stove and flipped through Ilse's photo albums. Family holidays, birthdays, anniversaries, weddings and school days – all easier times and happier memories than the problems that lay ahead.

I especially admired her wedding pictures. I didn't know the word for *more than happy*, but whatever it was, that's how she and Johannes looked. She showed me her wedding dress, folded neatly in a box on a shelf. Running my fingers along its cool yellowing whiteness, I pictured myself twirling around a grand ballroom at my own wedding, the centre of everyone's attention.

Ilse pointed out a photograph of a young Ilse, her older brother, and their parents. They were informally arranged on a low stone wall in the garden of a large and prosperous-looking house.

Though younger, she was still unmistakably the Ilse I knew – a pretty and open face, perfectly oval with a high forehead and twinkling eyes. She wore dark lace-up shoes, ankle socks and a dark-coloured dress with a round white collar. Her two thick plaits were tied with big bows and she shared the same mischievous smile as her brother – a gangly, straight-backed boy with a flop of thick fair hair. In contrast, her parents looked dour and imposing, dressed in very formal and slightly out-of-date clothing. I wondered why she never spoke of her parents.

Other times I went looking for fresh hiding places to fill the cold unfolding hours. I investigated spaces under beds, inside cupboards, under the stairs. I made a game of it. I'd make myself as small as possible and Ilse had to find me. She was so patient, and I often ended up giving in to the suspense and exposing myself. But what else were we to do to fill the hours?

We were playing this game late one morning before

Ilse went out to find bread and potatoes to supplement our paltry food stocks. While she was upstairs layering on woollens and her overcoat, it was my turn to hide and I squeezed myself under a shelf, behind a wooden storage bin inside the small *Küche* pantry.

It wasn't at all comfortable back there and I thought of giving up, but the pantry door slammed shut, causing the wooden slats to clatter and rattle, so I continued with the game. I quickly became aware of another noise, a scraping, but this time from inside the bin. Mice or rats? Maybe Beatrice had managed to climb in without my noticing. I opened the lid a crack, ready to lift her out, but instead an odd little giggle cut through the gloom.

I dropped the heavy lid on my fingers. I had become so used to speaking in a low tone and keeping on top of my emotions that I didn't even whimper. But as the lid inched open, I backed away as far as I possibly could and pushed against the pantry door, working hard to contain the urge to scream for help. The door was shut fast and now I wasn't sure if the heavy breathing was mine. I rattled the pantry door, clawing at the wood, trying as hard as possible to get Ilse's attention. Long delicate fingers appeared over the rim of the bin, then the top of a head.

I was about to pound on the door and call out for Ilse – I didn't care who heard me.

The lid sprang back, and Adelena sat there, a look of triumph on her face.

'You!' I reeled backwards, slamming my head against the wall. Shock and fear meant I didn't at first feel the sharp pain or realise I'd torn my fingernails. 'What do you want with me?'

She sat back, giving me one of her long cool looks.

'I'm just trying to talk to you, that's all,' she said. 'Why do you think you're so special? You never paid me much attention at all in the "out there" and now that you're in here, you still hardly ever think of me.'

'It's not my fault,' I said. 'You never showed much interest in joining in and getting to know anyone. You just hung back waiting to be noticed and appreciated for being Adelena.'

'How can you say that?' she almost hissed. 'I was there every single day. You took me for granted. But you'll come with me one day. I know that. One way or another.'

'What's that supposed to mean?' I demanded. 'Go where? When? Do you know when this is all going to be over? When I get to see my parents again?'

'Not necessarily,' she said. 'Anyway, I better go. She's looking for you.'

'No, wait. Don't go yet,' I called, as she shut herself back in the box.

But I lifted the lid and she'd vanished, just as Ilse unlatched the pantry door.

'How did you manage to get locked in here?' she asked. 'I thought I heard the door banging.'

'I think there was a draft,' I said, my heart

thudding. 'Anyway, you've found me.'

I wasn't going to tell her about my encounter with Adelena. She'd think I was going mad. There were times that I wondered if I was becoming unhinged with too much time to think, taking too many risks and showing little regard for the outcomes. But I would never share these thoughts – not with anyone.

As the days rolled on, the weather remained cruel and cold. We wore as many warm clothes as possible and during the day huddled around one small stove, slowly rationing the remaining bits of wood and coal we had in the house.

All I could think about was the tunnel and when I would get back there. Where did it lead? How long had it been there? Did anyone else know about it?

I began to feel trapped in a way I hadn't before when I was sneaking out on my own to take in fresh air and enjoy the open sky. Though limited, it was nevertheless a freedom of sorts.

On those long dark nights, as the rain hammered down and the wind howled in the eaves of the house, we went to bed early to preserve our meagre heat supplies. Ilse often helped me lug my overstuffed eiderdown along the narrow hall and let me snuggle up with her in her soft feather bed.

With our heads burrowed against the great fat pillows, we told one another stories to pass the time. She liked me to read from my *Tales and Legends* book, or we studied my atlas.

I liked to hear about her years growing up. She had wealthy grandparents on her father's side who, with their old aristocratic blood, didn't much like Ilse's mother. They lived in a beautiful old chateau in the hill regions of the northern Rhine country. That must have been the place in the old photographs.

'They felt my father had married beneath him and had a hard time accepting my poor mamma,' she explained one night as she fluffed the pillows behind my head.

'How sad,' I said, snuggling in.

'It was all right in the end. When my brother and I were born, it somehow made my mother more acceptable.' She rubbed the bridge of her nose. 'Then my baby cousin came to live with us after her mother died and our family was complete. She was a happy addition to the tribe with her big blue eyes and golden curls – she looked like an angel. That was all it took for my *Oma* and *Opa* to cave in. They doted on us and let us get away with all kinds of mischief, especially the baby.'

'I would love to have a baby sister or brother,' I said. 'Especially one that looks like an angel.'

She threw the bedclothes back. 'Let me find a photo.' Her footsteps pattered down the hallway and she soon ran back with a small box in her hands.

'Look, here she is – you can see the look on my *Oma's* face.' Ilse thrust a photo at me and there indeed was an angelic-looking child in the arms of a beaming old woman. On either side of her skirts stood two impish-looking children, identified by Ilse as herself and her brother.

I examined the four faces, noting the characteristics that had crossed the generations, the oval face shapes the most obvious, followed by a good head of hair. They also shared a mischievous glint in their eyes.

'The things we got away with – to the horror of the housekeeper,' Ilse said, fluffing the bedclothes. She rubbed the bridge of her nose. 'We were actually allowed to race our tricycles through the corridors, throw balls inside the great hall and slide around the ballroom in our stockinged feet.

'There was an old cook. Frau Strobel. My grandfather teased her, saying she was "as old as the palace itself".' Ilse smiled, twisting her wedding band. 'Frau Strobel did have a face like granite, but a heart of buttercream. It was the same every Christmas without fail. She and my grandfather would lock horns over something stupid, and Frau Strobel would quit every Christmas Eve, so that she could go spend it with her sister.'

'So, what did they do for their Christmas feast at the chateau after being left in the lurch like that?'

'My grandparents had a deputy on standby in the village who was always ready to traipse up and fill the breach – mind you, she was paid very well indeed. Then Frau Strobel and my grandfather would make up and back she'd come to her post. It was the same until they closed the place just before the war broke out. My father died not long after.'

I loved Ilse's stories, of which there was an endless repertoire. And as food supplies grew leaner and the weather harsher, I often pressed her to recount the story of the magical pot that cooked endless porridge supplies on command.

At last came a break in the weather and Ilse spent the following few days of the thaw on short trips to help neighbours, some of whom had homes damaged in the storms. Some were ill with the cold and from lack of proper food. Frau Van Der Berg went into labour during the blizzard and her new baby was sickly because there had been no heat and her milk wasn't coming in.

Once our own repairs were seen to and the garden paths cleared again, Ilse would leave me for an hour or so. She'd act as a nursemaid for local families who had to leave their children or elderly parents while they went about the city hunting for tradesmen to repair roofs, fix their burst pipes or look for food to replenish their own dwindling stores.

As soon as she was out the door, I'd wait a few minutes and then run down the back steps and fly past the pond with such speed that the gulping fish swished with a startled *plink* back into the dark depths. Finally, I would stand at the tunnel opening. But anxiety that Ilse would soon return always prevented me from taking the longed-for next step.

It was over breakfast one pretty and cloud-free morning when Ilse announced that she would open the house again to her students and that she was being pressed by Officer Kaufmann to return to her lessons with Gerda.

'We've been together such a lot lately. Will you manage on your own again when I have to go out?' she asked.

All I could do was reassure her that I'd be fine alone, that Beatrice and I would putter around the house; I'd do some reading and drawing, and everything would be all right. Just as it always was.

Once I was sure she had gone and, when I gauged she would be at the end of the road and on her way to Gerda's, I dashed to my room and changed into outside shoes, noted the time, then bolted through the garden to the back wall.

My hands shook as I groped in the dirt for the wooden plank concealing the tunnel entry. It didn't take long and, pushing it aside, I dropped into the opening, thumping heart in my dry mouth. The lamp and matches were still where I'd dropped them the day of the storm. They were damp and I struggled to get the lantern lit. With only two matches remaining, I succeeded. My eyes began to adjust to the gloom as the packed earth walls, floor and ceiling came into view.

Squatting down on the trolley and sitting back on my haunches, I pulled myself along the tunnel. There was no time to waste. I made such quick work of the short journey, my thin arms ached with the effort and my old shoulder injury flared and protested at being so severely pushed.

Reaching the end of the tunnel, I gazed at the wooden overhead hatch, heart pounding so hard it banished any other rational thought. All of a sudden, the walls seemed so close that I struggled to breathe. It was hard not to gasp for air as the walls closed in. I managed for a moment to quieten my breathing just long enough, and with little consideration as to what I was about to do, I placed my hands against the coarse wood.

All was still and deathly silent.

Wincing, I pushed up a millimetre.

But nothing happened.

Nothing. No response. It was still as quiet as the grave.

Biting my bottom lip, I dared to push another fraction.

The only sound was my own fast breath and the blood rushing past my ears. Hunching my shoulders, I pushed up again, ever so slightly against the hatch.

It didn't budge.

'What a waste of time.' Adelena sounded disappointed too. 'It's just a dead end. Goes nowhere.'

In a flash, all the anxiety I had felt earlier rushed over me. I felt entombed down here in this small dark space where not another living soul knew I had ventured. I could be buried alive and no one would ever find me.

I had to get out. Fast. What had I been thinking? Such a stupid fantasy to think the tunnel led somewhere mysterious and exciting.

There were no mysteries. This was life. I was living like a ghost inside the walls of Ilse Graaf's pretty house, separated from my parents and my friends. Maybe I would live like this for the rest of my life. What if something happened to Ilse? What would happen to me? I felt the tunnel shrink around me.

I had to turn back now, before it was too late. But in a blind panic, I knocked the lamp over, sending it clattering to the ground and shattering the glass bulb.

'No.' The word jumped from my mouth before I could stop it.

From above came a muffled scraping sound. I froze. I imagined all kinds of terrors on the other side of the hatch.

The scraping continued, followed by a dragging sound.

My heart pounded explosively, stifling my breath. I hadn't considered the next step. I shifted my position on the trolley and reached for the rope. My one thought was escaping to the safety of Ilse's.

No time.

I cried out in surprise as the trapdoor was flung open.

I don't know what I expected, but it wasn't this.

A ring of goggling faces stared back down at me, illuminated from behind by a single hanging globe.

Some faces were misshapen, heads were out of proportion on short necks, others' eyes slanted upwards; some had small chins, flat noses and tiny ears.

The rising murmur was interrupted by an animal-like shrieking. I had to escape.

Before I could act, though, a pair of strong hands reached down and hauled me up through the hatch, dumping me down onto a bare earth floor.

The cackling and roaring continued. I burrowed my head between my knees. I tried to shrink from all the bodies crowding around, curious hands running along my spine and fingers tangling my hair and clawing at my limbs.

'*Mein Gott*, get away from me.' Fear suffocated the words before I could utter them.

I wanted my mother.

I shut my eyes. Shaking and sobbing, I wanted to be somewhere else. I needed Hetty. Hetty and Adelena – they would know what to do in this terrible situation. I dug my fingernails into my folded forearms and rocked side to side as the noise faded. I felt myself floating, like that day at Zandvoort, as the waves tumbled me against the sand bed.

Chapter 15

The clamour that surrounded me was interrupted by three snapping claps. A short, sharp whistle broke the whirling hysteria.

'It's all right, children,' the female voice said, firm but pleasant. 'Hush, everyone. Let's make some space please.'

Feet shuffled away.

'What do we have here?' the voice asked. 'Don't be afraid.'

Feeling hot and sick, I opened my eyes before lifting my head, an action that seemed to take an eternity. I was in a low-lit space and all I could see was a scatter of rugs across a dirt floor.

'Stand up,' she commanded me in Dutch.

Legs weak with nerves, I rose.

I was encircled by a small gaggle of children. But they were children of a kind I had never seen. One child had only one good eye, another balanced on crutches, and one child's face was contorted and twitched uncontrollably.

Some sat in wheelchairs; one boy had a great hump on his back, so that he was bent almost double and had to look up to see what was happening; another had stumpy little arms and legs and grinned, while others made strange guttural noises. A one-armed boy smiled widely, and he stood next to a pair of girls who communicated using frantic hand signals.

The scream froze in my chest and I wanted to run, terrified by these twisted and broken children. I pulled my head into my shoulders, afraid to breathe the same air, fearful that the underground miasma would envelop and infect me.

I had heard that such people existed. 'Poor unfortunate freaks of nature', my grandmother would say, but I would not have believed it had I not seen for myself.

Fascinated, I used to hang on to every word as she recounted stories of a wealthy relative's trip to America before the turn of the century. He had attended a circus freak show featuring displays of children with no arms and legs, a man covered in fur, perfectly formed miniature men and women, and a girl with two sets of legs.

My recollections were interrupted when a girl with strawberry blonde curls and a small doll-like face put her nose right up to mine and said confidently, 'Don't be scared. We won't hurt you. I promise.' She grabbed at my hands with her own short, fat little fingers. She wore shiny red patent shoes, and her socks bunched around her ankles.

Then I saw someone else – the tallest woman I'd

ever seen and the owner of the strong firm voice. She had a rectangular-shaped face and the sleeves of her rolled-up shirt revealed powerful arms and a pair of square hands, fingers stained with nicotine. A few mousey-brown tendrils escaped from her messy bun and she tucked them back in as she side-stepped the small crowd.

'Let me through please, children.' She towered over me but crouched to my eye level, shrinking herself down so that she could look into my face. The way she placed an oversized hand on my shoulder was somehow reassuring.

'Who are you?' I squeaked.

'I'm Marta and I live here with the children. What is your name? How did you find the tunnel?'

I noticed a heavy wooden club hidden amongst the folds of her long skirt. 'Please, please don't hit me,' I pleaded.

She looked down at the club and shook her head, as if she was seeing it for the first time.

I glanced around the dim room. There were no windows, a low ceiling, and the earth floor was covered in thinning but cheery patterned rugs. Rows of neat beds lined two walls, a colourful tapestry hung overhead and a bank of wardrobes ran the length of the third wall. There was something akin to a Brothers Grimm fairytale about its quaintness and yet also there was an unnerving sense of dread. I hoped my story would end in a more positive way than most experienced by Grimms' characters.

'Will you please answer?' She was direct – firm, but somehow kind. Her tone reminded me of Fraulein Gerber, my kindergarten teacher, whose neatly coiled bun was always half undone before the morning was out.

'Yes, tell us,' the doll-faced girl pleaded. 'Where did you come from? Would you like to play with us?'

'Thank you, Clara,' Marta said. 'Leave this to me, please.'

Everyone's eyes were on me.

Then Adelena, who I had not even noticed until this moment, whispered clearly, 'It's too late, stupid girl.'

This was it. The game was up. I had blown it. 'I need to go.' My voice, strangled by fear, sounded foreign to my ears. I glanced at the hatch, only an arm's length away.

'You're not going anywhere,' Marta said. 'Not until I know who you are.'

'Greta Dietrich,' I lied. 'That's my name. Please, I want to go.'

'No, you don't get to go anywhere until I know more.'

I could not have regretted giving in to my curiosity more than I did at that moment. I would never make it out of here alive, never see my parents again, let alone Hetty.

'What do you want?' I asked.

'I want – I need to know how you got here, Greta.'

'I live not far from here, in the blue house behind the wall.' I paused, breathless with the same anxiety that had suffocated me when being chased by Fritz. 'I found the tunnel – before the storms. I wanted to see where it went. That's all I wanted. I don't mean any harm. Let me go.'

'You live with Ilse, the teacher? Ilse Graaf?'

'You know her?'

'Of course. She is my neighbour. She's a good neighbour, too. And I know then that your name is not Greta.'

Well, that's it, I thought. She had caught me in a lie. 'No,' I confessed. 'My name's not Greta.'

'I know who you are,' Marta said. 'Ilse has told me.'

'What?' Ilse had betrayed me? It made no sense.

'Look,' Marta said. 'It's okay, we're on the same side.'

'Yes, Ilse has taken me in.' I spoke fast. 'I don't know where my parents are. I mean, I'm not an orphan or anything. I live with her in secret – I'm Jewish.'

Everyone continued to stare. Their silence drove me to explain myself, to fill the heavy silent space with some sound. 'If the Nazis find me, they'll take me away, you see?' I looked right at Marta.

Her eyes softened and she lowered herself into a straight-backed chair.

'Because, like I said, I'm Jewish – understand?'

'I understand. I told you, we're on the same side. We're against Germany.'

'I see. Please, you can't tell anyone you've seen me. I get so bored. I know I shouldn't have disobeyed the rules. But I live like a prisoner and I can't stand it some days. I'm not supposed to go near the windows or even step outside. If anyone finds out I will be in terrible trouble, and Ilse, too.'

Marta nodded, listening to every word.

'Please, please, don't tell anyone,' I begged. 'I'm not supposed to be here – or there. I don't belong anywhere at all and Ilse has no idea I found the tunnel. In fact, she has no idea I've been sneaking out on my own.' I looked around the circle of faces and blurted, 'She can't find out about this.'

Marta laid the club on a low table. 'It's all right.' She gestured around the room. 'You are safe here. You're like these children. Looked down upon, misjudged, discarded.'

I was nothing like these children. My top lip curled at the idea. These children, with their crooked, swaying bodies and mumbling, flapping mouths and dragging legs, were nothing like me.

As though able to peer inside my rushing thoughts, Marta said, 'No – you are not like them. Not physically. These children have been tossed on the rubbish heap. They're like you because you, like them, are considered different and unworthy.' The way she said 'unworthy' made it sound like a swear word. 'They've been rejected, through no fault of their own. Like you.'

Rejected. The word hit me in the pit of my stomach.

'Are these all your children?' I asked, turning my attention back to the scene before me.

The story put about by the Germans, Marta explained, was that all these children were to be taken from the local orphanage, or from their parents, to be sent to the safety of a hospital institution somewhere in Germany. She knew the Germans would never take them to any such hospital.

Her worn black leather shoes kicked up dust from the floor as she paced. The children didn't take their eyes off her, not for a moment.

'My husband heard increasing rumours that the children were being herded up and housed somewhere in the Jewish ghetto.' Her large hands clutched her long skirts.

'But Ilse has said the ghetto is overflowing with people. Where would they put them?'

'It was. It's all but empty now. Jodenbuurt is a ghost town.'

'Empty?' I asked. How could it be a ghost town? I knew plenty of people in the ghetto – the Apfels, Henzels and Elbaums. It was bustling, a close community. Everyone knew everyone's business, the gossip, the tragedies and the small everyday comedies of one another's lives.

'Yes, quite so,' she said. 'To see the empty buildings, the open windows, curtains hanging in the wind – it is quite eerie to pass Jodenbuurt.'

'Where is everyone?'

'Camps – they call them labour camps.' She stopped and retied the apron that had become loose during the earlier melee. 'Franz, my husband, is a tailor. He has been accredited by the Dutch royal family.' There was a hint of pride in her voice. 'He was recruited by the Resistance before me. One of his customers is a city official who told him about these children. We rescued those that we could over two nights.'

It turned out the ghetto had been a collection point for children who were being brought from all over the Netherlands before being sent to camps.

Marta sank down on the edge of a bed and gestured me to sit opposite. She and Franz had been involved in helping the Dutch Resistance in the Jewish rescue efforts since the earliest days of the Occupation.

'But how did you do it?' I asked.

'Not without a lot of difficulty and planning.' She smiled. 'As you know, the terrain is flat with few forests and no mountains for cover, so we decided to turn our home into a safe house – an initial stop on the Resistance underground railroad. We helped arrange fake passports for Jews.'

I sat, transfixed, shooting the occasional glance around the circle of children.

'Like real-life spies,' I said.

'Yes, you could say that.' Marta laughed, scratching the side of her nose with a nicotine-stained finger. 'In the beginning, we also helped to equip the Resistance fighters. There were a few times I ran radios, guns, even explosives, hiding them in my bicycle. My longest journey was fifty miles. Let me tell you, with that cargo, I felt every single one of those miles too.'

'Fifty miles?' I was astounded. 'That's as far as Zwolle in the north-east. We went there to visit Papa's cousin just before the crackdown. I remember because I had to pee, but Papa didn't want to stop the car. It took us more than an hour to get there. How was that possible with a bicycle?'

'With a lot of determination, creativity and no shame,' Marta said, taking a sip from a cracked teacup on top of a bookshelf. 'It was dreadful.' She reached into her skirt and produced a tobacco pouch. 'But at the funeral of an elderly relative, I rifled through Dutch mourners' coats and stole any papers I could find, knowing they would not be penalised. We knew of people who could enlist the help of train station pickpockets, who stole travellers' papers, passports and documents.'

She answered my raised eyebrows with, 'All for the cause, Lena.'

Marta cocked her head around the room and began rolling a cigarette. 'This cellar and all the tunnels leading from it were built by early city shipping merchants for storage and security. They were mostly filled in after many began sinking and caving in. But a few links, like the one between here and Ilse's garden, remain. They are ideal escape routes.

'The tunnels were discovered by my son, Pim, and his sisters Bep and Anke.' She exhaled, wreathing herself in a blue haze. 'The children heard kittens. We looked high and low. They were trapped under the floorboards of the storage bins over there.' She pointed 'Right there in the corner. Under the boards, we discovered the tunnel hatch and we pulled them all up to expose the earth floor.'

Like a thunderbolt, it dawned on me.

Her husband was a tailor, accredited to the Dutch Royal Family. She had two daughters Bep and Anke. A son named Pim – a common family pet nickname for boys named 'Willem'.

This woman was Willem's mother.

The boy who played so beautifully and who had a brave and daring mother and father was Pim . . . my friend Willem Walsma was 'Pim'.

The shock sent the blood rushing to my cheeks and yet I felt light-headed and giddy. Giddy, giggly and a little ill all at once.

This was Willem's house. I had been living – hiding

– next door to Willem all this time. How had I not made the connection?

I knew he lived in an older district, but had never been there as my parents didn't allow me to visit boys' homes.

I knew that Willem's father was a tailor and that Willem was an accomplished musician, but the Pim who came to Ilse's sounded different to the Willem I knew. Pim's voice was deeper, more like a man's than a boy's.

Hetty and I never called him Pim – no one at school ever did. He wasn't the kind of person you used a nickname for. He may have been Pim to his parents and big sisters Bep and Anke who fussed over him, but to us he was Willem.

My head whirled. I was thrilled to know the stories of the secret tunnels had been true. And now I knew who Pim was!

It was only then I thought to let my eyes sweep the crowded cellar looking for Willem. There he was at the back of the pack, holding hands with the little doll-faced girl, taller and more handsome than I remembered, or had ever noticed. Willem Walsma.

'Willem?' I asked. 'Willem, is that you?'

He stepped forward and Marta said, 'This is my son Pim – Willem.'

'You are Pim? Pim who takes lessons with Ilse?' I was ecstatic and we ran at one another. I hugged him close, feeling his arms wrap around my back as

I clung to the rough wool of his sweater.

'Pim's been my nickname since I was a baby.' He rolled his eyes and we laughed.

'So, you have to tell me.' I couldn't hold back. 'Do you know where my parents are? And what about all our other Jewish school friends, Willem – Jacob and the Smeltz twins, Ruth and Johanna? What about Hetty? Any news?'

Willem opened his mouth to speak, but it was his mother who answered, drawing hard on her cigarette, which caused its end to glow fiery orange.

'All I know is that I understand your parents were helped into Belgium, almost one hundred miles from here,' Marta said, gesturing for me to sit at a small chair she dragged forward. 'This was their plan. Risky, but sound. They had thought it would be safer to hide you here in the city than try to move you. They had planned that if they made it over the border, they would send for you.'

It was like having a bucket of ice water poured over my head. My parents had not sent for me. What if something had happened to them?

'But,' she said, 'it doesn't mean they didn't make it. They could have realised that it's just too difficult to get a message out, let alone to move you now.'

I tried to take hold of this possibility, but couldn't ignore the other strong likelihood that they were dead, and my heart sank.

'The Caslers seem to have disappeared into thin

air,' she said. 'The Breslers and a few other Dutch families are working closely with the Germans, toadying themselves into a feeling of false security by supplying information and black market materials.'

She also said that in some cases, women were even giving themselves in 'that way' to the German soldiers.

At first, the stories were just a tangle of terrible words. But my mind slowly unravelled them.

How could otherwise good and normal people – people I knew, mothers and fathers of my classmates, women who came into our shop, how could they do such things?

But even worse than this, was Marta saying some people had even offered to hide Jews in their homes only to give them away . . . that people were opening their arms to the desperate and afraid, only to stab them in the back.

I was taken back to the moment I sat blindfolded in Ilse's *Küche*, flinching and waiting for the sound of a cocked pistol or the cold steel of a knife blade at my neck.

Could anyone be trusted ever again?

Uncertain of what to do next, I turned to Willem and asked the obvious. 'You've been here the whole time? Next door to me?'

A cheeky smile and nod.

'I didn't know it was you coming to the house,' I said. 'I listened to you playing. I should have realised.'

'I knew you were there – I can see you when you sit up in the tree canopy. I can see you from our top floor.'

'And you told no one?'

'Of course I didn't.' He sounded offended.

I was almost lost for words and all I could say was, 'Willem. Willem Walsma – you are Pim.' And after eyeing him closely, 'You look different. I used to be taller than you – and your voice! You sound like a man – almost. And look at your jumper. The arms are so short.'

'And you have changed too. You used to be flat-chested.' He grinned and I punched his arm.

Desperately pulling my thoughts together, I told Pim and Marta I could never have imagined this was what lay at the end of the tunnel.

'Would you like me to show you around?'

'No,' I stammered. 'Yes – I mean, I don't know. I have to go. I have already been away too long. Ilse could be back any moment.'

Clara and the hunch-backed boy, who I learned was Aldo, came forward. Aldo grabbed my sweaty hands and begged me to stay.

'No,' I said, twisting my hands from their grip. 'Don't touch me. Let go.'

'Lena,' Marta said. 'I am sure that Ilse will understand. I can tell her if you like – that you have discovered us. That we have all found each other.'

'No!' I shouted this time. It was the first time in a

year that I had yelled out and it took me aback.

Adelena slapped her hand over my mouth, but I brushed her aside to speak.

'No, please,' I said, bringing my tone down. 'She will know that I have lied. She has risked so much for me. Please, please don't tell. I have to leave.'

'We won't say a word,' Willem said. His hand on the small of my back, he guided me towards the hatch in the floor. 'Don't worry.'

He helped me drop back through the hatch and onto the trolley where the little lantern still flickered in the dark.

'See you,' was all I said.

I heard the hatch close and latch softly behind me as I trundled back along the tunnel, my head spinning and my heart dancing and aching all at the same time.

Arriving at the other end, I stared at the broken ladder. How was I going to make it out?

Chapter 16

A fine misty rain had fallen during my visit and the tunnel entry was musty and damp.

I planted my foot on the first available rung, but it slipped on the wooden tread, worn smooth with age. Gripping the ladder's side rails, I stepped at the same time, pulling myself up. I was about to take another foothold when the rung snapped and I ended up on my behind, collecting a painful splinter on the way down.

The ladder resembled a toothless grin with only a few remaining rungs, unevenly and inconveniently spaced.

There was no other way out.

Was Ilse inside, searching the house for me? Would she be hunting through the cellar? Tearing open cupboards, looking under beds or up in the attic?

How would I explain my disappearance to Ilse?

I pushed the panic away and tried jumping, hoping to grab the lowest rung, but after several attempts gave up, alarmed at how weak I'd become.

I searched hopelessly for anything that could serve as a step up and out of the hole. Nothing, not a box nor a rock nor a stump. I was stuck. I'd have to go back. But then I was struck by an idea.

If I dragged the bottom of the ladder forward as far as possible, keeping the upper end anchored to the entryway's opening, it acted like a bridge of sorts and I could use the side rails to crawl up.

At the top, I hoisted myself up and peered over the rim of the ditch before emerging and racing back to the house. A mixture of disbelief, guilt and excitement pulsed through me.

Ilse wasn't back, but Beatrice was sitting in the *Küche* and shot me a stern look, as if upset I'd left her behind. I grabbed her, ran up to my bed and drew the curtains.

So, the Walsmas had no news of my parents beyond their suspected flight to Belgium, or of the Caslers. I wondered how true this was. They seemed to have good knowledge of what was going on. Maybe they didn't want to give me any bad news.

I should have pressed them more. I wondered if Ilse spoke to Marta often and if they shared information.

Realistically, if I were in their shoes, I wouldn't be telling someone in my situation anything terrible and demoralising. It was like being tossed again in the waves at Zandvoort, back and forth, up and down.

As I tried to sort through this new information, I heard Ilse's return. She called quietly up the stairs, asking me to come down.

As soon as I entered the *Küche*, I could see she was

deep in thought, standing at the sink, gazing through the sheer curtains out towards the chestnut tree and the wall beyond. Her drumming fingers tapped out her anxiety on the cold porcelain sink.

She knew. I could tell with every tap of her fingernails.

Guilt and shame coursed through me.

I was like Herr Bechtel, who had lived two doors down from us. I had overheard my parents speaking about how 'poor Herr Bechtel' had become 'captivated and addicted' to schnapps and beer. Frau Bechtel died after her second baby was born the winter before and Herr Bechtel had built up lots of credit at Papa's shop.

'You should stop giving him credit,' Mutti said. 'He can never pay it back, we know that. Think of his family.'

'That is precisely why I give him the credit, Vera,' Papa replied. 'He has to feed those children. They have no mother. They have no one here.'

'True, but giving him credit just lets him keep on with the gambling and the drinking. He is captivated by it, addicted. It will ruin them.'

Later, I asked Papa what 'addicted' meant.

'It means, *Schätzchen*, that you cannot stop doing something that is bad for you, even though you know it is wrong. Even though you know it will bring pain and suffering, you will risk everything.'

This had made no sense to me then. But now I knew

differently. I, too, had been captivated and addicted to the idea of doing what I pleased and sneaking around behind Ilse's back. I had become addicted to my short periods of freedom, even though I knew I was doing wrong and risking so much.

Ilse told me to sit. She looked me squarely in the eye. 'Are you feeling all right?' She put her cool hand to my forehead. 'You feel warm and you're flushed.'

I was burning hot, but not because I was sick. 'No. I feel fine, really.' I could hear my thumping heart through my lie. 'How did it go with Gerda?'

'Oh, it went fine – the same as usual.' Ilse sounded uninterested. 'She's quite a pleasant girl – straight forward, sincere and diligent.'

I couldn't wait any longer. 'Are you all right? You look angry.'

'Me? No. I'm not angry. I'm a little tired, but not angry. But I do have something to discuss with you, though.'

'My parents?' I jumped to my feet. 'Papa, Mutti? Are they dead? Tell me!'

'No, no, not your parents. I've had no news of your parents.' She placed her hands on my shoulders. 'It's Hetty. The Caslers.'

'Hetty – did you see Hetty?'

'No.' She could not hide her impatience with me. 'On my way back, I saw Anika De Wit. I know her quite well and she knows my neighbours here – Pim's family, Marta and Franz. They are all involved in various ways in the Resistance. As we walked along, we got to speaking – you know, about things. The progress of the war and that kind of thing.'

'Just tell me,' I cut across her, shifting my feet, my hands clasped tight.

'I'm sorry, yes – she has been helping to hide the Caslers and some other people over on Keizersgracht, on the canal, not far from the Westertoren clock.'

In that instant, everything changed. The room sparkled, glassware in the dresser glittered, the pattern all but jumped from the red check tablecloth, while the snowdrops in a small vase on the windowsill filled the space with their fresh scent.

'So, they are alive?' My intense joy was sharpened by the fact I'd not been caught out as feared.

'Yes, isn't it marvellous?' Ilse said, glowing. 'We couldn't speak for too long. But I knew you'd want to know.'

'Did you tell her about me? Did she have news of my parents?'

'I said nothing about you. Poor Anika has enough secrets to keep. It would be a burden to add yet more to her load. She said nothing about Vera and Jacob. It wasn't relevant to our discussion. I'm sorry.' She paused for a moment. 'But we can have hope that there are Jews secreted away all over the city, right under the noses of the Germans.'

The very idea of this wonderful subterfuge, this blatant trick, cheered us considerably.

'Ha ha.' I grinned. 'They think they are so clever, so superior. But they're not!'

That night I lay bundled in my bed, content as a curled cat, my guilt having faded to the point I could almost ignore it. Though I was dead tired after everything that had happened that day, I could not sleep, and I didn't want to. Sleep would mean not being able to relish this wonderful news about Hetty and the renewed hope for my parents.

I could hear the distant Westertoren clock, faithfully marking out the time on the quarter-hour. It took me a long time to get used to the regular chiming through my first long, dark nights under Ilse's roof. Now I drew comfort from its regularity. This night as I lay awake it was even more the case, because I knew that somewhere out there, Hetty could hear it too, just as local citizens had for the past three hundred years.

Hetty was still safe. She had not been found and sent to some dreadful camp. She was alive and still living here in Amsterdam, under the same sky as me, listening to the same clock chimes in the dark night.

Maybe my parents, my aunty and uncle and Double B were all out there somewhere over the border, being well looked after too.

Maybe everything would work out after all.

Maybe.

Chapter 17

The whitewashed wooden door squeaked as usual when I entered the *Küche* the following morning. Ilse turned to greet me and placed a small piece of wood on the corner stove fire, sending a flurry of dancing sparks through its open door.

Taking a blue and white patterned cup and bowl from the open-shelved dresser, she smiled and gestured me to my place at the table. 'Just in time,' she said, and spooned a ladle of steaming hot watery milk from a pan on the stove into the bowl.

I cut myself a slab of hard rye bread and dunked it into the milk. 'Will you ask Anika to deliver a letter to Hetty for me? I know Hetty will want to know where I am. I have to let her know.'

To my surprise, Ilse looked incredulous and shook her head as she sank into the seat across from me.

'Why?' I demanded.

'You can't mean it?'

'Of course I mean it,' I shot back. 'I need Hetty to know that I know she's alive and that I'm alive too and that I'm thinking of her. What's wrong with that? We promised we'd always keep in touch if we could. And now it's possible.'

Ilse breathed deep, looking at me across the top of her steaming cup. Deep in thought, she set it down and pulled her thick cardigan around her shrinking frame.

'Nothing, there's nothing wrong in that.' She slipped an escaped piece of lank golden hair back into her bun. 'But it's ridiculous. Can't you see?'

I thumped the table so that the milk spilled from my bowl.

Ilse pushed herself back. 'Quiet,' she hissed.

'Why? Why is it ridiculous? What are you talking about? I thought you wanted to help me.'

'You need to stop and be quiet.' She moved towards me with outstretched hands.

Unable to control my temper, I slapped my hand down on the tabletop again, upsetting my cup and making the crockery clatter.

Ilse stood over me, all at once looking angry, sad and tired.

'You will not behave like that.' Her eyes were dark. 'Take a hold of yourself.'

'I can't believe you won't help me get a message out.'

Ilse clapped a hand over my nose and mouth. Deep in shock and unable to breathe, I flailed and tried to pull her hand away.

'You need to be quiet, you little fool,' Ilse whispered in my ear, loosening her grip so that I could at least inhale. I nodded so hard my head might have fallen off.

She released me and I sat back in my seat, my tears mingling with the spilled milk.

'All I am asking of you is to pass Anika a note to deliver to Hetty,' I pleaded. 'She goes regularly. It's not like we'd be asking her to do anything out of the ordinary. Please, Ilse. I've not asked one thing of you this whole time. If you don't do this for me, it means you don't care. You don't know what it's like being trapped like this and kept away from the rest of the world.' I cried softly, my fists balling and unclenching.

'Stop. Enough.' It was clear Ilse was taken aback at my sudden passionate outburst. 'Go to your room and pull yourself together. I will come up later.'

I pushed my chair back from the table and ran from the *Küche*, taking the stairs two at a time. I slammed the door behind me.

I listened as Ilse cleared the breakfast dishes and sat waiting on my bed. Would she come and scold me for making so much noise? Did I go too far? Perhaps she would send me away to hide out with some other sympathetic family. She wouldn't turn me in, would she?

I didn't care. I was suffocating, I had no voice, no presence. I left no footprint on this world. It was as though I no longer existed anymore, any way. The war would never end.

I would not let her in, I decided. I wasn't interested in anything she had to say.

She didn't really care about me at all. Even Adelena agreed. If she did, she would have done this one simple thing for me. What's more, last night she'd said my parents weren't relevant. She hadn't asked Anika about them because it 'wasn't relevant'.

Hetty was my best friend in the world. Why couldn't I send her a message? Just one small, harmless message.

My anger and disappointment simmering, I still felt a prick of shame. Had I not already risked enough with my secret wanderings and visits next door?

Soon I heard Ilse's tread on the stairs. She tapped on the unlocked door.

'Lena,' came her gentle call.

Despite my softening mood, I dug my heels in and ignored her, even though Adelena poked her elbow into my ribs, egging me to let her in.

She knocked again and I huffed, 'Go away. Leave me alone.'

'I have to go out soon to the infirmary,' she said. 'Will you be all right?'

'Yes,' I answered, sniffing. 'Of course. Aren't I always?'

Hearing the click of the front door lock, I got up

and went to wash my hot face in the bathroom.

Staring in the mirror, I noticed yet more changes in the features gazing back. I studied the new planes and angles, the arch of my brow and the quality of my skin, which had become quite fine and paler than ever. What boy would ever love me looking like this? I would have to fatten up once this was over.

All I could think of was Hetty, so much indeed that I didn't take this opportunity to steal away into the tunnel, or even to take out my violin and soothe myself by pulling the bow across its strings.

Instead, I sat at my desk and wrote another outpouring to Hetty.

> Dearest Hetty
>
> Ilse saw Anika! I can't believe how close by you are near the Westertoren! I can hear it chime at the same time as you. It's like being connected by a silvery thread.
>
> I am looking plainer than ever and I am sure that no one will ever be able to love me, looking the way I do now – all scrawny and pallid.
>
> But still, I suppose I am luckier than the children I've discovered living next door! You wouldn't believe it, I found a secret tunnel running directly between Ilse's house and the one next door – and what's more, it's Willem's house. His parents are hiding all these damaged kids

in their cellar. Even though they spend just about all their time down there, they seem to manage.

When will this all end? Some days my spirits are so low that I have no energy at all. Not helped by the fact that there's barely anything to eat with everything going to the war effort and the Germans closing down transport routes. Ilse does her absolute best and manages to get hold of contraband butter and cream from time to time. But we eat so many root vegetables. And a salad of potatoes and edible flowers last night – can you believe it? I'm waiting for her to serve me tulips for breakfast any day now.

I am so glad to be able to hear a little of the outside world on the radio service and every report seems to carry both good news and bad news, but overall, we have to believe that the Allies are inching forward.

I often wonder what you do to pass the time. I suppose for one thing, you're doing more reading than ever.

Anyway, all the best and I can't wait to see you again – I hope it's soon.

Your best friend in the world

Lena

As always, I folded the letter neatly and put it in my desk drawer along with all the others that I knew wouldn't get to her because no one would help me.

I flipped through a dog-eared magazine and sometime later heard Ilse trundle back with the infirmary trolley. I threw myself down on my bed and waited once more.

Soon enough, she was back at my door. 'I'd like to speak with you.'

'Come in,' I said in a way that channelled Frau Achterberg on her highest of high horses. As soon as I saw her tired face, though, I began to weep.

Her own tears sprang forth. She ran to me, wrapped me in her arms and we nestled like this, wordless, as the minutes ticked by on my bedside clock.

She broke the embrace first and looked down into my face. 'Look at us.' She smiled, passing over a handkerchief. 'What a pair of sillies. Just as well we don't have any plans with Clark Gable tonight.'

She always knew what to say.

'I know you want to reach Hetty. I would like nothing more than for you to be able to communicate with her. It's not that I don't care for you or love you. That's why I said "no" earlier.'

'Then why? Why can't we ask Anika to pass on a letter – just one note?' The words spilled out almost before the thoughts had formed. 'One note, one letter, to tell her where I am. To say I'm alive and that I know where she is and that at night, I can hear the Westertoren clock strike, just like she can. That's how close by she is. But if you won't let me write to her, then she might as well be in Africa – or dead.'

'Stop it.' Ilse looked appalled.

'Well, it's true,' I said, dropping my head. 'I know how happy she'd be and then perhaps she could get one back to me.' Looking up again, I grabbed Ilse's hand. 'And you can be assured that if ever I am caught by the Germans, I'd never give up my secrets. Especially when it's life and death.'

'And so, it is life and death in this case.' She took my face in her hands. 'And that is why we cannot ask Anika to deliver any notes. Apart from the fact it would mean entrusting Anika with yet another secret when she already holds so many, it would be unfair to add another. Revealing – even to Hetty – your whereabouts is a risk to you.'

'And to you?' I asked, not hiding the sour note in my voice.

'Yes.' Her tone was matter of fact. 'And to me. But that's not the only reason I have refused you, don't you see?'

Of course, yes, I could. But that didn't make it any better. However, I knew that for now at least there was no point pressing her further, so I apologised and said I knew that she had already risked her own security in helping us – me, Mutti and Papa.

'But you did say my parents were irrelevant – that hurt me.'

'I did not say that. Don't make things up.'

'You said last night that you didn't ask Anika about Mutti and Papa because they weren't relevant.'

'Oh, don't be ridiculous. Anika doesn't know you are here, so why would I bring them up? They weren't relevant to what we were speaking about. That's what I meant.' Ilse stood and rearranged the small glass animals on my dressing table. She straightened a framed print on the wall and turned to face me.

'You must realise with things as they are, we must be very careful about who knows what and how much. Does that make sense to you?' She paused. 'People are living on their nerves. There are more people happily willing to turn on their neighbours than I care to admit. I don't want you to feel afraid, but I don't know how to make you understand.'

So, it was true and not just Marta's perspective or a couple of random traitors. People on the outside, people you'd think were good and decent, were turning against one another, remorselessly betraying one another to ingratiate themselves with the Nazis.

I knew with all my heart that the Germans were not my only enemies. I also realised that Ilse was risking her life to protect mine with a guilty pain.

She looked so frayed and pale. It gave the impression of being able to see through her, like the four beautiful ladies in the architecture window at the Rijksmuseum.

I felt in that moment that Ilse regretted taking me in. She probably thought it was going to be for just a short while. Instead, she had become encumbered with me and the responsibility of me – keeping me fed, warm and safe – to keep me alive. And on top of it all, she had to put up with my moods.

Everything she said, though, did make sense and I knew well enough that each word uttered outside this house had to be well-considered and minutely orchestrated so as not to attract attention or arouse suspicion.

'So, let's forget this spat then,' she said. 'Your punishment for being so horrible is to help me boil the latest batch of infirmary sheets. There's a few days' worth to catch up on and my hands are red and dry like an old washer woman's. That's your job for tomorrow.'

Chapter 18

Just as the nightly mist that settled on the canals dissolved with the sunrise, so too did our recovered good mood vanish on entering the cellar the following morning to begin the task of washing the sheets.

At first, all appeared usual with everything in its proper place. The big square blocks of soap lay in their dishes; two stout vats sat in the middle of the room; the mangle for squeezing out the water stood in its usual place and the two laundry batons, used to drown the laundry in the vats, sat propped in a corner.

But over on the other side, storage bins had been overturned and corners and shelves disturbed. To my horror, this included the preserve shelves concealing my hiding place.

Someone had broken in.

I thought I knew what fear felt like. But this was different. I felt naked. Exposed by the intrusion. The palms of my hands prickled, my breath caught in my chest and my bowels went to water.

I pressed myself against a damp wall, hands pressed

over my mouth, eyes darting, seeking out the intruder.

The pile of shattered glass and an old sack flung over the sill of one of the two small cellar windows gave away the entry point. The intruder must have surely been a child. No adult, no matter how small and thin, could have squeezed through that opening.

It wasn't uncommon for Ilse to return from her lessons with Gerda, or from one of her other errands, with stories of desperate people resorting to stealing and cheating, competing for their share of the diminishing resources across the city, where soup kitchens and long food queues were regular sights.

And now some desperate soul had broken into our cellar. But how had we not heard? How had the culprit been able to break in with such stealth they didn't disturb our sleep? The idea was beyond frightening. The tight lines around Ilse's mouth and the way she twisted her wedding band relayed her worry.

'I don't understand.' She wiped her hands on her clean apron. 'Surely we would have heard this and you certainly would have known if someone had been in the house when I was out.'

The shock had sent blood rushing to my face and beads of sweat pricked my top lip.

I hadn't heard anything because I wasn't there when it happened. I was in the midst of my discovery at Pim's when Ilse had left the house.

Even if I had been here, I tried to ease my guilt, I couldn't have done anything to stop them. Not without giving myself away.

'The glass is old and brittle. It would take little to break it.' Ilse's eyes swept the room.

'It doesn't look like they took much,' I said. 'Not that there's much to take.' I bent to help pick up the glass and a small shard pricked the tip of my finger, making me cry out.

I watched the tiny red blob grow on the end of my finger, tremble for a moment and then splash to the floor.

Ilse managed to prise the sliver from my finger, causing a fresh bubble of blood to spring up.

Before we could get much further with our clean up, the scrape of the gate announced the arrival of Frau Voskuijl, the pastor's wife.

'Good news,' she called out in her loud clear voice. 'Frau Graaf, are you in? It's good news.'

I scuttled towards my dark corner, leaving Ilse to deal with the visitor.

'One moment,' Ilse called, ensuring I was safely out of sight. 'Let me just dry my hands.

'Frau Voskuijl,' Ilse finally greeted her. 'How are you? Everything well with Jan?'

'Marvellous, everything is marvellous. I've just come from the church,' Frau Voskuijl said. 'Jan heard from his cousin. Italy has surrendered to the Allies.'

My heart leapt and inside my hidey-hole, sucking

on my bloodied finger, my face scrunched into a smile. I pressed my ear against the top slider.

'It's such good news,' Frau Voskuijl continued. 'This just could be the start of something. Look, Jan and I are hosting a small and discreet gathering of thanksgiving at home this afternoon. Please come if you are able. I must be off. There are a few others to see.'

The scrape of the gate indicated Frau Voskuijl's departure and I relaxed a little.

Ilse tapped on the slider, signalling the coast was clear.

'Sounds like good news?' I said, emerging from my hiding place, smoothing my skirt.

'It does, but who knows anything anymore?' Hands on hips, Ilse looked around the cellar. 'Come, let's finish this.'

She clambered up a ladder and I handed her a shelving board to cover the broken window. We set things back in order, uprighted the overturned bins, tidied the empty preserving jars and swept away the remaining glass shards.

'Apart from almost frightening us to death, there's no damage done, I suppose.' Ilse cast her gaze around the space. 'There are break-ins all over. People have to eat.'

And with that, we turned our minds to the original task of the infirmary laundry.

***

It was as though things were taking a positive turn and from there on the war against the Nazis seemed to progress in the background as I took any opportunity to visit Pim and the hidden children in the Walsmas' cellar. As my friendships developed with them, I poured my descriptions into letters to Hetty.

> There are two girls called Cornelia and Renate who are deaf and use sign language to communicate. They've taught me to say 'please', 'thank you', and 'I have to go home'.
>
> Another girl, Clara, who I think is just a little younger than me, but is more like Double B in the way she acts, has a funny little sing-song voice, and is constantly asking questions. There's a boy called Aldo who is never still and has a big hump on his back. I feel bad for saying it, but he repulsed me at first. But I'm getting used to him and just have to be patient with him.
>
> I think my favourite is a little boy, a German-Jew, named Tomas. He's blind but he can still play the flute. He has such a sweet nature that reminds me of Double B. I tell him about all the places I'd like to visit one day – Venice, with waterways instead of streets; the pyramids, that

hold treasures and the bodies of ancient kings; and queens and Australia, where they have strange animals that carry their babies in pouches.

So my days seemed to pass by smoothly enough and in November we were sure a large Allied air raid on Berlin was going to be the thing to quickly bring the Germans to their knees.

But it didn't.

Christmas 1943 came and went. Ilse went to church and marked Christmas Eve with friends from her bowling group, while I sat by the *Küche* fire and worked on my latest knitting project.

1944. Would this be the year? Would 1944's arrival bring evening walks through the city in summer, afternoon picnics with my parents and the Caslers in Vondelpark, a trip to Zandvoort and rides on packed trams? If we were liberated, I promised myself I would take Double B to the park to look for fairies without question or resentment. I would keep up with all my chores around the shop and never complain about French grammar again. If only I could walk through the front door of Ilse's house, go safely into the world without a care.

This time there were no answers of 'for certain', 'to be sure', or 'it'll be over by summer'.

In February, Pim said word on the street was that Britain might invade the Netherlands. 'Yes! At last,' I said to Adelena as I sat cross-legged on my bed one evening, brushing my lank hair while fantasising I had a curtain of lustrous blonde tresses.

'Freedom will bring swathes of Allied troops to the city, all of them suave Englishmen and handsome Americans,' I said, watching her closely. 'They will sweep through the city and send those Germans running home to Hitler, their tails between their legs and sorry they ever started this stupid war.'

Using my hairbrush, I took aim at an imaginary enemy. 'The first thing I'll do is find Hetty. Pim will lead all the children from next door out into the fresh air and we can all go to Vondelpark and lie on the grass in the sun.'

I ignored Adelena's eye roll.

'The best thing,' I said, putting down the hairbrush, 'is my parents will come back, and Ilse will marry a square-jawed American who will love her and look after her, and we will put all this behind us.'

'Don't count your chickens,' Adelena said, in that smug way that made me want to round on her with a stinging slap across her self-satisfied face. 'You really have no idea, do you? You've been cooped up way too long.'

'Who asked you?' I scowled to show her I meant business. 'Why do you do this?'

'Why do I do what?' She looked perplexed.

'Don't play stupid. Why do you have to say those things? Whatever happened to you to make you so mean and sour and hateful?'

'I'm not hateful. It's called being awake and realistic.'

I lay down and turned my back on her.

'Not like you,' she went on. 'You have no idea. You're here safe and sound and you dream about handsome soldiers and glamorous film stars and when the war's over and how everything will go back to normal.'

'Well, why wouldn't it?' I asked, rolling over to face her. 'The Germans will be beaten, and they'll run away. They're like Willi Smeltz. You remember him, that boy who moved here from Poland? He was big and brave, too, picking on that small Binder boy. He'd smash him in the nose or dangle him over the canals if Binder didn't keep good on his promise and bring Willi a guilder note each week.

'Remember that? Remember how scared we all grew? We'd scatter when we saw him on the street. And then Binder's big brother came back from Austria. He boxed that Willi good and proper. Sent him packing and he never bothered us again. We didn't have to worry about him or where he'd be or what he'd do. It all just went back to normal.'

Adelena shook her head slowly. 'You are such a simpleton.'

'Go then. You know the way out.'

Chapter 19

Ilse had to go even further afield for food and that meant cycling out to the farms once a week.

Farmers were having ever more problems getting their produce to market, thanks to the cutting of transport routes and blockades on normal trade by the Germans.

'It's as though they're trying to starve us out,' I said.

'We're lucky. At least we can still get good food if we make the effort,' Ilse said, always trying to find the bright side.

But it was still hard to imagine that while city people were half-starved, the farmers had mountains of grain, potatoes and sugar beets they couldn't sell.

Food collection was the task of women, children and old men. Ilse's food runs took almost a full day, which I of course, ignoring my still-present nagging guilt (often in the form of Adelena), took full advantage of.

As I told Hetty in my letters, it was during these frequent long absences that I soon forged friendships with the children next door. But in the weeks following my initial visit, some of the more severely afflicted children began disappearing, eventually leaving behind just Tomas, Aldo, Clara, Renate and Cornelia.

With his sisters and mother on a food collection mission one morning, I asked Pim, 'Where are they? All those others, they're not . . .'

'No, they're not dead,' he interrupted. 'They need medical care that we can't give them. My parents have allies who are doctors. They've been sent there.'

Some days Beatrice watched as I left, her ears flopping in a forlorn way, so I began to take her along. Aldo, the hunch-backed boy, was fascinated by her twitchy nose and stumpy little tail.

Marta reassured me that he meant no harm, but I did not like the way Aldo grabbed at Beatrice. When she tried to struggle from his grip, he only tightened his hold, clutching her closer to his chest. One day, in obvious distress, she began to snort.

'Stop, Aldo,' I said. 'Marta! He's hurting her. He will crush her to death.'

'You show him,' Marta said. 'You show him how to be gentle.'

So I did. I took charge and made him sit quietly, showing Aldo how Beatrice liked to be stroked and fed any tiny vegetable scraps that had escaped the cooking pot.

'You see what a little patience will do?' Marta said. 'Things have a way of working out.'

'Do you think so?' I sounded glum, even to my own ears. 'I thought being patient would have brought all this to an end by now, but it hasn't.'

'Don't be so down,' she said. 'When I was a girl all I wanted was to be able to keep up with my older sister Johanna. She was a champion show jumper and our bedroom was full of her prizes – ribbons and trophies everywhere. She was set for the Olympic Games. As for me, I just couldn't stay on a horse for more than five minutes. My weak little legs dangled on either side and off I'd come.'

'And did she go?' I asked. 'Did your sister go to the Olympics? Did she meet Jesse Owens?'

Our school's gymnasium teacher used to tell us all about the Berlin Olympics in 1936 and how the African American athlete won not just one, but four gold medals.

'Jesse Owens is a hero,' Tomas piped up, his elfin face beaming. 'He showed Hitler!'

'He sure did.' Marta smiled. 'No, she didn't meet him. She didn't get to Berlin.' Her smile faded. 'Her horse fell at a jump. It snapped Johanna's neck so that she felt nothing below her shoulders.'

Marta's voice caught in her throat, and when I put my hand on her shoulder, she covered it with her own warm fingers. 'My mother never quite got over it,' she went on. 'I'd spoon food into Johanna's open mouth, wiping her tears and the spilled food as I went. Eventually she was put into a home and she only lived another year. She stopped eating.'

'Oh, I'm sorry.'

'I made up my mind that I would keep trying to master the horse,' Marta said. 'I made my legs strong by cycling every day and walking up and down the stairs at home until I drove my father mad. I was never as good as Johanna, but I was as good as I could be.'

I was taking all this in when Pim took over. 'I know how this goes,' he said. 'I hear this all the time when I don't want to practise, when I would rather go to the cinema or to Vondelpark. What she is saying –'

But it was my turn to cut in. 'I'm not stupid you know, Willem. Your mother is saying that sticking it out brings rewards.'

I poked my tongue out and he said, 'You can just call me Pim if you like. Everyone else here does.'

'I'm so used to calling you Willem, I forget. I like "Pim" better though.'

Pim rolled his eyes and added, 'Well, I hate it.'

His mother ruffled his hair.

He ducked away and said, 'But I figure when I'm a famous musician with the respect I deserve, everyone can call me Willem.'

We laughed, just as we used to over some shared amusement. Only this time I was aware of the gap in our gang created by the absence of Hetty and little Double B, who'd been ever trailing in our wake. Not to mention Fritz and his big broad head and bright eyes.

Riding the wave of good humour, Marta announced, 'I have a surprise,' and reached into her apron. Everyone gathered around excitedly, moths to a flame, as Marta's hand reappeared with a bar of Swiss chocolate.

'Where did you get that?' an awestruck Pim asked.

'That doesn't matter.' Grinning widely, Marta handed out smooth, creamy squares of chocolate. I held the precious square between my fingers and inhaled its sweetness before popping it in my mouth. I fought the urge to consume it immediately and allowed the chocolate to rest on my tongue for a moment, the hair rising on my arms as it melted.

Just when I thought no more surprises were possible, my heart jumped on hearing an old and familiar husky yelp and brisk clip on the stairs.

'Is that . . .?'

Pim interrupted me before I could finish my sentence.

'It's Fritz!'

Seconds later, my four-legged friend was licking my face and nudging my empty pockets with his nose.

'Calm down, Fritz!' Marta laughed. 'Look how happy he is.'

He was beside himself, as was I. Dropping to my knees, I nestled my face against his warm neck.

'He has been with friends of Herr Winkler's. They

can no longer care for him so they asked us to take care of him,' Marta said.

'Where did he go?' I asked, picking myself up off the floor after being knocked backwards by Fritz.

It was Marta who answered. 'We aren't sure where he is.'

'I like Herr Winkler. I hope he's safe,' I said.

By now, without my mother's hovering protection, I had lost much of my former shyness. Clara, Aldo, Tomas, Pim and I became special friends with the two deaf girls – Cornelia and Renate. Together, we were quite a unit.

There was an old book in their small library, and it was full of old-fashioned children's games, silly rhymes and pictures. Clara's favourite rhyme was Playtime ABC.

'M is for Mutti, dearest of all, who wipes baby's tears when she has a hard fall.' She'd say it over and over until Aldo slapped his hand over Clara's mouth, igniting an almighty squabble, pulling hair and causing tears.

Meanwhile, Tomas learned by heart, 'T for the trumpet, the troops hear its call, and join their bold captain to stand or to fall,' which he recited while marching back and forth and saluting.

I often found myself watching Tomas move carefully around the cellar, sometimes bumping into furniture or stumbling on a discarded toy. He and

Willem on occasion performed together to everyone's delight, filling the cellar with light and air, even if the sound was a little lifeless.

One afternoon, after putting his flute aside, Tomas grabbed for my hand. 'When the war's over, Lena, my *Opa* is going to take me to a concert in Vienna and to visit Vivaldi's birthplace in Venice.'

'Lucky you.' I ruffled his dark hair.

'If your parents allow it, you must come. And Pim, too.'

'That sounds like an outstanding plan,' Pim said, smiling at me over Tomas's head. 'I'll start packing my bags.'

Tomas's pale face beamed as though lit from within as he placed his flute back into its case with great care.

I was wondering if his blindness made this confinement harder for Tomas, but my train of thought was interrupted by a high-pitched squeal. Clara and Aldo tussled on the floor by the old oil stove. They had been playing with a bag of marbles.

'Stop it, you two.' Pim intervened, pulling Aldo away from Clara. 'That's enough.'

'He called me a *dummkopf-baby*.' Clara wiped the tears from her pale eyelashes. 'That's what the doctors said, too. But I'm not.'

Pim distracted Aldo by taking Clara's spot in the game of marbles. I plonked down on a low settee, patting an adjacent cushion. Clara accepted the invitation and sat down hard.

Clara had been taken from her parents when a German doctor said she was 'feeble-minded', couldn't be educated, and had to go away to be 'fixed up'.

I tried to comfort her. 'It's not fair.'

'No. But they sent me to the hospital with a lot of other children and babies. I liked cuddling the little babies. But the nurses were mean. They didn't feed us much and they let the babies cry all night long. It made my head hurt.'

She held her hands up to cover her ears and shut her eyes against the memory. 'Every day the doctors came. "*Todesärzte*. Doctors of Death", some of the children called them. They stuck a few of the children with needles and gave them medicine to make them quiet.'

A pit opened in my stomach.

'One day a baby with one eye had an injection to go quiet and he didn't wake up.' Clara swallowed. 'And my friend, who was just like me, had an injection and never woke up, either. Then, there were no more babies crying. Instead, at last, there were only happy babies.'

The pit in my stomach widened as Clara's story continued and her hands twisted in her lap. 'I ran down the hall one day to play with them but all their beds were empty.' The confused memory of the sad discovery showed in her light brown eyes. 'They had stopped being bad crying Jew babies, one of the nurses said, so they were sent home to their parents.'

I pulled a clean handkerchief from my skirt pocket and handed it to her. 'Well, I suppose that's good,' I said. 'Good they went home again.'

'Someone else said it wasn't true, though. That they didn't go back home. Some of us saw an ambulance driving in and nurses pushing wheelbarrows with small bundles towards it.'

She buried her face in her hands and I drew her close, just as I did when Double B was upset about something.

Soon after, Clara told us that the older children, including herself, were loaded onto a bus with painted-out windows. She scratched her fingernail against the glass to make a peephole but could only see a few houses and trees.

By the time the bus stopped, it was growing dark and they got out at a square brick building with a tall chimney stack. There was a fearful thunderstorm and the terrified young passengers were herded into a small room and left to wait.

'It was dark, and the thunder was so loud. I cried and someone wouldn't stop screaming,' she said. 'But Marta and Franz came, dressed like doctors and nurses in long white coats.'

Clara said the children grew even more terrified at the sight of them, not knowing what new pain these doctors would impose on them. 'But they didn't hurt us. They took some of us away with them and that's how we got here,' Clara finished, and I noticed how much older she suddenly looked. 'I'm tired. I have to lie down.'

And she did, right there on a rug in the corner, leaving me on the settee, confusion and disgust rising throughout my body. I felt sick to my stomach. Where might I be if it weren't for Ilse?

Chapter 20

That evening, after another meagre supper, I flipped through my atlas while Ilse picked up her darning basket and set to work on several pairs of worn-out socks. I was happy to sit in silence under the glow of a table lamp and listen to the static of the radio.

As was the norm, the radio announcer shared news of the terror taking place in the real world, beyond the borders of my seclusion.

Without a word, Ilse leaned over and turned the sound right down. 'I can't bear it.' Her shoulders dropped. 'I saw another German woman today, in the square. She has Catholic relatives in Germany, like me. Things are not good there, either. There are Nazi rallies – total loyalty is expected and questions are asked if you don't attend.'

'So it's not just happening here with Jewish people?'

'Not just here. At these gatherings, she told me, everyone must rise to applaud the speaker. Everyone. It's deafening, she said, and it goes on and on. No one dares to be the first to stop clapping. So out of sheer terror, the applause continues until their arms ache and hands sting. She was at a rally and eventually one man was the first to stop. The next day, he was arrested. His fate is still unknown.'

I twisted the front of my pullover. 'Anyone who doesn't follow their rules is doomed. If they got their hands on us, we'd be doomed, too.'

'That's been obvious for a long time.'

Was it my anxiety or was Ilse staring at me a little too long?

Finally, she looked down at her darning and we sat in silence a moment longer before she asked, 'Are you sure you're all right on your own when I have to leave? Not too bored or lonely?'

'At first I was.' At least this was honest. 'But it's okay now.'

'What's changed, do you think?' She gazed at me over her stitching.

Why was she asking? Why out of the blue? Had she seen Marta in the square? Had she caught me when I didn't think she was home?

'Hmm?' she prompted, my silence stretching too long.

'Um, I don't really know.' My cheeks burned with the lie. 'I suppose I'm better at finding things to keep me busy, that's all.'

'What's your favourite thing to do to pass the time when you're on your own?'

My thoughts whirled. 'Read or write in my journal. Sketch.' I curled the edges of the atlas page

I was on, turning it into a scroll. 'I like to practise my French – I'm getting much better – and I study my music texts. I've started a movie star scrapbook, too. The time passes.'

'Do you know what I think?'

I couldn't tell if her mouth was shaped into a smile or a sneer. My stomach churned and my thoughts scattered like ash on the wind.

'Hello?' Ilse tapped a finger against my temple. 'I said, do you know what I think?'

She knew everything, I was sure of it. She knew I was a liar.

'No?' The word sounded small and strangled as the floor opened beneath me.

'I think you are maturing.'

'What?' I slapped the atlas shut in surprise. 'Maturing? Is that all?' I exhaled and laughed in sheer relief.

'Don't laugh. It's an important thing. You are no longer a child who needs to be occupied one hundred percent of the time. You know how to fill the space and that makes me happy for you, but I still worry when I am away for any length of time.'

'You don't need to worry about me, really.' I tried not to sound too desperate, fearful she would plan to reduce her time away. 'You are quite right. I'm able to fill my time quite well on my own.'

'Well, you see, that is proof you are certainly becoming more mature. But I can't help but still think of you as my Little Lena sometimes.'

Maturing. It was all I could do not to collapse with relief. All the thoughts I was unable to string together moments earlier now washed over me. I could not bear to think she should ever hate me for the lies I was telling. That she would forever look at me with disdain for being so untrustworthy.

But I had to crush the feelings back down, so turned my mind to the word hanging in the air. Maturing.

***

Perhaps it was true that I was 'maturing'. I certainly felt a responsibility towards the children at Pim's and because they couldn't get outdoors often, keeping everyone occupied wasn't easy. Squabbles and disputes often broke out over toys and space and whose turn it was to go be 'it' in hide and seek games. Fritz whined when this happened and he'd hide away under a bed, or would be found in a corner with his snout between his big paws.

Pim kept tadpoles and a black and yellow fire salamander in a glass tank in a corner. We were all fascinated with the transforming black wrigglers, observing their tiny budding legs as they morphed into frogs.

But for Clara it was Solomon, the salamander, that held a special allure, and she didn't stop pestering Pim to let her hold him. Fed up one afternoon, he gave in and gently placed Solomon in her small, cupped hands. But when he wriggled and squirmed, she squealed and dropped him on the floor. Aldo darted in, grabbed Solomon's tail, and the whole thing came off in his hands.

Everyone screamed and jumped around. Fritz growled and his ears folded back.

'Be quiet, will you?' Pim hissed. We all closed in to watch Solomon's detached tail wriggle and twist at our feet.

I stared down, agog at the jiggling tail, wondering if it could still feel anything now that it was no longer part of Solomon.

'Is he going to die?' I asked. 'The poor thing.'

Aldo opened his mouth, but Pim clapped his hand over it and signalled for everyone to quieten down.

'What did you do that for?' I scowled at Clara. 'Why did you just drop him like that?'

'I didn't think he was going to be so slimy,' Clara said, hunching her shoulders and hiding her face in her hands.

'It doesn't matter, Clara,' Pim said as he retrieved Solomon and returned him to his tank. 'He'll grow another tail.'

I scoffed at the absurd idea. 'Don't lie! He won't grow another one. That's like saying Hitler will end his hatred for Jews,' I said. 'Why even make things up like that? You always must know more than us. You and Hetty were always like that.'

I could see he was hurt, but no one was more shocked than me by my nasty shot at him and at Hetty, and my cheeks burned red as proof. I put my hand to my mouth, but it was far too late to take back the petty barb.

'It's true,' he said. 'They evolved that way to escape predators. He'll grow another new tail within a few weeks.'

'This would be a handy thing for me to be able to do, should I ever get caught by the Germans,' I said. 'Imagine if they grabbed me and my arm came off in their hands and I could run away!'

'Don't say that,' Pim said, the frown on his face a sign the image of my detached arm disturbed him – a fact that deeply pleased me.

'Anyway,' he continued, 'it's true about Solomon's tail. Lots of things in nature find a way to adapt. I can show you in my animal encyclopaedia.'

'No need. I believe you,' I relented, grinning broadly. 'You always sound so serious – remember how Hetty would make fun of you for that?'

At that point I so wanted to tell him I knew where Hetty was, but I liked knowing something he didn't. Instead, I suggested another game and something we all enjoyed – dressing up and performing our own plays.

The Walsmas had an impressive collection of theatre costumes, props and wigs, inherited from an old aunty and former local actor of some renown.

'My turn to choose and I say we do *Hansel and Gretel*,' Tomas said.

'I'll be the witch.' I especially liked to dress up in a grey-haired wig, with a long black sweeping robe and black pointed witch's hat.

'You were the witch in *Snow White*, though,' Clara said. 'And in *Sleeping Beauty*.'

'Lena makes a good witch,' Pim said, running his hand through his fair hair and making it stick up at the front. His eyes crinkled as a cheeky smile spread across his freckled face. 'Why don't you play Gretel, Clara, and you get to eat all the sweets from the witch's house? Tomas can be Hansel since it was his idea and I will be the father. Renate, would you like to be the mother?'

Pim communicated her role using a variety of hilarious miming gestures, including sticking his chest out to indicate a large bust and walking around the cellar, hips swaying.

'But I want to wear the Viking helmet,' Tomas said when we had all recovered. He jutted his angular chin in defiance. 'I've changed my mind. Can we be Viking raiders today?'

'You can be a Hansel who wears a Viking helmet, okay?' I told him.

He didn't look convinced, but Tomas placed the helmet on his head and Clara took him by the hand.

With roles settled, I swept around the space, poking at the caged Hansel and Gretel.

Pim, the children and I were mid-performance when Fritz, who had recently incurred the wrath of several residents for harassing their pets and digging in their gardens, began whining.

'No going out just yet, Fritz,' Pim said.

'Maybe he wants to have a part,' Cornelia signed.

'He was the Big Bad Wolf in *Red Riding Hood*,' I reminded them. 'He can take a break. There are no wolves in this story. Let's continue.'

But Fritz wouldn't let up.

'Maybe he needs a pee,' Tomas said, making everyone snigger.

'Fritz,' I scolded. 'I was just getting to the best part.'

'All right, Fritz,' Pim said as he led him up the cellar stairs. 'Do you need the toilet, boy? I'll let you out, but don't go getting in trouble, understand?'

'Hurry back. You can get him when we've finished.'

Pim returned, and I resumed my role as the witch menacing the caged children. We were so immersed in the fantasy that we didn't hear the knocking on the front door.

'*Hallo*,' someone called out in German. '*Jemand zu Hause ist?*'

The owner of the voice was standing in the front hall!

Who would just walk in like this?

Fritz was barking madly. Frau Achterberg called, 'Frau Walsma, you need to control your animal. And you must lock your front door. Anyone can just walk right in here.' Annoyingly, she clapped her hands together, as though this would make Fritz stop. It only seemed to make him more furious.

We froze. Pim, who was still wearing his *lederhosen*, called up the stairs, 'One moment.' He frantically signalled to us to hide.

I flung the hat off, removed the rug from the tunnel hatch in the floor and motioned for everyone to pile in.

I had just led Tomas down and closed the hatch when I heard Pim speaking to someone in the cellar.

'Where are your parents?' the German voice asked.

'Out, Officer,' Pim said, curt but respectful. 'What do you want?'

'And when will they be back?' came another German voice.

'She will not be long.' Pim sounded calm enough.

Germans in the house. I was done for. Me, and all the other children also cowering in the tunnel. Pins and needles prickled across every surface of my skin and my breath came in short, sharp gasps as I tried to stop myself from screaming.

'I've told you people before,' Frau Achterberg started. 'My poor Gustav, he can't take anymore. The dog is a nuisance. I was just bringing him back here when I saw the officers and they asked if I needed help. So kind.'

I could hear her grovelling tone as she went on. 'I

didn't want to take them away from their important work, but they so generously offered to escort me. See how you are wasting their time?'

'Frau Achterberg has reported your dog is a nuisance,' one German said. 'She said he has been coming on to her property and fighting with her cat.'

'I am sorry,' Pim said.

'You should be, young man. Creating a public annoyance,' Frau Achterberg complained. 'Come, Officers, let us get out of here.'

'Please, madam,' the other officer said in a clipped voice. 'We will handle this.'

'We will keep him tied up then,' Pim said. 'I will tell my parents when they return.'

There was a short silence.

'I will see you out.' Pim's voice sounded strained.

'This is an interesting set-up down here,' one of the offciers said.

'Oh, yes. Sometimes my cousins come from the country come to stay with us. They are very messy.'

'Ah, a salamander tank,' one of the officers said. 'I had one of these when I was a boy. He's lost his tail. No matter, he'll grow another.'

It was pitch black in the tunnel and the children breathed heavily after the rush to the hiding place, but more so I guessed from fear. Fear I shared as I scrambled to find the oil lamp and matches.

Someone whimpered, causing someone else to hiss, 'Shhh.'

I thought I would pass out. I was barely breathing at all.

On the other side of the hatch, Pim sneezed, something he sometimes did when nervous. I could imagine his dread as they were sure to be taking in all the tell-tale signs of inhabitants in the cellar.

'You have been preparing for a play, I see. All these costumes and props. A witch's hat. Where is the witch? Flown off on her broomstick?'

Fritz growled, long and low.

'It's okay,' the officer said. 'You have been a bad dog. The neighbourhood is getting tired of your games.'

'I promise,' Pim said. 'We'll keep him under control from now.'

'That's what your father told me last week,' Frau Achterberg said. 'And look, today he's out again and back in my garden, harassing my cat and digging up my flower beds. If these officers hadn't been passing by and stopped to ask if they could be of assistance, he'd have torn my new beds to pieces. Officers, I feel I am going to faint with the stress of it. Please, will you take me out of here for some air?'

'Please, madam. Quiet one moment,' an officer said.

I had managed to light the lamp, turning the flame down low so as to be almost ineffective. But the children's wide-eyed faces were just visible in the gloom as I put my fingers to my lips.

The damp sat heavy in my lungs and I realised I was breathing in tiny shallow gasps, so that I became lightheaded and had to drop my head down for a few moments.

From our hiding place in the tunnel, we heard the squeak of the German officers' leather boots as they trod around the cellar.

Clara's fairy wings rustled as they crushed against the wall and Tomas's Viking helmet horns lightly scraped the ceiling. I removed the helmet, squeezing his hand as reassurance.

'Where are you, witch?' the officer cooed.

Oh no, we were done for.

'You can go, madam. We will wait for the boy's parents' return and we'll sort this problem with the dog. Hauser, go and see the Frau home safely.'

'But I need to speak –' she began.

'Come with me, madam. I will see you home.'

She puffed and muttered something I couldn't catch.

'Now, young man, we all have better things to do with our time, no?' the remaining officer said.

'Yes, sir,' poor Pim answered, his voice shaky.

'Don't be concerned about the dog,' he said. 'Try to keep it under control, though, or this woman will give no one any peace.'

'Yes, sir.'

'Very cosy down here,' he said. 'Like a little dormitory.'

'Yes, sir, for my cousins from the country, as I said.'

'So you said. There must be a lot of them. They keep plenty of things here. These wardrobes are full of clothing.'

'Yes, sir,' Pim said. 'My mother has many brothers and sisters.'

I began moving the children along the tunnel towards Ilse's garden, eternally grateful I had taken a pot of grease from the cellar and used it to coat the axles. I sent three away in the trolley and using the oil lamp, signalled the twins to follow behind with the others.

Praise be. Renate was such a good teacher and I a good student. I signed to her to collect everyone at the other end and keep them quiet. I promised I wouldn't be long and that all would be well.

Off they went but I hung back at the hatch, listening, unsure whether to leave Pim on his own with the officer.

'And what role are you playing today?'

'Ah, I'm Hansel's father,' Pim said.

'From *Hansel and Gretel*. I should have guessed. That's a good German fairytale.'

'Yes, sir, it is.'

'So, where are Hansel and Gretel? Where have they got to?'

No answer.

'Under the beds?' he asked. 'Hmm, no. Not there.'

Silence. Sweat pricked my brow, my hands bunched into fists.

Be strong, I repeated over and over in my head. You can't be fragile Little Lena, not a scared little mouse anymore. You must be Adelena. You must.

'Maybe they're in this wardrobe over here,' he said. 'Not here either.'

His tread drew closer to the hatch.

'Perhaps they are down here?'

'No!' Pim shouted.

Before I had time to react, the lid was lifted, and the officer's eyes looked directly into mine.

It was Officer Hass.

I didn't flinch. I didn't scream. I looked him dead in the eye, not with pleading, watery Lena-eyes, instead with Adelena's fierce and certain gaze.

He held my regard for the briefest moment, and I knew he recognised me under the grey wig.

Gently, he closed the hatch.

'No, no one down there, either,' he said. 'Your other cast members are very good at making themselves scarce.'

I leaned my head against the wall and exhaled.

Pim stammered something that made no sense

'Ah, yes, no, I don't know . . .'

'So, you like German fairytales, young man?'

'Yes, sir.'

'I'll tell you something,' he said. 'My best friend

was a Jewish boy. His grandmother read us Jewish fairytales and made us chocolate *rugelach*. Friends are important. Be a good friend, young man. I think you are.'

'Yes, sir.'

My pounding heart went out in overwhelming gratitude to that boy and his grandmother. Maybe their friendship, fairytales and chocolatey pastries had saved us all.

'I must go – and remember – you keep an eye on the dog.'

'Thank you, sir.' Pim's voice cracked. 'Yes, sir.'

Once we were sure the coast was clear, we all emerged from the hatch in silence. An overwhelming sense of confused relief enveloped us and it was several moments before we could utter any hushed or excited words about what had just happened.

I was certain of one thing, however, and announced it simply. 'From this day forward, never call me Lena again. I am Adelena. Like it says on my birth certificate.'

Chapter 21

My announcement after the incident in Pim's cellar was a turning point.

Of course, not everyone remembered to call me Adelena all the time, and I didn't always remind them when they slipped up. But there had been a small interior shift that brought with it a thin silvery armour.

In April, heading towards the end of spring, just to pass the time, Pim and I sometimes gave the others rides on our underground railway.

But today we were alone. Pim returned to Ilse's garden with me before I retreated inside.

As though sensing it would soon be called elsewhere, the sun tipped itself towards the earth, giving the last of itself to the gardens and fields before leaving. I wandered and picked a few bits and pieces from the fading spring flower beds for pressing between the pages of my books.

Walking back towards Ilse's house, we whispered of how our world had changed. Who would ever have thought it just a few years ago when we played in Vondelpark, laughing behind our hands in choir at someone or something, that we'd be having secret meetings in Ilse Graaf's garden, or thinking up games in a cellar to occupy a group of hidden orphans?

'Do you ever wonder about Hetty?' Pim asked. 'Do you ever wonder if she is alive or where she is?'

'Of course – always. I think of her always,' I said right away. 'And Double B. I thought about her the other night, during the thunderstorm. She hates storms.'

'Me too,' he said. 'Do you think they're dead? I think Hetty must be dead, or she'd have somehow let us know –'

'She is alive, Pim – I know for certain she is alive,' I blurted. 'Ilse told me. They are over on Keizersgracht – at the back of her father's office building.'

After all this time avoiding the topic, I couldn't help myself. I told him what Ilse had entrusted me with, about Anika and her involvement with the Caslers' hiding place.

I enjoyed the look that spread over Pim's face and relished the power of revealing such big news. The glow that spread over his freckled cheeks confirmed, in my mind, the suspicions that he had a crush on Hetty. It stung.

'Then if Anika knows, my parents must know, too,' he said. 'But why haven't they told me?'

'Because it's too dangerous – don't be so stupid.' I didn't tell him I had also asked the same questions myself.

Pim frowned but ignored the dig.

'But now that we know – we have to get a message to her,' he said. 'We must set up communication. Surely you've already tried?'

This was a surprise. It was not like Pim to be a risk-taker. That was more Hetty's style. He must have it bad, I thought.

I happily squashed his hopes and informed him just why it was so dangerous and could not possibly be risked.

'The adults are dead set against the idea.' I watched the glittering fish flash to the pond surface as we passed. 'They won't hear of it. It's far too risky, so forget about it.'

Even though I too desperately needed to speak to my dear friend, jealousy stirred and unfurled itself somewhere inside my chest. I wanted Pim to have those feelings for me, for his eyes to shine when he thought about me the way that they did whenever we spoke about Hetty.

'Anyway, if she wanted to get a message to you, she could have done it before this,' I said. 'She doesn't know where I am, but she must know that Anika speaks to your parents.'

'Shut up, Lena. I mean Adelena,' he said. 'It's not risky if we plan well. We just have to think about it. And how can you talk about risks? What do you think you've been doing lately? Playing it safe?'

Of course, he was right. I had been taking

increasing risks and, with the passing of time, had grown dangerously complacent.

But I wasn't going to admit that to Pim, not now.

'I've been very careful – no one would know. Ilse has no idea,' I snapped in a bid to deflect him. 'And how are you going to get your message to Hetty? Walk up to the front door and ask to speak to her?'

With that, I turned my back on him and went inside. The uncomfortable internal conflict came with a metallic tang at the back of my mouth and salty tears coursed down my face. I paused to catch them with the tip of my tongue before silently closing the door behind me.

Chapter 22

I barely slept that night. Not just because I had been horrible to Pim, but because now I had someone else on my side, a co-conspirator who wanted to get in touch with Hetty as much as I did.

And with his relative freedom as a Dutch boy, he had opportunities that I did not.

But how were we to execute our plans? That was the question that kept me tossing and turning throughout the night. I had no doubt that just over the garden wall, Pim was probably spending a restless night thinking the same thing. Each time the Westertoren chimed, it thrilled me to know that at that exact same moment, Pim, Hetty and I were all hearing the same thing. I saw it as a code that we all remained united despite the dark.

As my bad luck would have it, Ilse came down with a bad cold and barely left the house the entire following week, which meant I was stuck indoors again.

She was forced to cancel all her students and several well-meaning parents dropped by to deliver small parcels of food. It was touching really, and

Ilse was humbled that at a time when so many had so little, they were still willing to share. She had to refuse several offers from would-be nurses, saying she did not want to risk passing anything on, especially as medicines were so hard to come by.

The truth was I made an excellent nurse, running up and down with hot cups of herbal tea, boiled onion and garlic broth and the other remedies delivered by kind friends and students' parents. Even Officer Kaufmann's wife dropped in to deliver a good-sized pot of chicken soup. We made the dish last a week by rationing watered-down servings.

Making sure Ilse was warm, comfortable, hydrated and entertained was my job and one I took seriously. I set the small radio up in her room, rubbed her feet and massaged her thin and aching legs.

Ilse was exhausted. Until now she had still been taking students and doing her infirmary laundry runs – plus she had the worry of me, keeping me fed and safe and hunting around for food and keeping up appearances so as not to rouse attention.

Even though it was a plan I constantly turned over in my mind, I was still no closer to answering the question of just how Pim and I would contact Hetty without help. I spent the week reviewing all the letters I had written to her over the months – now perhaps I would get to send them after all, if only we could work out how. I went through the magazines Ilse had bought me and tore out the photos of our favourite Hollywood stars. I decided to send her a parcel. I made a card and included some of the pressed flowers from the garden.

When Ilse was finally feeling better, she went out on a Saturday afternoon to replenish our supplies and post a letter to her mother. I waited impatiently for half an hour before daring to step foot outside again, somehow fearful she may have forgotten something, or would feel ill again and decide to return.

I snatched up my parcel of letters and pictures for Hetty and tore through the garden and into the tunnel, tapped on the hatch and climbed up into the cellar.

Immediately I was surrounded by Clara, Cornelia and Aldo, demanding to know where I had been the past week.

'You can't just leave us like that,' Clara scolded.

'I would have thought Pim told you,' I said. 'Ilse's been unwell.'

I brushed her away and asked after Pim. He was with Tomas and Marta in the Walsmas' cramped back *Küche*.

I leapt up the stairs and found him cutting beets at a table in front of a narrow window that overlooked the private back courtyard.

The room was similar in size to Ilse's, but not nearly as neat and tidy. A pale oak dresser was stacked with newspapers; two meat safes stood side by side, one open, displaying its empty shelves. Two large cast-iron pots bubbled away on the black iron stove. Metal buckets containing shrivelled vegetables, smelling earthy and musty, stood lined up along one wall and the bare wooden floorboards were in need of a good sweep.

I cleared my throat and apologised for being sullen the last time I saw him.

'That's okay.' He smiled and wiped the back of his hand against his brow.

I knew I wouldn't have been as understanding and told him so.

Tomas stood close beside Pim and was washing the beets in the sink. He took great delight plonking them in a big iron pot. He dried his hands and felt his way along to the sink and to the end of the table to where I stood.

'Lena,' Tomas said.

I reached for his hand and gave a squeeze. 'Adelena. Remember?'

'Sorry.' His grin was crooked. 'Adelena, we've been talking about you.'

'Oh really?' I was taken aback. 'And what have you been saying, Tomas?'

'We think it's time you told Ilse what's been going on,' he said.

'Thank you, Tomas.' Marta pulled rank on him. 'Look, Adelena, I know I feel very bad keeping this from her and at times I actually think I should never have encouraged your visits.'

This made me wonder whether the suggestion sprang from her own real sense of guilt or for wanting to soothe mine, which came and went, not unlike Adelena, depending on the day and the occasion. While I increasingly felt focused and determined, there were still times I was very much Little Lena, groping my way around in the dark.

'You have been taking very big risks and I have allowed it,' Marta said, setting her knife down and resting her forehead briefly in her hand. 'Many of us in the city are taking risks at this time to help other people, so I'm sure she would understand.'

'No. Please, no,' I begged, somehow feeling rejected, unwanted . . . and like an intruder. 'We can't tell her – I can't tell her that I have broken my promise to her, and to my parents, to be good and obedient. Please don't tell, Marta.'

'I think maybe you underestimate her,' she answered, getting up from the table, its oak surface scarred and marked by years of heavy use.

'Don't tell.' I was close to tears. 'If it makes you feel better, I will just stop coming here at all. That will be easier, won't it? I only came to give you this, Pim – it's for Hetty.'

I thrust the packet I had tied with the ribbon I'd kept from my parents' birthday parcel at him.

Without another word I headed home, picking my way through the garden and back inside, where I threw myself on my bed and quietly wept.

It was weeks before I went out again, even with Ilse, into the garden.

As the food on our table diminished further, my hips and ribcage became prominent. We both grew thinner by the day. I knew Ilse was worried, but I felt so flat I could barely even try at pretending otherwise.

I heard Pim come and go for his lessons. Pim and the others. How I envied their freedom – coming and going, leading a normal life. Normal in comparison to mine at least, where I couldn't even post a letter to my best friend, sing out loud or go to the cinema on a Sunday afternoon.

I hated the Nazis more than ever. I wanted them smashed and punished and felt that the world had forgotten me and all the others like me were forced to hide year after year, season after season, cooped indoors like insects, to exist beyond the reach of their punishments for simply not being one of them.

I skulked around in the shadows, behind the walls, under the windowsills, behind the curtains. When it all got too much, I just lay in bed all day.

Early one evening Ilse asked if I needed a doctor.

'I know someone I believe I can trust,' she said. 'Pim's mother mentioned someone to me. You can take valerian drops quite safely. It will help you sleep and calm you, Lena – sorry, Adelena. And I'm sure I can find some brewer's yeast to boost you up.'

'You mentioned me to someone?' I asked her.

'Not directly, but there is a woman and I know she

is someone I can trust. Someone nearby.'

'No, Ilse, it's all right,' I said. 'I don't need anything. I just feel hopeless and forgotten. Will it always be like this? Will it ever end?'

She snuggled in next to me and we spoke into the night of this and that, about the war's progress, and that there was news through the Resistance that the Allies would be in Europe by the summer.

And so, the weeks until June passed easily and ordinarily enough. But at the start of June came the news that the Allies had landed in France. Surely, it wouldn't be much longer.

Ilse and I danced around the *Küche* like two fools who'd drunk too much cherry schnapps. We sat up much of that first night as the news began to filter through on the radio set.

The following day was crisp but clear. Sleepily, I made the effort to get up, wash and dress.

When I went down to the *Küche*, Ilse made me sit and shut my eyes – just like she had in the early days. But this time I was not waiting for something bad to happen.

'Put out your hands,' she said and obediently, I did so.

She placed two soft chicks in my cupped hands. They were past the yellow stage, but still twitchy, small chirping bundles of feathers.

'Maybe we will have eggs in a few more months,' Ilse said.

'But where did they come from?'

'Let's just say they fell off the back of a farm truck on the way to a German supply *Küche*.'

I spent the morning playing with the chicks and helping Ilse make flatbread.

That afternoon, Pim arrived for his lesson. It was hard not to run down to the *Stube* and sit while he played.

At the end of the lesson, he stood at the foot of the stairs speaking of nothing of importance, asking Ilse if she had a busy afternoon ahead and even commenting on the mild weather.

Sensing he was stalling, I paid closer attention.

'Frau Graaf,' he said. 'My mother told me she has been speaking with Anika De Wit.'

'Yes, Pim?' Ilse asked. I could tell she was wondering where this was going. 'I know Anika.'

'She is a very good person and would be willing to help anybody – no matter what.'

'Yes, I know she is a very good person – we are lucky there are people like her in this world at times like this. Off you go home. I have work to do. I will see you next week.'

On the face of it, the exchange was a little odd, but not meaningless to me at least. I knew immediately that it was Pim's way of telling me that Anika would get our messages to Hetty. And hopefully she would be bringing some back to us.

Joy of joys! Could things get any better?

I wanted to throw open the windows and shout. I needed to run down the stairs and out into the street all the way to Herr Casler's offices on Keizersgracht.

But of course, I could not. I had to wait out the next couple of days before Ilse went out to take lessons with Gerda.

The minute I felt it was safe, I flew out of the house and headed for Pim's.

I had a terrible fright, though, on opening the tunnel hatch when I heard a noise coming from the other end.

It was Pim making his way to me. He had a small posy of daisies. On her way out, Ilse had stopped by to deliver some tutorial notes to him and he knew the coast was clear.

I was so happy to see him. We stood in the ditch at the tunnel entry and I threw my arms around him, almost knocking him off his feet.

'Shhh,' he said, placing his hands on my shoulders, frowning so that his sandy-coloured eyebrows drew together comically. He seemed to have grown several inches in the past weeks so that now I felt dwarfed. Even the sleeves of his checked shirt rode up his forearms.

'I know what you are going to tell me,' I babbled. 'I heard what you said to Ilse the other day – this is the best news. When do we start?'

'We already have. Anika has said she will deliver your parcel to Hetty.'

'When?' I demanded. 'When will she take it?'

'Soon. We haven't seen Anika for a week or so – but I'm sure it will be soon,' he said. 'But there's more. I heard my father tell my mother he knows a Resistance family living at Westermarkt overlooking the back part of Herr Casler's building. They told my father a young girl peeks from the high windows after business hours. She watches the birds in the chestnut tree in the courtyard garden. Anika will tell her to stay away from the windows or she might be seen by the wrong people.'

'Wouldn't it be wonderful if you could get up there, to Westermarkt and see if you can spot her?' I asked. 'Do you think –'

The clattering din of Ilse's gate being shaken made us both stare in wide-eyed terror at one another.

As the struggle at the front of the house continued, I gripped Pim's arm.

Noiselessly and probably stupidly, he followed me as I dashed towards the back of the house and zeroed in on the exterior entry to the cellar.

If we squeezed up, we could both hide together in my hidey-hole under the shelves.

But before I could undo the trapdoor, a long scraping noise told us that the gate had been opened.

'She needs to fix that,' a woman said in German. I heard two sets of footsteps coming up the short flight of steps to the front door.

'Mamma, I'm cold. I want to go home,' a girl's voice said.

'Yes, Gerda, right after this. We have more carrots than we need, and Frau Graaf has been very good in helping you with your lessons. We'll just leave these and go.'

It was Frau Kaufmann and Gerda.

With no time to get to Ilse's cellar, Pim and I flew through the back door and into the *Küche* – just as Gerda and her mother pressed the buzzer.

I knew that hinged *Küche* bench would come in handy one day, I thought, tossing Pim's posy on the table. I lifted the lid, and we both tumbled inside.

'There's no one home,' Frau Kaufmann said. 'We will leave this here with a note. Let me get my notebook.'

'Hurry, Mutti,' Gerda complained. 'I need to pee.'

There was only just enough room for us both inside the storage space, which smelled of old newspapers and wet earth.

'Get down,' I said. 'Move over so I can get in.'

I stopped lowering the lid as we heard Frau Kaufmann exclaim, 'Ahh, here she is. Good afternoon, Frau Graaf.'

Oh no! Ilse was home already and here I was trapped inside the storage seat with Pim.

'Please, won't you come in?' Ilse said. 'I was on my way to your house when I met your housekeeper on the street. She told me you were on your way here. Is something wrong?'

I carefully closed the lid. I could tell they were standing inside the hallway outside the *Küche*.

'We will stay for a moment. I'm sorry I didn't let you know – but with the landings and – well, things are changing again,' Frau Kaufmann said. 'I am so very sorry. Gerda will have to stop her lessons as we – she and I – will be going abroad shortly. To Switzerland, perhaps. We have been packing up the house and I must run some errands before we leave. It's all happened very quickly.'

She sounded as anxious as any mother would be having to relocate at short notice. I recalled Mutti's face when she and Papa broke the news of our changing circumstances.

'I see,' Ilse said in a measured tone that was both thoughtful and worried.

'I have come by some lovely carrots, Frau Graaf – far more than we need and I thought you might like some.'

'That is most kind,' Ilse said graciously. 'Won't you step into the *Küche*? It's the only room I keep warm and it's where I spend all my time when I am at home these days – what with the restrictions and all.'

Frau Kaufmann gave a little cough, before offering, 'Yes, it is all madness. Dreadful madness.'

This was rather generous, I thought, considering her status as the wife of a senior German officer.

'Indeed,' Ilse agreed. 'Please sit – I don't have much to offer. There is some coffee I have saved for special occasions. I think this qualifies.'

There was a clunk on the bench above us.

Had Gerda and her mother planted their bottoms over our heads? I felt light-headed, letting the trapped breath leak painfully from my lungs in slow snatches. If I had the ability, I would have stopped breathing altogether at that moment.

'Thank you,' Frau Kauffman said. 'No coffee. We have to get on. I will just leave the carrots here on the bench. I don't intend my visit to make things difficult for you – I saw that dreadful Achterberg woman as we passed, peeping out through her curtains. No doubt news of my visit will be all over the street by now and you will be a collaborator before supper time.'

Ilse chuckled and I could imagine her nodding in agreement.

'Mutti,' Gerda bleated.

'Excuse me, Frau Graaf,' the German woman said. 'May Gerda use your bathroom for a moment?'

'Of course,' Ilse replied. 'This way, Gerda. Follow me.'

My eyes widened in the gloom. This was a ploy, I thought, a trick and the German woman was going to search through Ilse's *Küche* for some clue to prove she was working against the Nazis.

Her light step told me she was looking out the

Küche window over the back garden. She lingered and I imagined her eyes admiring the pretty little plot. The heels on her shoes indicated her moving back, towards the bench.

Surely any moment, she would lift the bench seat and be gazing down into our terrified faces.

There was silence and the creaking of the wood over our heads told us that Frau Kaufmann had instead taken a seat.

I was sure my heart was about to stop. I squeezed Pim's hand and we pushed the tops of our heads together for comfort.

She sighed deeply and hummed a few lines of something I didn't recognise, drumming her fingers gently on the bench.

Then came the approaching voices of Ilse and Gerda.

'I hope you will keep up your practice, Gerda,' Ilse said. 'You are coming along very well.'

'I promise,' Gerda said. 'I wish we didn't have to leave, though. I will miss you. Most people have been very mean to me here.'

I heard the little girl's voice catch and felt a flutter of sympathy.

'Oh, Gerda, don't be sad,' Ilse said. 'Who knows what the future holds? Maybe we will meet again some time when all of this is over.'

The girl's mother interrupted. 'Come, Gerda. We have a lot to do to get ready.'

Their voices drifted from the small entry.

'Thank you,' Frau Kaufmann said. 'From the bottom of my heart, thank you. I know that it must have been difficult for you to have associated with us.'

'Please. It is enough that we are all still here – that we have made it so far through this chaos. *Bis bald*,' she said, using the informal German for 'goodbye' and wishing them safe travels. She saw the visitors out and I heard the door click as she locked it behind them.

All the while, Pim and I remained as still and alert as cats about to pounce on a baby robin. We listened as Ilse stepped briskly up the stairs and along the hallway. She would be looking for me.

I bustled Pim out through the back, silencing his attempts to speak, and met Ilse on her way back down the stairs.

'Oh, there you are. I was looking for you.' She smiled.

'I was hiding under the *Küche* seat,' I said.

'Not the cellar?'

'No time.'

'So close,' she said. 'You know they sat down for a moment?'

'I thought so.'

'Come on, I've managed to scrounge up some cream, cocoa and butter and a solid bit of wood that should burn well for a while.'

The news made me so happy, I almost skipped after her into the *Küche*. I stopped in my tracks though, when Ilse picked up my tossed-aside posy she had obviously overlooked during the unexpected visit.

She frowned. 'Where did this come from?'

'Perhaps from the visitors?' I lied.

'No,' she said.

The word fell flat to the floor.

My heart thudded so hard it must have been visible beneath my sweater.

The seconds stretched agonisingly. Unable to still my mind, I busied my trembling hands by folding some cotton napkins on the table, but I dropped the pile to the floor.

'No,' Ilse repeated. 'No, they didn't bring them.'

I wanted to throw my arms around her and beg for mercy, but Ilse may as well have been a thousand miles away from me.

I stood frozen with flaming cheeks, red with disgrace.

I blubbered and cried and blurted the whole thing out. Everything about the tunnel, Marta and Pim and the children and how it was good to have friends again and breathe fresh air and lie in the grass and sit in the branches. That I would have gone mad by now without the small freedom I had taken for myself.

Ilse didn't say a word, just walked back and forth around the *Küche* table. Her face was pale and tight, her mouth an angry slash in an otherwise blank oval.

'Have I not done enough for you?' she asked, pinching at her bottom lip, the fury-laced hurt clear in her voice so that I did not dare correct her. 'I thought I knew you better than this. Do you know how easy it would have been for someone to find out? Do you know what would have happened to us? To the Walsmas and those children?'

She didn't have to say anything more.

I knew I had let her down. I knew I had let my parents down. I had behaved like a selfish, arrogant fool. 'Ilse . . .'

She rounded on me with a raised hand and dropped it just as suddenly.

'Don't speak to me,' she said.

Tears coursed down my cheeks. I hung my head.

She was about to leave the room when there came a firm knock at the back door. We were both startled, gazing owl-eyed at one another.

There had been none of the usual prelude to a visitor – the warning grating of the gate, footsteps on the path or the jarring of the buzzer.

Someone had snuck up with the stealth of a thief.

Finally, I had undone all the careful planning by my parents and by Ilse to keep me safe and alive.

I deserved whatever came next, Adelena said. But Ilse did not.

Ilse lifted the lid on the bench seat and was momentarily stunned that I did not take the hint and move. Angered by my slowness, she shoved me down and silently shut the lid.

The next thing I heard was Marta's voice.

'Ah, Marta, Pim,' Ilse said. 'This is a nice surprise.'

'Look what I have.' I could hear something solid being placed on the table. 'It's coal. Don't ask me where it came from. Just accept it.'

'That is very kind and such a treat. I will ration it out carefully.' Ilse sounded a little stiff. 'I would ask you to sit, but I have things to do. I am behind in my laundry for the infirmary.'

'It's all right, Ilse,' I heard Marta say. 'You know my secret and I know yours.'

There followed an uncomfortable silence and Pim broke it with, 'Come out, Adelena.'

Of course, I remained bundled in fear and confusion. I bit my bottom lip and refused to move. All at once, the lid was lifted and I could only imagine the look on my face.

It was Marta who moved first. 'Come out,' she said. 'It's time to come out.'

With the radio crackling in the background and a pot of weak coffee before us, it was well into the evening before both women had exchanged full details of the happenings under each of the rooms and within the walls of their homes on either side of the common garden wall.

Ilse had known something of the goings-on at the home of Franz and Marta Walsma, but had never revealed the fact of my presence under her roof.

'Didn't you feel you could trust me with your secret, Ilse?' she asked.

'It's not that,' Ilse said. 'I promised Adelena's parents I'd protect her with my life and that meant telling no one.'

I felt a prickle of shame at this blatant reminder of the commitment she had made.

'Not only that, Marta,' she added. 'In entrusting me with their only daughter, they knew they were handing her to me indefinitely and into an uncertain future. I see her as my own.'

This made me well up and I blinked back tears.

'I felt that Johannes sent her to me for safe keeping,' she went on. 'Little Lena's given me a sense of purpose when all else in my life felt so pointless after – everything else.'

She didn't have to specify for me to know she meant after Johannes' death and her subsequent miscarriage. I knew she had taken herself to the attic with a plan to end her suffering.

Pim and I listened to these two fearless women speak of past, present and future. They laughed, cried, sat silently and at times spoke over one another as they probably enjoyed the first uncensored conversation either had truly shared in years.

As they exchanged news and information and joined bits and pieces of old tales, rumours and local folklore, Pim and I learned that a great and important old home had once taken up the site of his house and Ilse's, as well as several others nearby. It was an estate that included medieval tunnels, created as a quick link for servants and messengers to dash and dart between its various sprawling parts.

Until I told her of my discovery at the end of her garden, Ilse had no idea it was there, and she had paid little attention to the stories of Johannes' great-grandmother.

Pim and Marta took her out to show her the tunnel.

Chapter 23

After Ilse left for her tunnel inspection, I retreated to my room, unsure how she would respond to the reality of the secret hidden in the garden.

As the time ticked by, my fears grew.

Maybe I would be forbidden from going out again ever. If that happened, my world would shrink unbearably. Or perhaps Ilse would decide I wasn't to be trusted and she'd send me away. I wouldn't blame her. I'd lied and risked everything she – we – had worked so hard to protect.

A tap on my bedroom door signalled my wait was over. 'Come in,' I said. 'You took so long I was getting worried.'

'That will be the guilt I suppose,' Ilse said, her tone blunt.

There was nothing more to add to what I had said earlier.

'Well, it certainly was a revelation.' Round-eyed and bewildered, she entered the room. 'It's hard to believe that the story of the tunnels is actually true. I never could have imagined it.'

She sat on the edge of my bed. 'I can see the

attraction, really, I can. But the danger – it's unthinkable. I asked Marta how she could allow it.' Her brow knitted tightly. 'You've gotten away with it but we all know that luck doesn't last forever.'

'Please don't send me away,' I interrupted. 'I beg you. I know I've been an idiot. I'll do better. You can lock me in my room if you want, but please don't give up on me.'

I had worked myself up into a state and Ilse looked at me with those kind eyes. 'I'm not sending you anywhere.' She reached for my shaking hand. 'And I am not locking you in your room – though I did think about it. You have Pim and Marta to thank for that.'

Relief flooded my body and I fell forward onto her lap.

'I'm not your jailer.' She stroked my hair. 'I'm here to protect you and look after you and ensure that you make it through this mire safely out the other side.'

I lifted my head and threw my arms around her. 'You are better than I deserve,' I said.

Ilse and Marta had mulled at length over the situation and decided that my visits could continue as they were good not just for my morale, but for Marta's hidden children.

But there were rules.

I was no longer to go when Ilse was away from the house and I had to seek her permission. If Ilse said no, there were to be no arguments as she would have a good reason for refusal. I could only go twice a week, on Wednesdays and Sundays.

The rules were more than acceptable and now that I'd been reprieved, I stuck to the boundaries.

To our great surprise and bitter disappointment, in the weeks and months following June 1944's D-Day landings in France, conditions worsened, with food supplies becoming more and more scarce across the country.

The heroic Allies had been able to liberate the southern part of the country, but their efforts came to an abrupt halt when their attempt to gain control of the bridge across the Rhine River at Arnhem in the east failed.

At the start of autumn, I developed a sniffle that turned into a cold. Ilse made me stay in bed and nursed me as best she could on our diet that consisted of bread, occasionally some cheese, lots of sugar beet and bulb, sometimes potato and carrot and very rarely, milk. She supplemented a basic thin broth with some pickled vegetables and jams that remained in the cellar, thanks to her judicious rationing.

I had been starting to feel a little better when I woke one night in a terrible panic. Clambering around in the dark, I called for Ilse through an impassable fog, clinging to the bed sheets to stop being swept out to sea on an ever-growing wave. I couldn't open my eyes. I held my breath, desperate not to inhale the water. The wave grew in strength.

I became aware of a presence in the room. I could make out a small crowd around me. I pried my eyes open but couldn't see clearly. Dressed in centuries-old style, with hats, bonnets and long dress coats and skirts, they stood around my bed. Still, speechless, shadows. Some of them looked like my parents, some like Hetty and Double B. There was no threat. It was more of a suffocating curiosity pressing in around me. I cried but I didn't feel scared, I felt sad.

A rushing noise, like wind, but no movement. Not a hint. The room was like an incinerator and then Ilse was there. She threw open the bedroom window. A screeching blast of frosty air shot in, cooling the hot watery salt running down my cheeks and dripping from my clinging hair.

I had a sweating sickness. A doctor came by once with Marta – a kind but craggy old thing with a battered black bag. 'She is very sick, delirious,' I caught the doctor telling Ilse as I drifted in and out of sleep, rising to the surface of the rolling ocean of confusion. 'This could be very dangerous. You are putting yourself at grave risk taking her in, you realise?'

'I know, but her parents, they entrusted me . . .' Ilse's voice trailed off as I was dragged back down through the layers of fever by grabbing hands.

'If they find what you are doing and that I know what you are doing –'

'Say not a word, doctor, I beg you. She's a harmless

child. Like the others – the different ones . . .' Her words petered out as I submerged completely.

The candle had almost sputtered out by the time the hands released me. I surfaced again to hear the doctor mutter, 'It's a devil of a thing. Truly. Now that I understand more fully, Ilse, perhaps were I younger, I might do the same. I will say nothing, but I cannot come again. You will have to manage on your own as best you can. I have written down these old recipes and you know where to gather the herbs and at what time of the day from your plot. That is all I can do. Without antibiotics, her chances are slim.'

He left without looking at me again, closing the door softly.

Ilse knew I had grabbed snippets of the exchange in the dim room. 'Forget what you heard. It means nothing. You've been dreaming again. You won't have to be concerned with it.'

She fretted and fussed and nursed me with herbal tisanes, compresses and broths amid my moments of fever, delusion, heat, chill, vomit and pain.

As the illness ebbed and flowed, Ilse sat by my bed each night until I fell asleep. I was in this twilight place for a very long time and oftentimes felt drawn to the restful, eternally calm place I sensed beckoning me. It was a fingertip's reach away and I knew that here there'd be no hunger, fear, cold or worry. It would be so easy to roll on to my side and into that warm peachy glow.

But each time I started to relent to the sucking pull, something held me back – a gossamer web tied me to the bed, the room, the house, to Ilse and everyone I had known. If I surrendered to the pull, I may never see their faces again.

I wouldn't know how it all ends.

Even Adelena looked surprised as I contemplated a peace-filled eternity.

'I didn't think it would be like this,' she said when I woke one night to find her watching over me. Exhausted, Ilse lay on the nearby camp bed.

'What? Like what?'

'That it would be under these circumstances you'd end up meeting our maker.'

'Shut up, will you?' I snapped. 'This isn't the end.'

Over the next few days, inspired by thoughts of Mutti and Papa, of Hetty and Double B, I used what strength I had to pull myself out of bed.

My legs had shrunk to spindles. My eyes could stand no light brighter than a single candle. I bathed and later went down to the *Küche* and sat almost on top of the stove, still feeling cold. I spent hours reading and received a visit from Pim at least once a day. He still couldn't get used to my proper name and often slipped back to 'Lena'. But I excused him. There were still times I felt very much like timid Little Lena.

Winter had come early, something the Germans took advantage of, making life even more difficult for us by restricting all kinds of transport movements. It was so cold our poor young hens perished in their outdoor coop, and with them the promise of fresh eggs.

One afternoon, on a day I had been feeling my best in a long time, Pim stepped into the *Küche* and stamped his cold feet in front of the stove.

Ilse was out, looking for anything she could find to burn to keep us warm. She took her never-used baby carriage on these foraging trips.

'I should put it to good use, no?' she said with a smile when I asked if she really wanted to pile it up with dirty odds and ends.

When Pim had finished his stomping, he stood stiffly, and I nodded for him to sit down. He pulled up a seat and plunked down on the opposite side of the little hissing stove. He held out a long white narrow sheet of paper, gesturing for me to take it. He held it by one corner, and I could see it had been concertinaed, folded over and over, like the little paper fans we used to make in the summer.

'It's for you,' he said. 'A letter. Anika brought it inside her bike seat.'

I set aside the cup of steaming nettle tea I had been cradling and reached for the paper, before my hand hesitated halfway.

'A letter? What's it about?' I asked Pim, almost afraid of the answer. Was this some awful correspondence about my parents? Had they been betrayed? Or maybe it was good news? They were coming to get me!

'From Hetty,' Pim said and pushed it under my nose.

I snatched at the paper.

'When? How?' But I didn't hear anything else he may have said. I spread the buckled and crackling paper across the *Küche* table, trying to smooth the bumps out.

I took it over to the window and in the thin light, read the words from my friend.

> July 31, 1944
> Dearest Lena
> How happy and amazed I was to get your letters and the beautiful pressed flowers!
>
> You are so lucky to have your own room – I share my small space with Fräulein Fischer! Can you believe that? I'm crowded in here with all these people and can't get a minute to myself.
>
> The whole idea of secret tunnels makes me so jealous! I knew you had it in you to venture out on your own. We have to creep around here like mice. We can't make any noise at all, or even flush the toilet or go near the windows.
>
> I'm so happy to know that you are

safe! I can't tell you how lonely I am and how much I miss you. I have Ursula of course and there is a boy, Walter, who is quite nice – but there is no one like my real friends.

How are you getting along with Fritz these days? I always wanted a big dog, but Mummy wouldn't let me. I don't care what she says, I'm getting one when we get out of here.

The longer this all goes on, the harder it is sometimes to believe it will ever end. Let's hope that the Allies get here soon and we can all be together again! Can you imagine the party we're going to have? I've told my parents that we must take everyone we know out for a special meal at the best restaurant in the city, somewhere like De Silveren Spiegel.

Like I'm sure you were, we were all so excited here last month when we heard that the invasion of France has begun – what better fifteenth birthday present could I receive?

So, to far more important matters. Have you kissed Willem yet? I can't believe he lets his family call him Pim – makes him sound like such a baby. I know you always had a crush on him – even

> though you never said. It was obvious to me. I hope that you have kissed him and if you haven't yet, then you had better hurry up.
>
> I've been keeping up with my lessons well – for one thing, it passes the time and it keeps the mind occupied.
>
> Enough of my ramblings and I will wait impatiently for your next instalment to hear what else you and Willem have been up to.
>
> Lots of love from your friend – and give my regards to Willem!
>
> Hetty C

I beamed at Pim and threw my arms around his neck, noting how he blushed but didn't pull away.

'Did you read it?' I asked, remembering what Hetty had said about kissing him.

'No,' he said.

'Good.' Relieved, I exhaled deeply, sparking a coughing fit – something that had persisted since my illness. 'I knew she'd do it. We promised we would, and we did. How clever are we?'

But Pim didn't seem to share my joy. He sat, staring into the mid-distance, swallowing hard.

'What's wrong with you? Why so grumpy and why did it take so long to get this here? It was written more than a month ago.'

There was no answer.

'Pim! Answer me, will you?'

'You were sick most of that time and Anika only brought it over to us last week,' he said. 'She found it among a whole lot of things left behind at the hiding place.'

'Left behind? Are they free? Is there news?' I held the paper to my chest.

'No. No news. Well, yes there is, but . . .'

'Yes, there is news or no, there isn't? Which one is it?'

'They've been found.' The words were simple, but I couldn't take them in.

'Found? What do you mean?'

'Just that – someone found out and turned them in to the Gestapo,' Pim said. 'All of them. They've been taken away.' He sniffled.

'No! Who? When did this happen? Where are they?'

'August,' he said. 'It was August twelve. They've been taken to one of the camps and I couldn't tell you. You were too sick, Adelena. I wanted to tell you, but they wouldn't let me.'

I looked at the letter still in my hand and watched the paper tremble. My heart raced and I curled up on the floor.

'Adelena, please get up,' Pim begged. 'I shouldn't have blurted it out like that.'

I didn't answer him. I didn't move for a long time.

He knelt beside me and stayed close in silence.

'Come on,' he said. I was so light, he lifted me with little effort and sat me on the *Küche* bench seat.

I asked, my voice a whisper, 'How were they discovered?'

'No one quite knows.' A deep line appeared on his forehead. 'After more than two years, Mother says they may have become a little less careful. Leaving a window open, the chink in a curtain, accidental noises – there are plenty of snoops around to notice these things.'

Of course, I thought about all my indiscretions and risk-taking. My carelessness had been astounding.

'But who would give them away?'

'There are suspects of course – Tony Alhers, he's a nationalist, Willem van Maaren from the stockroom in the warehouse, or even one of the cleaners.'

'What does Anika say?'

'She's in a bad way,' he said. 'She stopped by one night. She has some papers and belongings for safekeeping to return later. But she gave me the letter to give to you when I thought you were up to it.'

I couldn't speak. Not a word. We sat side by side in the cold room and re-read the letter together. I didn't care that he would read what Hetty had said about me having a crush on him. That was childish stuff. And I was no longer a child.

'July thirty-first – that was when she wrote this, less

than two weeks before they were found.' I waved it in front of Pim's face.

In the following days and weeks came terrible guilt and constant dread. I felt guilty about being alive and for every breath I took, guilty for all the risks I had taken, guilty for putting my own whims and curiosities above Ilse's safety, guilty for not thinking about my parents more often and guilty that I had never said a proper goodbye. I feared discovery and every sound; both the well-known and the unfamiliar made me jump. Where once I felt comfortable in my darkened room, I imagined it hid dark shadowy threats, or that it harboured spies and collaborators.

If Hetty could be betrayed, then so could I.

Chapter 24

That September the railway workers went on strike, bringing all transport, including food trucks, to a standstill.

'Why?' I asked Ilse, still grappling with the news Hetty and the others had been betrayed. 'Why are people turning on each other when things are so close to ending? Why are our own people making it worse by stopping the trains?'

The Allies by now had liberated the south, but the Germans still had a grip on the rest of us.

'It's to slow the Germans' movements,' she said.

'So we can catch them and smash them once and for all, I hope.'

But it didn't work so well. The Germans had reacted by freezing all food and medical transports to the western Netherlands, including, of course, to us in Amsterdam. Ilse said she had been at the market when the news came out.

'Adelena, if the news wasn't so terrible, it would have been comical for a moment. Frau Achterberg stood in the market square, her basket stuffed with as much as it could hold, and she shouted, "They are determined to kill us. Kill us all. Starve us to death, they will. You will see". She was throwing her arms around and was clearly enjoying the attention. I couldn't help but exchange a smile with Marta. But then you can't guess what happened.'

'Go on.' I pressed her hand as we sat huddled together in the living room. 'What?'

'A German soldier, he looked quite young and pale and tired, pushed to the front of the small crowd gathering around Frau Achterberg. He walked right up to her, "*Halt die Klappe*. Shut your mouth", he told her. She redirected all her shouting and ranting at him. People just froze and then someone from the back started to join in. People shouted things. Terrible things.'

'Like what?' I asked.

'Shocking things, Adelena, like "baby killer, rapist, Nazi pig". They went on and on until the soldier held his rifle up and told everyone to be quiet. Frau Achterberg spat at his feet.'

'Oh no! She didn't?' Even I knew what a stupid thing this was.

'He fired a shot in the air above our heads and knocked the basket from her hands. Everyone lost their senses, Adelena. People grabbed at the food on the ground and ran off in all directions. Frau Achterberg lunged at the soldier, but Frau Bresler slapped her face and dragged her away. Within seconds, the square was all but empty.'

'Why didn't he shoot her? Why didn't that soldier shoot everyone?'

'I don't know. Maybe he's had enough, just like us.'

We felt the harsh effects of the German retaliation to the rail strikes in other ways almost immediately. Our food supplies were already sub-standard, and the weather had also started to turn in the previous months, but we couldn't have guessed that it could get any more serious.

By the time the blockades were partially lifted in November to allow restricted food transports over water, an early winter had already set in. The canals froze over, as did water pipes and fuel lines. So, there was next to no food, the gas was shut down and there was no coal for heating because all supplies were still cut off.

It was as though the gods of winter, war and revenge – Hoor, Thor and Vali – had stepped out of my favourite myths and legends stories and formed an alliance against us.

With no gas for cooking and no coal for heating, people started to burn any wood they could get their hands on. People scavenged through the empty ghettos, tearing houses apart for wooden doors, windowsills, floorboards – whatever they could carry that was combustible. Ilse said even the wooden blocks between the tram rails were pulled up for fuel.

People moved their entire households into the

living rooms, beds and all, so they would only have to keep one room warm – something Ilse and I had also done in the past few days. She found a small table-top stove in the cellar which we used in the daytime for heat and food when it was so cold our breath was visible.

I became frighteningly weak from lack of food and rarely ever went next door where Marta, Pim and my other friends were in the same state.

Half-starved themselves, Marta and Ilse cycled once a week, against freezing headwinds and across open country, wearing pretty much every warm piece of clothing they had, in search of food.

Ilse said people were dying by the truckload. There had been no sugar, no butter, no cheese, or meat – though Ilse did say she heard that the staff of De Bijenkorf department store managed to sneak a horse into the basement where it was slaughtered, and the meat shared around.

'Poor animal,' I said when Ilse told me.

'People are desperate, I suppose.'

'I wouldn't be surprised, you know,' I said, in one of my frequent darker moments, 'if the Germans engineered this savage winter also, just to make us suffer even more. Where are the Allies? Why aren't they here?'

Even Ilse couldn't summon the enthusiasm for one of her upbeat and sensible explanations. She shook her head, stared at the little blue and orange flame on the stovetop and stirred the bubbling pot of tulip bulbs.

The Nutrition Council had distributed copies of sugar beet and tulip bulb recipes. There were recipes for purees, mash, biscuits and cakes – all made from tulip bulbs.

In December, temperatures dropped below freezing. People on the streets were referring to the current situation as a state of famine.

Pim turned up one afternoon. He had been sick, he said. He'd had the runs. 'Too many bulbs and sugar beets.'

'I know. Me too.' I made a gagging gesture. 'Pureed, mashed, baked, grated, boiled. Yuck.'

'Mother tried something new yesterday – bread,' he said. 'Bread made from tulips is not very good, I can tell you that. And I have Ilse to thank for it. She shared her recipe.'

I laughed. It was all but inedible and it sat stone-like in the gut. The skin of the bulb was removed, like an onion, and so was its centre. The rest was dried and baked in the oven. Ilse ground the bulbs to a meal-like consistency. She mixed it with water and salt, shaped it like a meatloaf, and baked it. It tasted like wet sawdust. But it filled our bellies for a while.

Tulip bulbs and sugar beets were usually thrown to the pigs, but people all over Amsterdam ate them now.

It was a bleak winter of ice, meat bone soup, bulbs and scavenging. It was famine. It was the Hunger Winter.

Chapter 25

So now, along with the lack of food and heat, power cuts were also the norm. Most dark afternoons, we took to the bed we shared in the *Küche*. Ilse and I hunkered down behind the shuttered windows, a lit candle dancing on the table next to us. We'd scour my atlas for rivers, mountain ranges and sweeping savannas in far-off countries where the sun shone all day and zebras grazed on wide open plains while lions stalked nearby.

We were lucky. Ilse had a plentiful stock of candles, courtesy of her great aunty, who had been fond of saying, 'A well-run household cannot function without a good supply of candles'. It was a family housekeeping motto passed down from her own mother. She had run the large family estate single-handedly after being widowed early, because her reckless young husband, having consumed too much good wine, decided to drive early one evening and came to grief on an ill-maintained mountain road.

By the New Year – 1945 – temperatures had eased a little, but power and food supplies were at best irregular. Ilse said there were still terrible sights on the streets. Scrappily dressed, barefoot children and old people queued for food, and there was relentless harassment from the occupiers.

Vondelpark had been closed to visitors since November, starving householders having regularly raided the park, cutting and hacking the trees for fuel. Ilse counted herself among the guilty crew of vandalising citizens.

Poor Beatrice was suffering too, her coat lacklustre; she was forced to forage around the garden beds for whatever she could find.

Having run out of our small supply of Vondelpark wood, I offered up the pages of my beloved atlas so we could stew a few bulbs one day, but Ilse refused. Instead, she broke the lid from the top of her oak jewel case and cast it into the weak fire.

'Stop. No, you can't.' I put my hand out. 'Not the wedding case from Johannes.'

Ilse looked at me with a sad smile. 'He would understand. He was a practical man. The oak will burn longer and hotter than paper. Besides, you will need the atlas for planning your adventures.'

'All right,' I said. 'But the next thing we put on the fire is my violin.'

'We'll see about that, and certainly not the Strad I've given you,' she said, before being struck by a coughing fit, something that had developed a few days earlier.

We sat close in bed and sometimes Ilse read to

me from her own childhood copy of *Tales of Hans Christian Andersen*. I adored the illustration plates, printed on glossy paper, and we spent time studying every detail. My favourite was *The Little Mermaid*, with her lustrous flowing hair, glorious tail and all the freedom to swim the vast undersea kingdom.

One evening, Ilse was warm and clammy. I made her set the book aside and fetched her a bowl of watery chicken broth. It was lukewarm, the stovetop having gone out some time ago, but she sipped it before resting back on the pillows.

'That's better,' she said. 'I will have a good sleep. That's what I need, sleep and rest. You are a wonderful nurse. You truly are very grown up now.'

Happy to be of use, I blew out the candle, pulled the bed covers up to my ears and buried my cold nose into the feather pillow. It was surprising how comforting a warm bed was at this time, when the rest of the world was cold and hard and unwelcoming.

Sometime later I woke in the dark, aware the wind was picking up and alert to its pulling at the shuttered windows. Disturbed by Ilse's restless sleep, I fumbled for a match and lit the candle, for comfort as much as practicality. Ilse's skin was hot to the touch. I padded to the *Küche* window and unhooked the latch, allowing a draught of icy wind to enter.

I paused to watch the full circle of the moon. Thin clouds rushed past its white face, not stopping to admire its pale beauty. Their haste to move on reminded me of our school visits to the Rijksmuseum, when we'd skirt past the Rembrandts, Vermeers and van Goghs, heading instead to the model warships, sails in full furl, to examine the trove of retrieved sunken treasure, or to scrutinise my favourite, the dollhouses, depicting perfect cross-sections of their miniature inhabitants' lives.

Mimicking something Ilse had done when I was ill, I rinsed a towel in the sink, the water so cold it burned. Nevertheless, I lay it on her fiery skin, mopping her brow, neck and shoulders. The action soothed her, and her twisting and turning began to still. Closing the window, I sat for a few moments, watching the rise and fall of her chest and wondering what to do next.

I made my move when the candle flickered out thanks to a whistle of wind forcing its way past the poorly sealed window frames, sending me scrambling again for the matches.

The blast had been the preamble to another storm that thrashed its way from above, and in minutes worked itself to a crescendo that left me torn, but in no doubt. I should go next door. The children would be hysterical in this storm and I needed Marta to come and look at Ilse, who had thrown off all the bedclothes, exposing her thinness to the icy *Küche*.

Covering her once again, I whispered my plan, made sure the windows were secure and the floor around the bed clear in the event she should get up. I placed the candle in the centre of the bare table, lifted Ilse's heavy coat from its hanging place on the back of the door and headed out across the garden, which swayed and shuddered in the storm. Adelena waited at the end of the path and the moon lit my way past the pond and along the path to the back wall. But nothing could protect my ears from the shattering thunder overhead. Hunched on the ground, I pulled Ilse's coat over my head.

What was I thinking? I'd be swallowed up by this storm or crushed underground. I froze, too terrified to move on or to run back to the house, only half registering that Beatrice had skittered past me, disappearing into the dark undergrowth.

I dared not chase after her. I knew she'd find her way back, as always.

'Get up,' Adelena urged. 'You've come this far.'

'No,' I shouted back. 'I can't. I can't move.'

We bickered back and forth until I felt a yank at the back of the coat that pulled me up on my feet, followed by a push in the back that almost threw me off my feet once more.

'Get up. Go.'

Rushing before I changed my mind, I pushed the planks aside, negotiated the ladder and paused to light the oil lamp. Thrusting the matchbox into a coat pocket, I trundled through the tunnel and tapped on the overhead hatch. However, there was not the usual quick response, eager hands and smiling faces above. I pounded again, longer and louder.

Still no answer.

A draught swept along the tunnel, extinguishing my light and leaving me entombed in the dark earth; earth and dirt which began closing in, attempting to crush and digest me.

With my eyes wide, I gasped and gulped, groping in the dark.

I pushed with all my strength against the hatch, sure that some diabolical hands were reaching for me, about to haul me into the black earth. The tunnel felt airless and I felt I was going to suffocate.

'Open up, open up. It's me – open up!'

Remembering the matches, I fumbled in my coat pocket. The first, then the second did not light. Crouching over the dead lamp, blubbering and panting, I managed to light a third and the lamp sparked to life.

There, just inches from my face, Adelena stood, smug-faced and silent.

'Help me!' I pleaded. 'This is all your fault. I shouldn't have come down here.'

'Help yourself,' she said.

I tapped and pushed against the hatch with renewed hysterical force and finally, it opened.

A grim and white-faced Marta met my staring eyes, the club of wood raised over her head, ready to strike.

'Stop! It's me!' I cried, one hand protecting my

head, the other gripping the handle of my lamp.

Pulling me up, Marta placed my lamp on the ground and turned to face me.

'You have never come after dark before,' Marta said. 'You gave us all a fright.'

The children emerged from their hiding places: under beds, inside cupboards and even up in the low hanging rafters.

Sobbing, I managed to tell her Ilse was sick, very sick. The room was half-warm and smelled of kerosene from a small heater.

The children crowded around. Dressed in their nightclothes, they reminded me of the innocent Halts Hummel figurines in Ilse's china cabinet, only these faces were thin and pale.

In the small crush, my lamp was knocked on its side. It rolled across the floor towards the bottom of the cellar stairs before coming to rest with a sharp glassy sound next to the kerosene stove, a trail of lamp oil snaking behind.

'Quick, Pim,' Marta said. 'Move that stove away, will you?'

I jumped to help. But my coat swept a candle from the low table onto the floor and set the oil trail alight.

I heard a loud bang in the distance, unsure in the confusion whether it was thunder or a door slamming above. At the same time, another wind gust swept along the tunnel. I had forgotten to secure the hatch. The draught fanned a narrow thread of fire fed by the oil trail from my lamp. A thin smouldering column reached up, and I backed away with Clara, Pim and the others.

Marta grabbed a pile of blankets and dumped them on the flames, quickly smothering the red and yellow tongues.

The pile smouldered and smoke filled the cellar, but the immediate threat was over. 'Everyone upstairs,' Franz called from the top of the cellar stairs. 'Adelena, Pim! Help me get Tomas and Aldo up. Clara, help Renate and Cornelia. Bep and Anke are up here with me.'

Ahead of us, Marta called back over her shoulder that all was well and no need to panic. Nevertheless, there was much screaming and fuss as children went in search of teddy bears and blankets.

I was no sooner up in the Walsmas' cold sitting room when Franz, who had gone to check the cellar, began shouting from below.

Marta and I rushed back down. The fire had flared up afresh in the blanket pile. Like a serpent, it hissed its way through the bundle and was making its way along the bottom edge of the wall tapestry. The space quickly filled with popping, fizzing and snapping sounds and the radiating heat was uncomfortable.

The room exploded with renewed chaos as curious children hovered at the top of the stairway while others – including Tomas and Clara, who'd followed us back down – were feeling their way around beds and in corners hunting for books and toys.

'Get out of here. Go back up.' Marta pushed them back towards the stairs. 'Pim, don't go over there! Stay away from the window.'

'I'm just letting the smoke out,' he said, straining against the cellar's narrow tilt window. 'There's no air in here. We have to let the smoke out.'

'Don't,' Marta shouted. But it was too late. Pim had forced the window open a couple of inches. It was enough to breathe new life into the flames and the whole place went up. The kerosene stove, boxes of books, linens, old newspapers, bedding and clothing all exploded in a burning flash that knocked me off balance.

Sprawled on my stomach, I watched the flames through a shield of interlaced fingers as Tomas and Clara, who had ignored Marta's earlier order to leave, stood frozen on the other side of a curtain of flames.

'Here, come here!' I screamed, my voice all but drowned out by the fizzing and roaring of the fire. I could see Clara, huddled in a corner and surrounded by flames, arms outstretched, her little mouth open in terror and pain.

'It's all right, wait, I'm coming. Don't be scared.' Terrified myself, the sight of their grasping hands forced me back onto my feet.

Clara screamed. 'I'm so hot!'

'Where are you?' Aldo cried out.

'Oh *mein Gott*, oh *mein Gott*,' I repeated over and over under my breath, willing myself to focus, reaching for Cornelia and Renate who I knew must be terrified. 'Listen to me. Say it with me, Clara. M is for Mutti, dearest of all, who wipes baby's tears when she's had a hard fall. Come on, say it. Say it with me Clara, you too, Aldo. Say it.'

Dazed and overwhelmed by heat, smoke and noise, I led the little group to the bottom of the steps.

Meanwhile, quick-thinking Pim tore the tapestry down so that it folded in on itself. Franz and Marta lifted a great basin of soaking sheets and doused the burning beds before swathing the floor with the wet linens.

Franz pushed me back up the steps, ordering me and whoever huddled next to me into the back garden before disappearing back into the smoky innards of the cellar. Marta slapped a wet sheet around the huddled girls' shoulders.

Her long skirts had great black-edged holes seared into them and her hands were blistered and raw. Steam rose from everyone's bodies as we stood, sobbing while a merciful rainstorm fell from above.

Marta, Pim and I made a whispered head count. Clara, Aldo, Renate, Cornelia, Bep, Anke.

'Tomas?' I looked around frantically. 'Where's Tomas?'

That's when Franz re-emerged, carrying a limp form – Tomas.

'I found him under a burning bed.'

'No, Tomas. Little Tomas!' A sound came from deep inside Marta. It was something I had never heard before.

Franz laid him on the grass at our feet and as the rain continued to tumble, he completed another frantic headcount. Everyone was present.

I threw the sheet off my shoulders and wrapped it around Tomas, whose frail body shook uncontrollably.

Dim lights from the back of the house cast a soft light over the garden and its low shrubs, stone-walled flower beds and the sterile vegetable plot.

In the shadows, he looked smaller than ever.

'Adelena?' he cried.

'Tomas, yes, I'm here.'

'It hurts,' he croaked into the dark. 'What happened?' His clothes were singed, parts of his hair and eyebrows burned off. I watched in horror as the soft skin on the back of his hands blistered and large bloody welts formed.

'Oh, Tomas, it's all right. Everything will be all right.'

In a desperate bid to keep Tomas warm and dry, I lay over him and tried to push my heart and soul into his chest. I was sure that if I willed it hard enough, I could pass some of my energy to him.

Clara and Aldo knelt by his side, their eyes staring, unable to understand what had happened. Marta tried to pull me off, as the other children crowded close, but I pushed them all away.

'He needs air,' I sobbed into the chaos and tried to place my mouth over his blistered lips.

'T is for Tomas,' Clara said. 'Say it, Tomas.'

Aldo and Tomas chimed in. 'T is for Tomas. T's for the trumpet, the troops hear its call, and join their bold captain to stand or to fall.'

And then . . . after a long low breath escaped his chest, Tomas stopped breathing.

Franz stumbled from the back of the house, covered in soot.

Pim tried desperately to fill a bucket from an old water pump by the broken-down summerhouse, its fallen-in roof and closed-up windows somehow sinister in the gloom.

'The fire's out,' Franz panted and everyone coughed and spluttered. 'Pim, it's out.'

I lay on my back, terrified – unable to move, unable to think or speak, letting the rain fall over me.

I don't know how long it was before I realised what was going on. But eventually, I was aware that Pim's sisters Bep and Anke were standing in the garden, in urgent discussion with their parents.

'Frau Achterberg is at the front steps, Mutti,' Bep said. 'She is asking questions about the noise and the smell. She thought it was coming from Ilse's and went to investigate. She says Ilse is delirious and she has sent for help.'

Marta issued a set of rapid instructions, and

everyone scattered into the abandoned summer house, including Franz, bearing the light burden of Tomas.

That left Marta and me, both soaked to the skin and shaking with cold and shock.

'You must go. Quickly. We'll tell Frau Achterberg and anyone who asks that we were taking wood from the old stores for the inside stove. And that one of our foolish, cotton-headed girls knocked the kerosene lamp over in the dark and started a small fire. You will have to go back home through the tunnel – will you be all right? Get out of those wet clothes immediately and get warm. Then keep out of sight. I'll speak with Frau Achterberg.'

'What about Tomas?' I asked, as tears pricked my eyes. 'We can't just leave him.'

'We will look after him. There is nothing you can do for him now. Please, we must appear as though nothing extraordinary has happened tonight. I have to go inside.'

'What about Ilse?' I asked. 'I don't know what to do.'

'I will come as soon as I can tonight. All you can do is try to keep the fever down and get her to sip water.'

I returned via my usual route, weighed down by my wet clothes and crushing guilt, my drenched hair stuck to my face and mingled with bitter tears.

Chapter 26

The ladder up from the tunnel ditch was slick from the rain and with great difficulty I managed to make my way along it. I knelt in the mud, making sure I'd covered the entry.

I slipped and stumbled through the garden, my clothes heavy with water and sweat.

'You think covering that hole matters now? Look at the tracks you are leaving, fool.' Of course, it was Adelena.

I swung at her but lost my footing in the wet grass. Crouching on all fours, I almost gave in to despair. I wanted to howl, and to wail over the betrayal of Hetty, the loss of Tomas, the injustice, waste and hardship that stretched before us all like a hall of mirrors that echoed sameness into a deep green infinity.

I didn't have what it takes to survive any of this and now had to somehow care for Ilse, who was lying incoherent back in the cold and sparsely-rationed *Küche*.

Panting and crying, I looked towards the house.

There, to my horror, were two bobbing globes of light.

Frau Achterberg's voice cut through my chaotic thoughts.

'Go fetch help,' she ordered someone, and the second light quickly bobbed away towards the street.

I crept as close as I dared through the darkness.

'Frau Graaf. Ilse,' she soothed, having dropped any formality as she entered the house. 'It's all right. You need help.'

It was over. At last.

I should have known this meddling busybody would be the one. She had been next door at Pim's earlier and had decided to stick her nose in here.

'Help is coming. Let me in,' she tried again.

I couldn't make out what, if any, reply Ilse made.

After what felt like an eternity, more lights gathered at the back of the house.

'Frau Graaf. Please open up.' It was Officer Kaufmann. 'Are you sure she is in there?'

'I saw her get up and stagger out of the room but since then, nothing,' Frau Achterberg said. 'She was speaking a lot of nonsense and came to the window.'

'What were you even doing here? There is a curfew, you know,' he said, no doubt aware of her previous and very public Marktplatz challenge to one of his soldiers.

'I smelled fire,' she answered. 'I thought it was coming from here. It wasn't – there was a fire next door as it turns out. But I can see inside, and I know she's ill.'

He ordered her to move aside. A sharp crack silenced Frau Achterberg and the bobbing lights moved inside.

I made it to the back wall of the house. Crouching behind an adjacent climbing rose planter box, I dared peep through the trellis just as Ilse was carried down the front path in the arms of Officer Kaufmann and towards a waiting military ambulance.

My first reaction, despite all the discussion and rehearsal, was to gasp at the shocking sight of Ilse's limp body in Kaufmann's arms.

He cocked his head in my direction and I pressed myself against the wall, the bricks cool against my burning hands. I didn't dare breathe as the seconds stretched on.

Frau Achterberg chose that moment to speak up. 'I told you. She looks very poorly. Let me take her to my home.'

'Please move,' Kaufmann said. 'She needs a hospital. I will take her directly to the infirmary.'

'You have more important things, I'm sure.'

'I asked you to move, Frau,' Kaufmann said.

Frau Achterberg made a disgruntled sound.

'Holtz?' It was Kaufmann again. 'What's going on at the Walsma house?'

'Nothing, sir,' came the reply. 'Just another accidental fire.'

With families crowded into single rooms, house fires and kitchen flare-ups were commonplace.

'Herr Officer,' Frau Achterberg said. 'As I said, I'm sure you have far more important things to do, and I know all the doctors.'

'Get out of the way or I will arrest you,' Holtz ordered. Frau Achterberg shuffled away, muttering.

'Go next door again, will you?' Kaufmann asked.

'It's nothing,' Holtz said. 'We've already been.'

'Do it.'

The sound of his crunching boots walking away signalled the end of the conversation.

I stood, as though riveted to the wall, for a long time, unsure what to do next.

We had covered surprise visits, air raids, house searches and illness, but this scenario of me all alone was one we had not prepared for.

Not daring a return to the Walsmas', when I was certain I was alone, I peered around the corner. The back door was closed but not locked, so I crept inside. I took off my wet outer clothing and hung it at the end of the bedstead.

Perched on the side of the mattress, drained of any emotion, I reached across and pushed my hand under Ilse's pillow, which still retained some of her heat. Knowing I had to get to a safe place, I glanced around for Beatrice, who would usually not be far away. But I had not seen her since she darted off into the garden earlier in the night.

Somehow, I knew it was the last I would see of my beloved and faithful little rabbit, who had brought so much comfort in those early days and months at Ilse's.

Thoughts of my parents, Hetty, Double B, Tomas and Ilse crowded my head. The room spun and a stunning burst of stars danced before my eyes.

I couldn't move. I allowed myself to fall on my side and drew my doll Lottie towards me, pulling up the blankets. I could still smell the familiar scent of my old room in her hair and in the candlelit room I sobbed out all my grief, fear, rage, bewilderment and shock.

I had so many questions yet no answers for any of them. But I was certain that Marta or Pim would come for me soon.

Chapter 27

I must have slept because when my eyes opened, it was well past first light.

No one had come for me. They would still be tidying up. What did they do with Tomas?

Marta, I expected, was probably at the infirmary looking for news of Ilse, or with Franz looking to get the children to a new safe house. Despite the sleep, my thoughts were still jumbled.

I dressed, pulling on a luxurious fur coat that had belonged to Ilse's mother. I finished the cold and thin broth sitting in the saucepan, and bit into a sugar beet as though it was a big juicy apple in my hands and not the bitter, sharp-tasting ugly bulb that it was. I chewed it, trying to pulverise its flesh so that I could swallow it, but its fibres stuck in my teeth and I spat most of it out.

Running upstairs, I washed my dirty tear-stained face, barely recognising the girl who stared back. This girl was not just pale, thin and tired looking. Lines of worry lurked under the skin of her brow and a veil of angst and sadness hung behind her eyes.

Marta would surely have had some news about Ilse's condition and would come, bundle me up and take me home with her. There was no point in going there. The cellar room had been ruined and she would have to accommodate me somewhere else until we knew what was happening with Ilse.

Someone would come. I had to be patient.

As I waited in my comfortless box bed throughout that day and into the evening, the hollow wind wailed around the eaves of the house. In the preceding months, increasing numbers of British bombers had flown low over the rooftops of Amsterdam on their way to their targets. I had become familiar with their very particular roar.

I collected a few things and put them in a small case. None of the clothes I arrived with fitted me anymore, so I packed a few things Ilse had given me.

I went to the *Küche* and waited, lighting a candle against the fading oyster-grey light.

As the darkness gathered outside, my hopes faded, and my thoughts turned to Tomas. Visions of his frail little body and the terrible burns on his neck and chest played against my closed eyes. Where was he lying now? Was he alone? Did they bury him in the garden? Where was everyone? Why had no one come? Were they waiting for the cover of darkness?

Two more days and nights passed and still no one came. Just me, alone with the low overhead droning.

I paced around the *Küche*. I stayed away from the pantry, not wanting to go too close to that dark little space.

I went upstairs and slipped into Ilse's wedding gown, the fabric cool against my skin was comforting. Twirling slowly before the tall mirror, I thought of my own wedding day. There at the end of the aisle, Pim would wait, a wide grin spreading over his face as Papa and I walked toward him.

I scolded myself for such stupidity and, embarrassed, I took the dress off. I would be lucky to see tomorrow, let alone my own wedding day.

I flipped through my atlas, wondering what people in Africa or Iceland might be doing at that moment. I envied the zebras and lions, the snow geese and reindeer. They roamed where they pleased and didn't have to think about war and Germans.

I glanced through Ilse's photo albums, my finger tracing the features of her pretty face. If I were ever to have a photo album, what would it include? Me on an ocean liner, or me and Pim and Hetty, the wind in our hair as we squinted into the sunlight. One of me at the top of the Empire State Building. A portrait of me on a magazine photo assignment in the jungles of Brazil and another one with my little baby boy, named Tomas.

'Stupid,' I said aloud, my voice sounding unfamiliar after so much silence.

When desperately hungry, I ate another sugar

beet, this time slicing it thin. I looked inside the bench box and found three shrivelled carrots and a soft potato that had sprouted long finger-like tendrils. The bread bin gave up a few dry bits and pieces and I drank the last bit of sour milk straight from the bottle. I felt sick – as much from the bad food as the knowledge that no one was coming for me.

Stuffing the vegetables and bread crusts into the pocket of my skirt, I returned to my waiting post. My teeth chattered and I closed my eyes, conjuring the image of the cooking pot from Ilse's repertoire of folktales and its promise of a never-ending supply of warm porridge.

Just as Ilse always did, I began out loud, 'Once upon a time in a faraway land, there lived a poor little girl who lived alone with her mother.

'One day they ran out of food and the girl went into the forest in search of something to eat. There, she met an old woman who gave the girl a little pot. She showed the little girl how it worked.

'"Cook, little pot, cook",' she said and the pot would fill with tasty, sweet porridge. When the old woman said, "Stop, little pot", the pot stopped. The girl took the pot home to her delighted mother and from that day on, they had sweet porridge whenever they needed it.

'One day the girl went out and when her mother was hungry, she ordered the little pot to cook and she ate until she could eat no more. But she did not know how to get the pot to stop and the porridge spilled over the edge, filling the entire kitchen and then the whole house, the house next door and eventually the whole street. The little girl returned home just before the porridge was about to engulf the last house in the village. She said, "Stop, little pot", and it stopped. Whoever wanted to return to the village after that had to eat their way back in.'

What would I have given for that little pot now? My belly was emptier than empty and it gurgled and gnawed.

Later, I turned the radio set on, careful to keep the volume down so low that it was just audible. I swayed to the tinny sounds of a jazz band.

I twirled around the *Küche*, around and around. I curtsied to my imagined partner, a handsome American GI. Raising my hand to his shoulder, I let him lead me on a joyous polka across the small room. I was warm again and the tip of my tongue licked a salty drop from my top lip.

Dizzy and light on my feet, I floated around the *Küche* with my eyes closed. For the briefest moment, I felt suspended in mid-air, only to fall onto the cold floor, my head buzzing and swirling as the room continued to spin.

The tinny jazz tunes were replaced by the rhythmic clackety-clack sound of a train passing over tracks. I saw myself in a stinking animal freight wagon, filled with grim-faced women and children. It smelled of cow dung and human sweat. There was an old woman crouched in a corner and next to her, a young woman tried to cover herself and the thin, nuzzling baby at her breast. No one noticed me except for a young girl with dark hair and owlish eyes.

Hetty.

Looking right at me, she placed her fingers to her lips and smiled. I had to tell her we must get off the train.

I opened my mouth to speak but the carriage dissolved around me as Hetty lifted her hand in farewell and disappeared into the carriage wall.

'No, come back!' It was my own voice which startled me out of my imagination.

Trying to rub the train wagon image away, I kneaded my aching head with both hands, struggling to stay awake and rooted in reality. As the evening drew on, I became more tired and anxious.

Where were they? Why had no one come? I lay my head on Ilse's pillow once more and slept.

***

I woke, startled, to the sound of panicked shouts. For a moment, I froze. Somehow, I managed to jump up and stumble towards the front *Stube*. I dared to peep out from a curtain and investigate. In the street, there was an altercation between three patrolling officers and two Dutch businessmen, whose names I didn't know, but whose wives used to come into our shop.

One by one, a small crowd gathered around the three soldiers.

'Get out,' one man ordered. 'Give in like your comrades in the south.'

'You're done for,' another shouted.

During much arm waving, jutting chins and pointing fingers, one of the soldiers fired into the air. A convoy of German army trucks passed the scene without pausing.

The Dutch scattered and the Germans hurried on.

I took this as a signal to get to my hiding place.

With the sound of another air squadron approaching, and the noise of raised voices outside, I sensed the tide turning. The Allies must have been pushing through the chaotic and crumbling defences, and the Germans knew it. In the meantime, I was alone and sensed I must not expose myself. Not yet.

'Where are you, Pim?' I whispered into my cupped hands. 'What's happened to you?'

He knew where I would be. I had shown him before, but not Marta or Franz.

I had to hope, then, that it would be Pim who would come. Maybe he had shared my secret with his sisters, Bep and Anke. It's the kind of thing he might do – just in case anything happened to him.

'No,' I told myself. 'That's silly, wishful thinking.'

I pulled on an extra pair of woollen stockings, wool vest and scarf and grabbed Ilse's winter coat.

I pushed my small case to the back of Ilse's armoire. I was as ready as I could be. My plan was to get to the cellar, to wait for someone, whoever that was going to be, to come for me.

I headed to my room, crouched on all fours and ducking under my desk, made my way down the secret hatch and into the cellar.

Chapter 28

Cordite. That sharp and strangely comforting smell filtered into my hiding place.

It had always meant fireworks to me. Fireworks and Sylvester celebrations in the square on New Year's Eve with Mutti and Papa, eating roasted chestnuts and skidding through the crowd, chasing Double B, trying not to slip on the icy cobblestones. The irony of taking part in a celebration that also happened to mark the feast day of the anti-Semitic Pope Sylvester was lost on me at the time, but I supposed no one wanted to be left out of the fun, so we all joined in.

How long had I slept? Had I in fact slept at all? Dreams and reality continued to merge as I lay hidden. There was more shouting and calling, more rushing feet and chaotic noise.

Someone was in the house. I was sure I was awake. The pain in my shoulder, the tingling in my fingers told me so.

'*Raus*!' It was a woman's voice.

'Out, out!' she shrieked again. I could only just hear it all through the small cellar window, never properly repaired after the break-in. 'Get out before I blow your brains out!'

The trampling ran down the side of the house and stopped suddenly at the low doorway to the cellar.

Finding the entry locked, the heavy wooden door was shouldered, once, twice, three times before the wood splintered.

Someone picked themselves up off the floor.

'*Sei ruhing*!' came a hissed command.

'You take that side,' a voice said. 'And you two, over there. I'll check the back. But be fast. We have to move out.'

My head was spinning. I held my breath. I was mere seconds, metres from disaster.

Now, whoever was in the cellar with me was no longer creeping around. Glass and earthenware jars and containers were being upended and smashed. I imagined the floor, a sharp glittering carpet of broken shards.

I believed the suspense would literally kill me.

I'm here! Down here! Come and take me, I wanted to scream but couldn't. I had no voice. The dark was suffocating, pressing in on my lungs, paralysing my ability to think, speak or move.

Something splintered, the sound reminiscent of the wood popping and snapping in Ilse's kitchen stove. They were close.

The time had come. This was the end, the event

I'd waited for and had fantasised about since the beginning.

I had imagined it differently. In more hopeful moments, I dreamed that news the Allies had arrived would reach us fast. Ilse and I would be breakfasting in the *Küche*, chatting about her chores, and I would tell her about some game or activity that Tomas, Pim and I were planning for the others that day. Shouts would go up across the city. The news would ripple in a joyous golden wave: the Canadians, Americans and the British were about to enter the city and the Germans were fleeing.

People would flood the streets, hugging and laughing. Joining them, my parents and Hetty would find me among the jubilant hordes.

But in the darkest, longest and coldest days of winter, when there were only small mounds of sugar beets and tulip bulbs to consume, my fantasies were darker. As Ilse and I had hunched around the small black stove at night, struggling to warm our fingertips and only just able to see one another in the gloom, I imagined the garden gate would scrape out a warning someone was approaching. But there would be no time for retreat as ten or more black-booted Stormtroopers swarmed through the broken back door, the jagged silver-grey 'SS' on their collars glinting in the torch light. Ilse and I would be marched at gunpoint through the dark streets, forced into the back of a truck and driven into the night towards some fatal horror.

It had not been either of these extremes. Instead, it had been a suspended wait for rescue or some form of death. I had risen and fallen out of thick sleep, penetrated by images, memories, smells and sounds.

My earth and wood hiding place muffled the intruders' movements, but in the dark, I was able to plot their progress through the upper storey. They had finished scavenging through the *Küche* for the food I knew they would not find.

Crash.

There it came again.

Closer.

They were in the cellar with me, moving around. They had taken the heavy lid off the laundry boiler; they were upending the preserve jars on the shelves concealing my hiding place.

My fate surely was only a few feet away. Like a game of hide and seek.

Should I give myself away? I wondered. What if it was Marta? Or Pim or Ilse? What if it was an American? Or a German?

Out of the dark came the teasing voice again. 'Done for either way. Fallen at the final hurdle.'

Adelena, I tried to call, is that you?

Nothing, just suffocating darkness.

Help me, I mouthed. Get me out of here.

The cellar was quiet. But I heard movement somewhere else in the house.

This time I summoned every ounce of strength and managed to call out, fearing whoever it was had given up looking for food and left. 'Help me.'

'Where are you?' came the question in German, so soft I was not sure I'd heard it.

'Down here,' I called, no longer caring who this German was. 'Behind the shelves.'

I could hear boards being moved and scraped aside.

I dared not breathe; I could not move. Was I dead already? Did I die months ago? Would whoever it was find my bones under layers of clothing and my little silver watch, its hands still like the rest of me?

The hatch began to slide, slowly inching away the lid to my long captivity.

I thought of that moment in the garden, when I first discovered the tunnel entry. What lay on the other side, I had no idea. I didn't want to know, but I couldn't wait to find out.

An inhalation of breath came from the other side of a yellow beam of light that hurt my eyes.

'Oh, *mein Gott*,' came the male voice behind the light.

More voices entered the cellar.

I could not lift my head.

The torch light shifted from my face and in its golden light, I look into the grey eyes of Freedom.

'Hurry, we have to get out,' a voice urged. 'What have you found there – anything worth taking?'

'Come on, this place has been stripped already. I'm not ending this war as a prisoner. Let's go,' another said.

'There's nothing of value here.' Yet another voice. 'Do what you like. I'm leaving.'

I stonily stared at the German, Officer Hass, the one who had let me off so many times in the past.

'Hass,' the voices at the cellar door repeated. 'We don't have time. What have you found?'

'Nothing,' he called back over his shoulder. 'Why don't you go check that safe in the attic again?'

'We don't have time. We already tried. Come on, Hass, we're going.'

'Okay, one minute,' Hass replied. 'There's nothing here. Let's get out.'

In one seamless move, he removed his fine woollen overcoat, now dirty and dusty, and spread it on the floor. Next, I felt myself lifted from the ground and wrapped in its folds.

'The pocket. Check the pocket.' That's all he whispered before turning to leave.

I rummaged as instructed. My fingers found an apple – it was to be my last meal in hiding . . . and my first meal as a free Jew. From that moment on, apples have always tasted of Freedom.

Chapter 29

I may have been released from the suffocating confines of my hiding space, but was far too confused, too frightened, and too weak to move. I looked towards the open cellar door, only metres away. Through it, the blessed comfort of daylight was visible. Even if I managed to crawl the short distance, what lay beyond?

Was it a trick? Were the soldiers waiting for me, or would they return?

Or maybe the war was over and outside, beyond the cellar, others were returning to their lives?

I tried to sit up, but my bones and joints were stiff and sore. I managed to roll to one side and with much effort, I pushed myself into a sitting position. Pulling the apple from the pocket, I took a greedy bite. But it stuck in my dry throat. Choking and coughing, I spat it out. My back against the shelves, I sucked the goodness from its red flesh, trying desperately to order my chaotic thoughts. Reaching back into the hiding place, I grasped the water flask Ilse had stashed there long ago. I knew it was long empty, but I still upended it in the hope of a last precious drop. I told myself it could be the difference between staying or getting out of the cellar.

But as expected, it was bone dry.

My gaze drifted to the ancient water pump by the washtubs. As I attempted to stand, it dawned on me that it may as well have been miles away. I couldn't even pull myself halfway up. Hunched down on all fours, urging myself forward, I crawled towards it, all the while keeping an eye on the open doorway.

It was like moving through molasses. The oversized coat was heavy around my back and shoulders, but somehow its weight was a comfort. My muscles and bones refused to work. I progressed just a few inches before ending up sprawled on my belly, panting against the earthen floor.

I must have slept. When I opened my eyes again, the daylight was fading, and the evening birdsong travelled through the cool May evening. Despite an overwhelming desire to beat the ground with my fists, I couldn't even manage that.

Amid this joyless freedom, I called for Mutti, Papa, Ilse and Hetty. 'I'm here,' I croaked.

Of course, there was no answer, only the rustle of the treetops.

I would have welcomed the return of Hass. I knew he would help me. Perhaps another German would come by and take his pistol from its holster to end my agony. I was past caring.

The wind picked up in the trees. I heard it move through each leaf and every blade of grass as though I lay under my own beloved tree.

The rustling soothed, hypnotised, and I fancied the wind whispered my name. So often in my hidey-hole I had imagined, along with the phantom smells of Mutti's cooking and old familiar sounds, that I was cuddled in my soft warm bed as the first winter snow fell. Or that Mutti was calling me to breakfast or to tell me that Hetty had arrived for a bike ride to Vondelpark.

'Lena.' The whisper cut through my fantasies. 'Adelena.'

I didn't even bother opening my eyes but lay flat against the cellar floor, hoping benevolent sleep would take me away again, an escape from this terrible reality.

'Adelena.' It came again. A thought struck me. Perhaps it was Hetty come to find me. Groaning, I opened my eyes and tried in vain to move.

'You're alive, thank God,' a voice said. 'Adelena, it's me.'

'Who?' I croaked. My heart quickened and my head spun as careful hands on my shoulders rolled me onto my back.

Pim's thin and worried face came into view, hovering close to mine.

Relief flooded my shaking frame.

'Shh,' he said. He was crying. 'Shh, it's all right. It's over. The war is over.'

'When?'

'Only in the last few days.' Pim bundled the coat

around me once more, easily lifting me from the floor. He carried me toward the water pump and set me down on a cushiony pile of Ilse's faked dirty hospital linen.

'I thought you were dead.' He pumped a clear stream of water into a tin cup. 'You were so still there on the ground.'

Cradling me and resting my heavy head on his shoulder, Pim held the cup to my sore and cracked lips. I drank, spilling a good deal of it down my front.

'Slowly,' he said. 'There is plenty.'

The first mouthfuls were excruciating. As the water flooded my starved body, I lay back in Pim's arms and continued to sip.

'I've been hiding in our cellar too,' he said. 'I wasn't sure what to do. Part of me wondered if it was all a trick and that the moment I stuck my head out, I'd be jumped on by the Nazis. I waited and waited and finally I came through the tunnel, just in case.'

I understood just how he must have felt, as I also had trouble believing any of it was true.

'Tell me,' I urged. 'Where is everyone else? Your family? The children?'

Pim's shoulders dropped and his head fell to his chest.

My breathing was shallow as he let out a long low sound.

'What?' I gripped his arm. 'Tell me.'

'Later that night, the night of the fire, it was chaos,'

he said. 'After Ilse had been moved to the hospital, the Germans found the children, even though they did their best to hide. They were rounded up with my parents and taken from the house. I don't know where they are.'

His face crumpled as he tried not to cry.

'It's my fault,' I said, fat tears seeping into my mouth and falling onto my lap. 'I am so sorry. I killed everyone.'

'Stop!' he shouted. 'Don't say that. Don't say my parents are dead. We don't know anything for sure.'

'What about your sisters and you? How did you manage to be missed?'

'It was a confusion, and Bep just grabbed me and Anke and we ran to the school principal Frau Eckert's house,' he said. 'She let us stay with her and in the next few days asked around in the circles about our parents. But no one knows where they are.'

He squeezed my hand and I squeezed back.

'Go on.'

'After a week or so, I couldn't stand not knowing anymore and I left Frau Eckert's one night.' He squeezed his blue-green eyes shut but couldn't stop the single tear that escaped. 'I wanted to come home in case my parents came back. I don't know, I've lost track, but it was the middle of April sometime. There seemed to be lots more Germans around here after the fire.' He rubbed his chin and sipped from the cup. 'There were stories on the radio, about things falling apart for the Germans with rebellions in the ranks and soldiers deserting. I felt hopeful. One night, I risked coming here to look for you.'

I could hardly believe he had taken this risk for me and I could not take my eyes from his face. He blushed and cleared his throat.

'I knew Ilse had been taken to the hospital. I came through the tunnel but when I got to the garden end, I heard that old bat Frau Achterberg. She was poking around by the back door with another woman I've never seen before. They had a small bag and they were whispering.'

When I looked back, it was as though I was watching through a curtain of water on panes of glass. I saw the memories clearly enough, but they were somehow unreal.

'What did they say?' I asked, hardly recognising my own voice, so soft and thin.

'I think they were taking things. The one I didn't know said, "Did you pack the silver brushes as well?" and that old busybody told her to hush up and said yes, she had the brushes.'

Anger boiled inside me.

'And then the other one asked, "Are you sure there's no one else here? Are you sure she wasn't hiding someone?" Frau Achterberg said, "Please, stop the questions, Rita. We have to go". And they left.'

I knew I was alive again at that moment, because

my heart blazed with rage. That woman had been here, poking around the house and stealing Ilse's precious brushes.

'I was afraid after that,' Pim said in a rush. 'I knew you must be in here. But I felt the Germans would be watching the area even more after the fire and discovering our children, and they'd take me away because we'd been hiding them.'

I buried my tearless eyes in his shoulder as a wave of shame and guilt washed through me. All the nightmares I'd endured while trapped in my hiding place returned.

'Shh.' Pim stroked my hair. 'It was an accident.'

But I knew that nothing anyone said or did would ease my terrible guilt over the fire.

'Come on, it's dark enough.' He lifted me in his arms again. 'Let's get you back to my cellar. I've been hiding out there, living on small beer and stale rye bread. It's not much, but it'll do you good. We'll work out what to do next.'

'If it's over, why are you hiding out? Where is everyone?' I coughed painfully; my windpipe parched.

'The radio says it's over, but no one has come to the house. It doesn't feel right. It's eerie. I just want to be sure so we still need to be careful. We'll use the tunnel – maybe one last time.'

He carried me through the garden and it was as though the space opened around me. I inhaled the fresh air, feeling as nourished as though I'd eaten a feast of fresh food of the kind I'd not enjoyed since before the war.

Dusk descended. As we passed the pond and my beloved chestnut tree, Pim said it was May seventh and the Germans had surrendered. I tried to raise my fist in the air, but it fell back to my chest and I realised I'd been in that hidey-hole for weeks.

'Free,' I whispered. 'No more hiding.'

Pim lay me down in the trolley and jumped on the front. 'I think it's safe to say that this will be the last trip we ever take underground. Let's just be certain.'

Tugging on the rope, he pulled us through the tunnel. Soon we were swallowed by the dark, the deadly oil lamp having been left at the other end the night of the fire.

We trundled on in silence, through the dark and the smell of rising damp. Even though I had a thousand questions swirling in my head, I didn't speak. Instead, I closed my eyes, rocking from side to side as we rumbled along.

At the tunnel's other end the hatch was open, and a weak grey light leaked in to meet us. Panic rose and I clutched at the overcoat's lapels, trying to pull my head inside the folds of material.

Pim entered the cellar ahead of me, reaching back down to help me up. The entry that was once so easy for me had become slow and painful, but finally I was back in the familiar room that held so many memories.

Looking around at the peeling, blistered walls and charred rafters, the smells and sounds of that terrible night washed over me. I crouched on the floor, much like the very first time I entered the cellar after being hauled through the opening by Marta. Only this time, I wasn't surrounded by curious, poking, crowding children, but rather by flashes of ghost-memories and the reassuring embrace of dear Pim. My eyes stung and my throat closed up as I struggled to hold back the emotional dam inside.

Pim led me as though I was some precious and rare museum exhibit to a chair at the trestle table, and poured a cup of beer from a keg. He tried to pull the coat from my bird-like shoulders, but I snatched it back, not wanting to emerge from its comfort.

'Okay, okay! Keep it on then,' and in the same breath ordered, 'Drink this. It will be good for you.'

And it was. Flat and warm, I sipped the beer and felt it fill my starved belly. Pim tore a small piece of hard bread from a loaf and dipped it into my cup. I suckled its goodness and looked around the ruined room.

He had tried to tidy away the debris, but there was no hiding the charred trail of lamp oil, burned wall hangings and bedding.

Pim had set up his base in this relatively untouched corner of the cellar by the keg. If my heart skipped when I saw the salamander had survived in his tank, it almost exploded when a thin and slow Fritz rose from a dark corner and approached, nuzzling my lap.

I craned my head to his. 'Fritz. We made it. Who'd have thought?'

I looked up at Pim and he lowered his forehead to mine.

'Where is everyone else?' I asked. 'Are your sisters here? What's happening in the rest of the city?'

'Sleep,' he urged. 'There's time for all that later. Bep and Anke didn't want to come back here. They're still at Frau Eckert's place.'

Exhausted, I let him guide me to his makeshift bed on the floor. Fritz lay next to me and I closed my eyes, burrowing my nose into the coat sleeve, inhaling the clean smell of the wool.

Waking hours later and feeling somewhat refreshed, I sat up on my own and saw Pim standing at the table with his back to me.

He turned. 'Look, two carrots,' he said, his glee undisguised. 'I don't know what made me think of it, but I checked the old vegetable patch and there they were.'

He helped me to the table. I sat in a high-backed chair as he cut the carrots into bite-sized pieces. I managed to swallow some beer-soaked bread and asked him when we could leave the cellar.

'I don't know. I'm almost too scared to leave – we don't know what's out there. What if the Germans come back?'

'But you said it's over. The war's finished, Pim. Do you think it could be a trick?'

'I still hear planes in the air sometimes. It could be a trick, I suppose.'

A deep sigh, one that had long been brewing in my bones, escaped my emaciated body. I asked him to tell me what he knew about everyone else. 'When can I see Ilse?'

'She's – Ilse is . . .' Pim stammered, looking down. Chills rippled over my skin and I grabbed his arm.

'Go on. Where is she?'

'The night of the fire – with her being so sick, Frau Achterberg raised the alarm and she was taken to the hospital,' he said.

'Yes, yes, she was very ill, I know that. But she's recovering? At the hospital?'

I wanted to shake him; he was so slow to respond.

'No, she's not at the hospital.' At last, he looked into my eyes. 'She died two days later from fever.'

I collapsed forward across the table, screaming inside. My saviour, my alternate mother, my friend, was dead? It wasn't supposed to finish like this, not after all her sacrifice.

I never got to say goodbye, to thank her for all her bravery, honour and love.

We were supposed to dance and sing and rejoice together when we had our freedom.

'Adelena.' Pim's hand on my back roused me. 'Breathe, will you? Say something.'

Pushing myself off the table, I began to sob.

'No, no, no.' I shook my head so violently I felt my neck would snap. 'You must have it wrong.'

'Listen to me.' He held my face in his hands. 'She was very sick.'

My head snapped away from his touch and my next thought was for my parents.

'What about Mutti and Papa?'

Pim's eyes took on a faraway look as his heartbreaking tale filled the room. According to the headmistress, Frau Eckert, they never made it out of Amsterdam, let alone Belgium. After leaving me with Ilse that night, they were stopped by a patrol. A near-hysterical Mutti had turned back to get me from Ilse's, forcing Papa to follow behind, pleading with her to see sense. A two-man foot patrol stopped my parents and demanded their papers. Papa handed over the documents, falsified by a man who had a printing press in the basement of our old shop and who had made a packet from desperate Jews in the early days of Occupation. By all accounts, he did an outstanding job.

But it wasn't good enough to fool this pair, one who struck Papa across the face in an act that sent Mutti into a frenzy as she rained down blows with her silver-handled umbrella. The German's retaliation was swift and brutal. He struck her across the face with the butt of his revolver, crushing her cheekbone and tearing her soft skin.

At the same time, there had been a commotion at Frau Achterberg's. Fritz had darted from the shadows, with the widow in howling pursuit. The dog lunged at one of the officers and my parents slipped into the darkness.

I sat, stunned, at the news.

'How does Frau Eckert know all this?' I asked.

'I guess it was that big mouth Achterberg,' he said. 'But who knows how true it is. She's a terrible gossip and always exaggerates. But Eckert also has connections.'

I didn't know if I wanted it to be true or not. I was terrified to think my parents had been intercepted and that they'd been attacked. But I was pleased to hear they'd got away.

'Try not to be glum. You are alive! You made it,' he said.

'But not Ilse, and what about everyone else? I need to find my parents. And what about your parents?'

He looked downcast for a moment, then poured us both a small cup of beer. 'We will find them,' he said. 'But a toast to us first.'

We clinked our cups and sipped.

'To our friends,' I said. 'And to your parents and Mutti and Papa and Fritz, Double B and Herr Winkler.'

After a short pause in which I turned the idea over in my mind, I offered, 'There is one person I'd like to remember.'

Pim raised his eyebrow in a silent question.

'Officer Hass,' I said.

'Who? I don't know that name.'

'Pim, he saved our skin so many times.'

Pim eyed the overcoat uncertainly.

'I never spoke about him. He's the one who let us off after pouring water out of the window at Hetty's.'

Pim started to show signs of recognition.

'I crashed into his motorcycle when Fritz first began to chase me. Remember that day?' I twisted my serviette. 'He let me and Double B off when we were out after curfew. He pretended not to see me in your cellar that day when Frau Achterberg raised a stink about Fritz getting into her garden.'

'Yes,' he said. 'I do remember. He told me he had a young sister who played pranks.'

'Yes, and that his best friend had been a Jewish boy,' I said. 'He overlooked much of our mischief that would have landed us in trouble. And then, when I had given up all hope of rescue in these last long days and nights, Pim, he found me, but again he didn't betray me. A patrol was in the house, looking for valuables, food, Jews . . . But he found me. Instead of giving me away, he wrapped me in his coat and left.'

'But you never even mentioned him.'

'No. I felt a strange connection with him, and I felt bad about it. I don't know – it sounds silly to say it aloud. But if not for him, things could have been very different for me.'

'I see. Yes, I see.'

We spent the next little while eating the carrots and speaking about nothing much apart from the few shared lighter experiences of the past year. He asked if he could put the long coat on and I handed it over.

He was tall now, Pim, but still not as tall as Hass. The coat sleeves hung to his fingertips as he walked around the room. He looked at me, deep in thought, and took the coat off, folding it and placing it next to me.

There was an unspoken understanding. We had each suffered and seen suffering.

Our conversation was meandering when he blurted, 'I have a confession for you, too.'

'Go on then. Don't keep me waiting.' I leaned forward. Maybe he was going to confess he had a crush on me.

'It's about that letter, the one from Hetty. You know the one?'

Of course I did – that precious, crinkled and fragile page that had gone everywhere with me had been my comfort and a reminder that Hetty was ever near.

'It wasn't really from her,' he blurted. 'It was a fake.'

'What do you mean?' I asked, trying not to fall into the pit that already lay open under my seat.

'I dictated it to my sister. To Bep. I did it for you, to make you happy.'

My face crumpled.

'Adelena, don't look at me like that. Don't hate me. I was scared. You were disappearing into a dark well. I knew I couldn't lose you, like we lost Hetty. I thought it would bring you back.'

Without a word, I rose painfully from my seat, and slapped him full across the face, leaving a stinging pink mark behind.

The full pain, confusion and betrayal of his revelation felt as if it would kill me on the spot.

'Lena,' was all he said, harking back to the old days when that was how he knew me – quiet little Lena.

'How could you do that to me? Why? It's been my little piece of her. And it's not even real.'

But my anger dissolved and tears fell freely, like small diamonds spilling forth.

'So, the whole letter was a lie then?' I stared at thc ground, reaching for the coat and fingering the silver thread of the shoulder boards.

'Not entirely.' He looked at his boots and chewed his fingernails. 'Anika said the day she delivered Hetty's parcel to Keizersgracht, she didn't have time to wait for Hetty to finish her own reply to me.'

So at least I knew Hetty had got my notes.

'She knew enough after spending time with Hetty

and the other residents with the Caslers to be familiar with Hetty's thoughts and experiences,' he went on. 'She relayed a lot of their news in conversation when calling in to the Walsmas' one evening with the excuse of collecting items left for tailoring.

'Anika said that there'd be a reply coming soon and spoke of life inside the Caslers' hiding place. I just knew that these were things she'd tell you if she could.'

He paused to breathe and shot me an uncertain look before continuing.

'So, I dictated the letter to Bep. I waited and waited to give it to you. I was relieved when I did, because then I couldn't take it back.'

I had no words.

I laid my heavy head down on the floor. Pim knelt next to me, but despite the protest of my malnourished bones, I turned my back and faced the wall. I shrank from his hand on my shoulder.

'I'm sorry. It was stupid,' he said to my silent back. 'I thought it would cheer you up, that's all. I didn't know.'

I don't know how long we sat in the difficult silence before he said, 'I'll get ready to go out and have a look around. It's time.'

I didn't answer.

'Will you be all right if I leave you alone for a little while?'

I still ignored him.

'Fritz will stay with you, won't you, boy?'

Fritz yelped his reply and I turned to face them both.

'I miss her,' I said. 'I miss Ilse and my parents. I miss everyone. I wish everything could be like it was before.'

'Me too.' He hugged Fritz around the neck. 'Everything's different, isn't it? Even us.'

He stood up, dusting off the knees of his pants. 'I'll try not to be long.'

Fritz sat back on his haunches in a way that startled Pim. The hairs on the back of his neck stood up as every nerve in our animal friend's body became alert. He whined and made for the damaged cellar stairway.

'Hello,' a woman's voice called.

Fritz yelped. Pim caught him by the collar and ordered him to hush.

'Anyone home?' It was Frau Achterberg.

My heart sank. Pim and I stared at one another, wide-eyed and slack-jawed.

Just when I had begun to think that maybe it was true – I was free, I had survived, it was all over – I began to fear that any moment, the Germans would march back in here, drag me to some camp, and shoot Pim on the spot.

Fritz escaped Pim's hold and took off up the steps. I hoped he'd tear his old adversary to pieces.

But no.

'Hello, Fritz. There you are,' she greeted him, as though they were old friends.

Surprisingly, he didn't growl at her and moments later he preceded her back down to the cellar. By this time, Pim had already scooped me up and piled us both inside a charred wardrobe.

Fritz led her right to us.

She swung the door open to see us cowering in fear.

'Please, please come out,' she said. 'There's no reason to be frightened. I promise you. Come. It's over, really it is. The Germans are retreating. They've signed the surrender.'

She looked different. Somehow less taut and thin-lipped. She was still pale-skinned, but not sallow and mean-eyed, the way I remembered her.

She held out her hand to me, but Pim stepped out of the wardrobe and stood between us, blocking my view of her.

'Why should we believe you?' he demanded. 'You gave Ilse away. You and your nosy ways almost gave Hetty away to the Germans.'

'And you looted Ilse's house when she was in the hospital. Why should we trust you now?' I added, craning my scrawny neck around the defensive Pim.

Frau Achterberg's shoulders drooped. She closed her eyes, probably trying to get her story straight.

'I know that's how it looks,' she said, with a reassuring tone. 'But the reality is very different. If

Fritz could speak, he'd vouch for me. Wouldn't you, boy?'

As though on command, Fritz sat back on his haunches and whined.

'You'd be able to tell them what's been happening.' Her brown eyes sparkled with an idea and she straightened the collar of her floral blouse.

'I know, let me show you something.'

Frau Achterberg clapped, then placed her hands on her hips. Fritz growled low, baring his teeth, and I was sure he was about to attack.

'How many times do I have to tell you? You must take control of this animal.' Again, she punctuated her words with a few short, sharp claps and instinctively, Pim's hand took Fritz by the collar.

'Shh, boy,' he said.

'Klaus trained him well,' she said. 'Klaus Winkler. I've been in Holland since the start of the war and met Fritz when he was a pup. And Ilse – she is my cousin. Like a sister, really, since her parents took me in when I was little more than a baby. Klaus trained him as part of our ruse, you see. Fritz has been keeping an eye on our people.'

'What people?' Pim interrupted.

'We are all – me, Ilse and Klaus, and even your parents, Pim – we are all in the Dutch Resistance. We have been working against the Nazis all along and hiding people in our homes and factories.'

Frau Achterberg smiled and wrapped her arms

around Fritz's neck. I looked at Fritz in disbelief, overtaken by yet another wave of betrayal and conflict.

'Liar!' I shouted with all the strength in me.

'It's true.' She thrust her chin forward. 'Come home with me, both of you, and I will explain everything properly.'

I looked her up and down, took in her feminine blouse, her brown lace-up shoes and neat but worn skirt. My mind went back to the hours I'd spent flipping through Ilse's old family photo albums – the stories of the mischief she, her brother and young cousin got up to on their grandparents' estate.

Examining her face, her hands, her straight back and thick head of hair, I noted there was something familiar in her features, the shape of her face and glint in the eye.

'This better not be some kind of trick,' Pim said. It was only then I noticed the revolver in his shaking hand.

'Put it down,' I told him. 'Please, just put it down. Maybe it's true. I don't think Fritz could be wrong. Let's just hear what she has to say.'

After several tense seconds, Pim placed the gun down on the table.

'All right,' he said. 'But I'm bringing it with me.' He placed it in an old knapsack, slung it over one shoulder and scooped me up.

'My coat,' I whispered, but he assured me he already had it.

I hadn't been out on the street in so long, the sights and sounds of freedom filled the air and made my head spin. The sun shone in a windless sky.

The buildings looked the same, but the people going about their business were not. Thin and poorly dressed, they sidestepped rubbish piled in the streets. Aside from household rubbish, there were bits of broken furniture propped against lamp posts or left at the bottom of front steps.

A pair of cats fighting over a scrap of food were shooed off by a woman sweeping her front porch. Music floated through an open window.

The smell of woodsmoke was comforting; someone had even set up a small drum and was offering handfuls of roasted nuts to passers-by.

'Free German contraband hazelnuts,' the nut roaster called cheerily.

Children played freely on the road and no one stopped them, their happy sounds filling the air.

It was as though the world was holding its breath and, in that moment, I let myself go and went limp in Pim's arms. It was the same sensation I'd experienced being tossed in the waves at Zandvoort all those years ago when I'd surrendered myself to the motion of the sea.

Only this time I let go of the fear, the angst and

anger, the lost years and the beauty of innocence that had been stolen along with them.

Pim reacted to the sudden wilting of my body in his arms by dropping to the ground and holding me close.

'What day is it again?' I asked, looking up and smiling into his eyes.

'Oh my God. I thought you were dead,' he whispered, lowering his forehead to meet mine.

'May seven,' Frau Achterberg said.

She led us the short distance to her home, Fritz bringing up the rear, and all the while we were greeted by familiar faces, all of who seemed to be heading in the same direction.

'Where are they all going?' Pim asked Frau Achterberg.

'Dam Square, for the liberation parties,' she answered, greeting passers-by as we continued.

Gasps and inquisitive glances met my bewildered eyes.

'Oh, my Lord. She is alive,' one woman said.

'Marise, shall I get Dr Peiter?' another man asked Frau Achterberg, who nodded acceptance.

'Yes, yes please,' she said. 'Send him to the house.'

Until then I had not known her first name and it softened her further in my mind. Marise Achterberg.

'What camp was she in? Or was she with her parents?' said another.

My heart leapt at the reference to my parents. But

I was horrified at the mention of a camp.

'Hush,' she replied to all inquisitors. 'Let me just get her home and we'll work things out from there.'

'Where are my parents? Papa and Mutti, are they all right?' I had to know, but all she said was, 'It's okay. Almost there.'

Moments later, we turned a corner and Pim, following Frau Achterberg, carried me through a front gate where three strangers waited on the steps.

An old man, somehow familiar; the woman, a grimace for a smile and a ghost-eyed child, clinging to her skirts with straw-like fingers.

'Marise!' the woman called. 'You found them?'

The woman reached for me. I recoiled in disgust and horror. She gasped.

'*Schätzchen*,' the old man said. I knew then it was Papa. But he wasn't as I'd remembered.

There was a moment of suspension, of lack of recognition, as though life before this moment had been a fiction.

Pim broke the spell. 'Shall we go in, Frau Achterberg?'

'Of course, of course,' she replied, leading the way inside.

Her home was nothing like I'd expected. Rather than being dark, old-fashioned and cluttered, it was light and airy, a blue-and-white tiled stove in one corner and the same china cabinet as Ilse's in another, complete with several similar delicate glass animals.

'Put her down here,' she told Pim. He set me down on the divan against soft pillows and covered me with a blanket.

Fritz settled on the floor beside me and I was suddenly aware of activity from the hallway.

All at once, Papa's face loomed close to mine and in that moment, the room and everything in it melted away as his face, wet with tears, filled my vision.

Gathering me in a painful embrace, we had no words. Minutes later, I said, 'Papa, you are hurting me.'

Everyone laughed and as he let me go, it was the woman I saw next. My mother. But not Mutti as I remembered her, with even, pale skin and a serene beauty. Her left cheek was caved in and a thick, ropey scar ran from the top of her cheekbone to the side of her mouth, pulling one corner down. Her beaming smile, as she moved towards me, was lopsided.

The small, thin child was introduced as my little brother Max. It was true then; they'd never made it out of Holland and Mutti had clearly suffered a terrible beating. So bad she almost miscarried the baby she didn't realise lay curled inside her dark womb.

But where had they been?

'We have been here,' Papa said. 'With Marise.'

This woman, who I now knew to be part of the city's brave network of underground Resistance members, was the most convincing of actresses.

Where I thought she was at best a busy body and at worst a collaborator, she was a heroine, cut from the same cloth as Ilse, Marta, Anika and all those others who had risked so much to fight our oppressors.

Her guise kept the Nazis at bay and allowed her to undermine their evil work with a degree of safety.

Hugs, kisses and tears, but few words were exchanged in those early moments of reunion. As the day wore on – a day that saw me undergo a medical check in Marise Achterberg's front room, glasses of salted water poured down my throat and thin slices of hard bread, soaked in watery milk offered at the end of a spoon – news came that there had been a shooting at the Dam Square celebrations.

Neighbours came to the house, their breathless voices filled with fear and consternation.

'Do you believe it?' someone said. 'The evil bastards set up a machine gun on the Groote Club balcony,' another man said. 'They started shooting into the crowd. We just got the hell out of there.'

It only ended after a small, combined force of Resistance and Germans convinced the rogues to give up, but not before they had killed dozens of revellers.

The noise and conversation in the room faded as a grating sob shook my body. I didn't care that people looked. I didn't notice the concern in their eyes or hear my parents scold them with harsh whispers not to discuss such things in front of me. I let it out and with it the terrible pain, fear, loss, frustration and bewilderment that had been my constant companion.

Afterwards, I noticed Adelena for the first time in what felt like an age. She stood at the back of the crowded room and let herself out the front door, smiling as she went. She inclined her head in a gesture that was somehow reassuring and left without a backward glance.

Mutti smothered me with hugs and kisses. But instead of being comforting, I found it annoying and had a dawning sense of a gulf between us, created by the years spent apart.

'It's all right,' she soothed. 'They've got them. They were drunk. It's all over. We are safe.'

'What about the Caslers?' I pulled away from her touch, breathing hard. 'Where's Hetty – is she safe? And what about Double B, Aunty Louisa and Uncle Eric. Are they safe too?'

'They . . .' Mutti began. 'I don't . . .'

But Papa cut her off. 'We can discuss all these things later.' Then he addressed the room. 'Dear friends, we are so happy to see you at last, but I think we need some time together with our little family. We will reunite again soon for a real celebration, I'm sure.'

'Indeed,' Frau Achterberg said. 'Come, Pim. Everyone, let us leave the family be. It has been a big day.' She placed a hand on Pim's arm and pointed him towards the door.

Everyone made understanding comments and gave well wishes as they filed quietly from the house.

'Well?' I looked up at my mother and gestured for her to sit opposite me. 'The Caslers and the Baums?'

My parents looked at one another over my head.

'Please, Mutti,' I snapped. 'I'm not a baby anymore.'

Mutti lowered herself onto the dark green velvet settee. Max clambered onto her lap and looked at me with big eyes.

'The Caslers – after they were found, they were sent to Auschwitz. Everyone in their hiding place.' She swallowed hard. 'Hetty's parents died soon after. The girls, poor Hetty and Ursula, were moved to another camp.'

The news winded me, so that I gasped for air. 'So Hetty and Ursula? Where are they?'

Mutti's hands was clammy as they sandwiched mine. 'They died sometime in March this year.'

This was only months before the war's end in Europe. Icy daggers rained down and I crumpled like a piece of paper.

'Double B? The Baums?' I rasped into my hands. I knew what the silence meant but still, I needed to hear the words.

'They were also discovered in hiding by the docks, but it was only a few weeks ago,' Papa said. 'Anika said Eric was shot during the confrontation, but somehow Double B and Louisa escaped. Louisa knew how to contact Anika through the underground and they've been in a safe house.

'Apparently a soldier in the patrol bundled Louisa and Double B into the darkness during the melee, telling them, "Walk, don't run",' Mutti said.

I knew who that was – it could only be Officer Hass. It had to be.

'Double B hasn't said a word since seeing her father shot,' Mutti said. 'But at least she and Louisa are alive. Poor Eric.'

All at once, I was numb. I didn't understand what or how I felt.

I lifted my face to find my parents focused on me – they seemed to be waiting for me to say or do something.

'What?' I asked, and Mutti again reached for me, but I pulled away. 'Don't stare at me. Don't touch me.'

'Lena,' Papa said. 'Don't be like that.'

'I'm not Lena. My name is Adelena.'

'She needs time, Jacob,' Mutti whispered and began clearing plates from the table, while Max trailed silently behind, like a small shadow.

They had left me when still a child and now, in so many ways, I was old. Old and tired and not understanding where I fitted into their lives, or they into mine.

From the moment the previous month when I stashed my small bag away in the back of Ilse's wardrobe, when I had accepted no one was coming for me and that something momentous was happening out on the streets, I realised my little hidden world was at an end.

The excitement of secrecy, the adventure of the tunnel, the danger of my visits to the hidden orphans and my closeness with Ilse – these were all things that had made me feel special and safe while the rest of the world fell apart beyond the safety of Ilse's small blue house.

I was unable to think in straight lines. A racing heart and darting pulse were constant features of my waking moments spent encapsulated in my dark hidey-hole under the preserving shelf.

***

I came to realise it was panic. It was panic I still felt, even reunited with Mutti and Papa and the sweet knowledge the war was over, that our tormentors had surrendered, and we had survived when legions of others had not.

We had survived the war, but how to deal with the peace?

No longer panicked about the fear of discovery by the Germans, I was fearful about the new and uncertain future in a changed world, filled with changed people. I had changed – I knew it and was afraid that I would not know how to live in a transformed world.

'Now' was the moment Ilse and I had so often spoken about in the evenings in her cosy *Stube*. It was the time that Hetty, Pim and I had so often dreamed of in those early months of the war; the moment that we always thought must be just around the corner, naively believing the war would be over in months rather than years. Now, it was 'after the war' and somehow it was anti-climactic.

Life wasn't as it had been; there wasn't an abundance of food and people weren't carefree. There were still queues of thin people at the poorly provisioned stores. The Germans and other vile opportunists had swept through the ghettos and other areas that were once home to the city's Jewish community. They pillaged what they wanted, leaving the abandoned buildings gutted and open to the elements. On our first excursion into the old ghetto, I lagged behind Mutti, listening to the sound made by her well-worn brown shoes clacking along the pavement and watching her coat swing from side to side. It had a hypnotic effect, like the metronome in Ilse's music room, patiently marking time as her young students persevered through their pieces.

A loud banging sound interrupted my daydream. I lifted my eyes to the building facades that were in shambles. As though pulled by a phantom hand, a single shutter thumped against the inside wall of an upper room. The light cotton curtains billowed out through the apartment's open windows as though lifted by the breeze on a warm, laughter-filled summer's day. As though it were days gone by, when families gathered together in these buildings. Behind those same windows, when women in light floral dresses sat in the front rooms, gently waving their coloured paper fans and sipping from glasses of lemonade, while the men played backgammon and we children ran free in the local gardens.

Once safe and proud in appearance, the derelict apartment blocks reminded me of the bent and toothless old men who gathered in knots on canal-side benches, sunning themselves and talking of days gone by. Now the buildings' doorways gaped open. Passers-by could peer inside the empty hallways and up the dark and ruined staircases that led to rooms which laid bare the minute details of people's lives, most of whom had perished in camps or were lucky enough, like me, to have been secreted away somewhere.

Others still had made it out of Holland and even Europe altogether, to America, Israel or Australia, abandoning what remained of once comfortable lives in cities and villages where they no longer felt safe, and where the faces of the lost stood on every street corner.

After a few more nights at Frau Achterberg's and several more doctor's visits, Mutti, Papa and I returned to what was left of our own apartment above the store. Anything of the slightest value had been carried off, especially during that last long cold winter when the desperate scavenged for heating fuel. Several solid wooden doors were torn off their hinges, floorboards taken up and even the small ornament shelf in my bedroom had been ripped off the wall. Mutti was devastated at the wreckage that greeted us. Her grandmother's mahogany sideboard had been axed to pieces, along with a grandfather clock and the picture frames containing portraits of long-dead family members.

If the bits and pieces had helped ease someone's suffering by providing warmth and comfort, I didn't mind, and I told her so.

'Don't be so insensitive,' Papa scolded.

I could make do without fine china and good silver. It was heartening that friends and neighbours rallied together to share their belongings in those early weeks and months of liberation.

Much to Papa and Mutti's horror, I insisted on hanging Officer Hass's overcoat in my own wardrobe. I would not, somehow could not, part with it, let alone destroy it. One afternoon, I found Mutti standing before the open wardrobe, tentatively touching the fabric.

'Only the best of materials for them, of course,' she sneered in a way that made her already damaged face look even more pained. 'They had the best, while everyone else suffered.'

I tried to close the door, but she refused to step back.

'What do you think people would say if they knew this thing was in our house?' she asked.

'I don't care.'

'Why keep it at all?'

'I can't explain.'

How could I tell her that when wrapped in its weighty layers, I was taken back to those days spent under Ilse's roof, those days of adventure, mystery and the sense of stalking danger that I never truly thought would ever catch up with me. I could never say out loud that I missed that time.

On sleepless nights when I lay awake listening for the Westertoren clock, or when disturbed by our neighbours' cries, torn from sleep by some terrible death camp nightmare, I often crept out of bed. I tiptoed to my wardrobe and took the bulky coat from its hanger. I wrapped it about me like a cape and scurried back to bed, where I would quickly fall asleep, holding the loose thread between my fingers.

I managed to hide this from my parents as we went through the motions of rebuilding our lives.

It took me some time to adjust to their stifling protection as we all struggled to piece our lives back to something that resembled better times. But even worse was grappling with the horror stories sweeping the world as the full terror of the treatment of Jews in concentration camps became clearer.

***

In the long months that followed, I learned that many of my school friends and neighbours were not coming back. Jacob Bresler, Anna Weis, Shem Olem, Regina Donner – the list went on and on. I went back to school and clung ever closer to Pim. Our numbers had diminished. We were discouraged from huddling in clutches to talk about our missing classmates.

Then there were the few that did return from the refugee and processing camps: Sylvia Spender, Marc Ishlam and Alfons Hoffman. They never spoke of their experiences, at least not in my hearing, but their dark eyes were filled with something I had never seen before or since. Sylvia was the only one who didn't hide the tattoo on her left forearm, a sure sign she had survived Auschwitz, a fact that earned awe and respect.

I'd eavesdrop on visitors' conversations. There was no real help for those who first returned, initially in a trickle and then as the weeks passed, the deluge of broken souls: orphans looking for parents, parents for children and husbands looking for wives, sons and daughters. The war had ended; the suffering continued.

With growing dread, I came to understand the roaring ache inside was guilt. A shame at having made it through. Why did we escape the mass murder when others had not?

In the meantime, all this turmoil added to the anger towards my parents, who insisted 'Things will return to normal soon enough. There is nothing to be gained by going over and over it'.

Even I could see that was a ridiculous statement. People and life would never be normal again – not as it was before.

If I dared raise the war or my time with Ilse, when gathered around the table or sitting together in the evening, Papa closed me down, with a fist on the table and a single barked word, 'Enough!'.

I realised how fortunate we were to have been helped by our Dutch friends, who had thought nothing of their own safety to save a few lives of people like us. While there was the odd story of other fortunate hidden individuals like us and the Caslers, and other stories of camp survival and miraculous escapes, there were also overwhelming tragedies of friends and families. They'd either been murdered or they had perished in the death camps from illness or a host of other horrors.

All this caused me frequent nightmares, and I came to dread closing my eyes at bedtime. More and more in the dead of night, I sought comfort in the folds of Officer Hass's overcoat.

Eventually Pim and I made a trip to De Silveren Spiegel Restaurant on Kattengat, about ten minutes from the Caslers' old hideout. The three-hundred-year-old dining establishment, with its original beams and elegant embellishments, was where Hetty had planned for us all to meet to celebrate the end of the war. We were shown to a window table. I felt so grown up as we made our way through the restaurant, and all around us the air was filled with the sounds of happy diners, jangling cutlery and a low hubbub of chatter.

Mutti loaned me a skirt, a short-sleeved blouse and a pair of low heels for the occasion. I had outgrown most of my clothes and anyway, they looked shabby and childish.

'A toast to Hetty,' I said, clinking my hot chocolate glass with Pim, enjoying the weak sunshine that came through the picture windows at the front. 'And Ilse.'

'To Hetty and to Ilse.' Pim smiled widely, his blue-green eyes sparkling in the dull sunlight.

'And we must not forget a toast to Clara and Tomas.' Glasses clinked once more. 'And to your parents and Mutti and Papa and Fritz, Double B and Herr Winkler.'

'What about Frau Achterberg?' Pim laughed. 'Shall we clink to her?'

'Of course – to the best actress in the entire world,' I said. 'There is one more person I'd like to remember.'

Pim raised an eyebrow in query.

'Officer Hass.'

'The German?' He looked uncertain. 'Okay, I suppose.'

‘I wish Hetty was here.’ My words hung in the air between us. ‘If only they could have hung on a bit longer. I have a rock in my stomach when I think of it – and that’s all the time.’

‘Hannah from our class – remember Hannah with the long curly hair?’ he asked. ‘She saw Hetty towards the end.’

‘How do you know that? Have you seen Hannah then?’

‘No, Anika told us. She knows the family.’

I nodded, wanting him to get on with his story.

‘Hannah was in a camp. She saw Hetty but they were divided by a barbed-wire fence. They both cried. Hannah said Hetty was in very bad spirits, very pale and ill. Hetty said that Frau Casler had died, and Ursula was sick.’

Pim sipped his chocolate. ‘A few days later, Hannah managed to throw a small parcel of collected food rations to Hetty over the fence.’

He swallowed hard, his Adam’s apple jumping in his throat. ‘That’s the last time she saw her.’

A fly on the window caught my eye and I swatted at it with my napkin, sending it into a crazed dance around my head and causing me to spill what remained of my hot chocolate across the table.

‘Let’s walk,’ Pim said, getting up and hooking his arm in mine. We walked down Koggestraat by the canals. With each step, the streets sparked to life with the war-time ghosts of people trying to live a normal life, despite the ever-present watch of the occupiers.

Then there we were – Hetty, Double B, Fritz, Pim and me. As my imagination drew on the comfort of the past, we materialised as more carefree selves. I whizzed past on my bicycle with Fritz close behind; across the bridge, I saw Hetty, Double B, Pim and me getting ready to board a tram headed for the cinema; at the corner of Keizersgracht and Passeerdestraat, we snuck past German soldiers, clutching our picnic basket on our way to Vondelpark.

Pim and I were sitting on a bench in the sun and instinctively I pulled my feet back to avoid them being trampled by an imagined passing German patrol. I looked up as the face of a passing businessman morphed into the familiar expression of Officer Hass. A barely detectable smile flickered at the corners of his mouth and he politely touched his hand to his hat.

I nodded and placed my right hand on my heart as he went by, a small gesture of silent thanks.

'You okay?' Pim asked.

'I'm okay,' I said. 'I thought I saw someone I knew.'

'I do that, too. We haven't made enough new memories to add to the old ones yet. Do you think of everyone often?'

'Yes. Hetty, all the children in your house, your sisters Bep and Anke, your parents, Officer Hass. But especially, though, of Ilse. I will never forget them.'

Chapter 30

One evening, after a pleasant supper at Frau Achterberg's, where Pim, his sisters and my parents also gathered and we all tiptoed around the subject of the war, I told Mutti on returning home that I would like to sit up and listen to the BBC World News.

'I don't think so,' she said. 'It's getting late and you still need your rest. Remember what the doctor said? Good food, fresh air, rest and routine – that's what we all need. It's what you need. Off you go and get ready for bed.'

I ignored her and instead, threw myself on a scrappy old lounge Papa had scrounged from somewhere.

I turned on the radio, kicked off my shoes and folded my legs beneath me.

'Lena.' Mutti sounded stern. 'I asked you to get ready for bed.'

'I don't want to go to bed yet,' I told her. 'Ilse used to let me listen. And how many times must I remind you that I don't want to be called Lena? Lena is a childish name. You named me Adelena, and that's my name.'

'I am sorry,' Mutti apologised. 'Yes, Adelena. But the doctor said –'

'I know, but I don't care what he said. I don't want to go to bed.'

My parents had become used to my frequent acts of defiance and soon gave in so as not to cause a scene in the cramped quarters of our new home – a two-bedroom apartment in a crowded building. It was one that had escaped too much damage, unlike so many others that were torn apart by people scavenging for fuel to burn during the bitter winter.

I learned that one way to get what I wanted was to make a fuss in front of Max, the little brother who had replaced me in the folds of Mutti's skirts. Max, so used to living hidden and under the cloak of constant hush, did not like raised voices or loud noises.

Papa, casting a long shadow in the doorway, told me not to be disobedient. That was all it took.

'You can't tell me what to do,' I shouted. 'It's too late to care now, too late after you left me with someone I barely knew. I called for you, I waited for you, I cried for you. But you didn't come back.'

My parents both looked dumbstruck, but their shocked silence spurred me on. We were strangers, who knew one another well.

'I didn't know if you were dead or alive. The moment I woke each morning and when I closed my eyes at night, I wondered about you and my heart would break.'

Papa found his voice first and ordered me to stop.

I spoke over him, and it was not until Mutti put her hand out and cupped it over my mouth in a gentle gesture against my violent tirade that I stopped.

With her free hand, she traced the cruel purple gouge across her face.

'I did go back.'

Yes, she broke away from Papa the night they left me with Ilse. She did turn back, and this was the reminder.

I hung my head in shame.

And we went on like this. Good days and bad days. We tried to work our way through, rebuilding and finding a new kind of normal. There was no formal support, not so far as I was aware. Not for Jews like us who had survived and who had a roof. It was as though having survived alive was enough and now it was just best to get on with it.

Mutti and Papa reopened the shop, though business was slow due to continued rationing. I kept to myself as much as possible and, despite their gentle prodding, revealed little of my life at Ilse's.

Towards the end of 1945, as the days shortened and the nights grew ever more bitter, I slipped into Officer Hass's overcoat most evenings, always careful to hide it away in the wardrobe before the rest of the house was up and about.

One morning, having overslept, I was startled awake by Mutti's voice.

'Have you lost your senses, girl?' Mutti asked.

My parents stood over my bed, appalled at the sight of me wrapped cosily in the overcoat.

Papa grabbed me by the shoulders, hauled me up and reached for the coat. 'What is this?' he hissed into my face.

I was dumbstruck and still sleep-drugged, unable to form words.

Next thing, a stinging slap on the cheek sharpened my senses. I grabbed at the coat.

'It's mine.' I snatched at the collar. 'Give it back.'

Turning to Mutti, Papa said. 'I thought I told you to get rid of this thing on that first day. Do you want us to be strung up in Dam Square for having this abomination in our home?'

Mutti tried to explain, but he was deep within his rage and unable to be reasoned with.

It was the first time I had ever been afraid of my father. Fearing he would strike Mutti for disobeying him, I came to my senses and put myself between them.

'Stop, Papa! Please, just stop.' I reached for his arm. 'It's not her fault. I wanted to keep it. He gave it to me, and it saved my life. He saved me so many times when he could have done otherwise.'

And so, we sat huddled together on my bed, the

coat over my knees, as I told them for the first time the details of my time away from them. They listened quietly as I laughed, cried, and raged.

When I finished, Papa wrapped me in his arms and kissed me on the head.

'Oh, if I could only change things,' Mutti said.

But of course, she couldn't.

Chapter 31

The coat's origins remained a family secret, hidden away in my wardrobe. My parents decided to turn a blind eye to its existence, realising, perhaps, all that it embodied for me.

One evening, after the shop closed, I heard Mutti walk up the stairs towards our modestly furnished *Stube*, with its little wood stove pumping out a warm glow. I'd already drawn the curtains, fashioned from a recycled bedspread by my clever mother, complete with a length of braid found in her sewing box.

But instead of entering the warm room as she normally did, I listened as she continued up the next creaking flight of stairs, and her footsteps told me she was heading towards my bedroom.

I called to her from the *Stube* doorway, 'Mutti, what are you doing up there?'

She didn't answer but was soon back on the landing with Officer Hass's coat slung across one arm.

My heart skipped.

'Mutti, what are you doing with my coat?'

'I've had an idea,' she said. 'Come.'

I followed her into the *Stube* and watched as she

lay the coat across her worktable among the needles, threads, scissors, and tapes. 'You need a winter coat.'

At first, I didn't understand but something in me sensed I should do as requested. I removed my sweater.

With a mouthful of pins, Mutti took my measurements and instructed me to put the coat on. Arms up, arms down, turn this way, turn that way. More measurements taken and recorded.

With skilled fingers, Mutti pinned the luxurious fabric and marked it with her tailor's chalk. While she worked, I realised I was ready to part with Officer Hass's coat, at least in its current form.

Mutti draped the coat over her arm. 'Follow me to the washroom, come on.'

'Where are you two going?' Papa asked as we passed through the *Küche*.

'Never you mind,' I said, happy to be part of Mutti's conspiracy.

In the laundry, she demonstrated how to mix the fabric dye and left me to carry out the task while she set herself up in the corner.

'Are you ready?' she asked, scissors poised over the material.

'Wait.' I left the big round dye vat and its swirling dark mixture and stood up. 'One more time please.'

Mutti held Officer Hass's coat up and I slid my arms in, enjoying the feel of the silky lining against my arms, the weight on my shoulders and the instant warmth as the material fell around my slender frame. I twisted the sleeve's loose thread between my fingers.

The moment triggered a flood of memories – pedalling away in terror with Fritz in hot pursuit; colliding with Officer Hass's motorcycle; Hetty's white face as I tipped water over the officer from the Caslers' front window; fairy-hunting with Double B; staring into the German officer's pistol barrel and the look in Officer Hass's eyes as he discovered me in the hidey hatch. All these and more passed, film-like, through my mind. Then I slipped off the coat and went to hand it back, before changing my mind.

'May I?' I asked, reaching for the scissors.

I turned the coat inside out and sat with it for a moment before carefully unpicking the lining, watching it fall away to the floor. Next, I unpicked the seams.

Mutti took over the job of mixing the dye.

Stitch by stitch, the past fell away. I said goodbye to Hetty, Ilse, Adelena and all those others I had lost or left behind.

When finished, I picked up the coat's individual pieces and took them to the large copper dye vat, pausing just for a moment before plunging them into the treacle-like liquid. I pushed it down, drowning it in the dark blue liquid, and watched as the dye soaked the fibres.

Hauling it back up, muscles straining under the weight, I wrung it out and plunged it back under, pressing it against the murky bottom of the vat, forcing it to take on its new shade.

The process was repeated several more times, stopping when my brow was damp and I could no longer lift my arms.

Mutti's voice broke my focus. 'I think you've finished.'

And indeed, I had. No longer the familiar light grey colour, the sodden fabric was blue-black, the colour of a fresh bruise or the dark glossy feathers of a blackbird.

By the end of the week, I was slipping my arms into the expertly lined sleeves of my new dark blue overcoat. Cut to the shape of my waist, with square shoulders, turned back cuffs and a tie belt, it had wide lapels and the coat fell to my knees.

No longer the cumbersome weight it had once been, I admired myself in Mutti's full-length mirror, with its yellowing glass and chipped corner.

'It sits well on you,' she said.

***

It came with us to Australia two years later, and I wore it often on the long sea voyage.

I hugged it tight around my thin frame while standing in the cool moon-lit air on the ship's listing deck. I drew the lapels up around my chin to keep out the sea mist, surrounded by the hushed conversations between the discreet couples dotting the railings.

The coat's deep pockets were somehow comforting as I craned my neck to observe the changing inky sky.

No bright shining North Star here.

I couldn't know that this unfamiliar, upside-down celestial atlas, sparkling over the southern hemisphere, was only a herald of the strangeness to come.

Fear has ruled my life. The suffocating, clawing fear of discovery, intimacy and remembrance. The thrashing panic of never having enough.

And though it no longer fits like a glove, the re-styled officer's coat remains hanging in my wardrobe. On those long cold nights when old dreams and a catalogue of memories crowd the dark hours, I reach for the coat and in the moon's pale light, drape it about my shoulders and remind myself I am home. I am safe.

There were many times during my hiding I thought I would never be free again. That I was going to die there in that tall, narrow blue house, or worse, alone, in a camp. The only choice I had, the one thing I could control, was when and where my end would arrive. So that day in the cellar with the Germans stomping above me, I was prepared to expose myself, to meet my end and get it over with.

But Officer Hass found me, and he spared me. That's when I knew I had to stay alive, had to keep pushing, breathing, to keep the blood flowing through my system, even though I was weak and there was no reason to hope.

So, I stayed alive. I stayed alive, because one day someone may find me in my hiding place and save me again. And he did.

A note from the author

This story germinated many years ago and is the knitting together of many threads. I grew up listening to my father's stories about his adventures and sometimes harrowing experiences growing up in WWII Germany. Born in a small medieval town in the south-west, close to the French border, Dad's seven-member family was Catholic and not members of the local Nazi party. Yet due to their religion and lack of major commitment to the party, they suffered their own type of persecution. Times were tough and my resourceful grandma got hold of a German officer's fine woollen overcoat. She dyed it, to disguise the material, and made clothes for Dad and one of his brothers.

At thirteen I read *The Diary of Anne Frank* – the same age Anne was when she went into hiding – and I always thought that under different circumstances, of course, we'd have been great friends. Her thoughts and the style of her reflections resonated deeply with me. I was utterly heartbroken by her story, which is one that has stayed with me over the years.

Several years ago, I wrote to Hannah Goslar, who

now lives in Jerusalem, aged in her 90s. She was a childhood friend of Anne and, unlike her, survived Bergen Belsen. I loosely based Lena on Hannah. She is one of the last living links to Anne – the young girl who came to symbolise so much Holocaust suffering and inhumanity. I wanted to tell Hannah I was planning to write a story and she supported the idea. She said that her parents raised her to be a proud Jew and believed it's important to keep the story of the Jewish WWII suffering alive for a new generation. She herself has spent much of her life speaking about her experiences to schoolchildren.

In order to tell my story, I knew I had to get real stories. I went on to conduct further research including interviews overseas and in Australia with former survivors and hidden children including Alice Sondike, Andrew Steiner and Eva Engel. I spoke with WWII historians and researched online archives of the Sydney Jewish Museum, and Jerusalem's Yad Vashem World Holocaust Remembrance Center. I spent many hours reading archived WWII newspapers and interviewed a nurse carer at Sydney's Wolper Jewish Hospital who was able to share the late-life impacts of the Holocaust that are often buried but become more prevalent with old age.

We are all survivors of something – perhaps bullying, a difficult family life, friendship or relationship issues. But among the lessons I learned from listening to these amazing people and reading their stories, was how important it is to keep putting one foot in front of the other during these scary times, to maintain a sense of hope – no matter how small – and to understand that looking ahead is a key to survival and recovery.